TRYIN' TO TELL A STRANGER 'BOUT ROCK AND ROLL

TRYIN' TO TELL A STRANGER 'BOUT ROCK AND ROLL

Selected Writings 1966-2016

Real-time observations and reflections on music and popular culture, from one of the nation's first rock critics

GENE SCULATTI

Swingin' 60 Productions

First Edition 2016
Copyright ©2016 by Gene Sculatti
for Swingin' 60 Productions
ISBN: 978-1535483827

www.genesculatti.com

Cover: Richard Henderson
Book design: Pablo Capra

Special Thanks to Daniel Weizmann

For George Davis and Miss Witte

Contents

The author, revisiting *Highway 61* in '65

Introduction

First off, about that title: *Tryin' to Tell a Stranger 'bout Rock and Roll.* It's, of course, from the Lovin Spoonful's "Do You Believe in Magic," but it may be a bit misleading here. Those first few of us who came to be called rock critics were initially a small bunch, wild about this music, itself already a decade old in 1966 but, like us, starting to turn some corners. But we weren't fishing for converts; we were kibitzing with the faithful about what was clearly the coolest game in town in those It's-all-happening-so-fast post-Beatles, pre-*Rolling Stone* days.

And another thing. I'm not especially fond of the term 'rock critic.' It works, I guess, but it carries a faint scent of pretense, a quality that's dogged writing about the music since the beginning, a defense tactic meant to compensate for R&R's low birth. My popping off about pop has generally been to convey the enthusiasm I have for the record or performance at hand. Negative reviews? I've done a few, but with so much worth celebrating, why bother? I had a hard time seeing our role the way fellow crit Richard Meltzer portrayed it: as dupe water-carriers for the music industry, pimping record-company product. To me we were cousins of the disc jockeys who so entranced me growing up; they were couriers, a kind of audio UPS that delivered fabulous gifts fashioned by others.

"There's no special merit in writing about a large number of topics," Dutch author Ian Buruma muses in the preface to his 2014 essays collection *Theater of Cruelty,* "as opposed to mining fewer veins ever more profoundly." "Profound" is probably another ill-chosen phrase here, but spelunking along a single vein is largely what I do: It's what's in the grooves that counts, though TV shows, radio personalities, advertising and media make their way into the mix too.

Here's what's here: a compendium of reviews and features, interviews, liner notes, and blog posts, published from 1966 to 2016, in *Creem*
and *Crawdaddy*, the *Los Angeles Times*, and *L.A. Weekly, Rolling Stone,
Phonograph Record Magazine* and *Fusion, Radio & Records*, the zines
Scram and *Ugly Things*, and a passel of expired websites.

The selections were chosen for different reasons. The earliest pieces
(which appeared in *Crawdaddy* and the *Mojo-Navigator Rock & Roll
News*) are journeyman efforts, but they're on-the-ground reports, prompt
responses to the work of the day. Other articles may dig deeper to, hopefully, reveal something previously undisclosed; that's where the annota-
tion for Madonna's *Immaculate Collection* comes in, and "Born to Run
Also-Rans," about Springsteen imitators, and "The Seventies' Fifties
Revival" and "Beguiled by Bruno: My Great Lost-Album Trip." (The
latter led Nick Tosches to tag me as "a true connoisseur of the bizarreries
that lurk beneath the stones of popular culture's forgotten back streets."
Guilty as charged.)

As the chronologically arranged collection rolls on, you'll probably
notice the emergence of a writing style, always conversational but grad-
ually aiming for greater clarity and conciseness, away from the obvious
Lester Bangs influence of the early Seventies that few of us were able
to avoid. Some of the reviews work themselves into a kind of baroque
hyper-drive, a signature tic from a certain time—which Ken Barnes perfectly savages here in his parody review of a fictitious Cat Stevens album.

It would be disingenuous to downplay the importance of right-time
right-place in informing this writing. Born in 1947 (in San Francisco),
I belong to what'd have to be called the first-generation rock audience,
those young enough to have been shook by Elvis, stirred by the Beatles/
Stones/Dylan Sixties, reanimated by punk and now, canes at the ready,
craning to make sense of what we hear this week—the only cohort to
have experienced it all in real time.

Music has always been my main emotional driver. My earliest memories are of being four or five, pestering my parents to buy me two hits of
the early Fifties, "Down Yonder" (I'm not sure whose version it was) and
Ralph Marterie's cover of "Caravan." By nine and 10, I saved allowance
money to buy, at the appliance store in our small Napa Valley town,
highly breakable 78's of Buchanan & Goodman's "Flying Saucers,"
Ricky Nelson's "Be-Bop Baby" and Little Joe & the Thrillers' "Peanuts."

Like many Italian-American dads, mine played accordion. His earnest attempts to pass on the talent failed big-time. The only thing I could
play was a phonograph, which, at 13 and 14, I sat by, tossing 45's on

and off, pretending to be a DJ at a Top-40 station (I still have the play-lists). The Beach Boys, girl groups and early Motown soundtracked my adolescence, the Bay Area rock scene my college years (UC Davis, San Francisco State)—which allowed me to write what's considered the first national-magazine piece on San Francisco rock (it's here). For three years I contributed a weekly pop-music column to the *Sacramento Bee*.

Music moved me from Northern to Southern California, in 1973. I followed fellow writers Greg Shaw and Ken Barnes to L.A., took over the Laurel Canyon closet-space vacated by Mark Shipper (the fanzine *Flash* and the Beatles sendup *Paperback Writer*).

In Los Angeles I interviewed Dion, Ben E. King, Frankie Valli (they're here), Brian Wilson, Spinal Tap and other luminaries, witnessed the Ramones' first West Coast show and the Pistols' last gasp (that in Frisco), and acquired enough credits to be invited to the Rock Writers of the World convention in Memphis in 1973. I became the first editor of the trade paper *Radio & Records* (where I interviewed John Lennon; it's here. Sadly, the *R&R* chat with Mick's brother Chris Jagger is lost to the ages), segued in the mid-Seventies to Warner Bros. Records, where I edited its house organs, then spent 12 years as Director of Special Issues for *Billboard* magazine (my *Billboard* history of record-company advertising is included in this collection) and closed out full-time employment in 2006 as Managing Editor of *Ice* magazine.

Music plays as a main theme in most of my books too—*The Catalog of Cool* (1982), *San Francisco Nights: The Psychedelic Music Trip* (1985), *Too Cool* (1993)—and books I've contributed to: *Bubblegum Music Is the Naked Truth* (2001), *Lost in the Grooves: Scram's Capricious Guide to the Music You Missed* (2005), and Jeff Gold's 2012 volume *101 Essential Rock Records*. That year also saw the publication of my first e-book, *Dark Stars and Anti-Matter: 40 Years of Loving, Leaving and Making Up with the Music of the Grateful Dead*. I helped curate the Rock and Roll Hall of Fame's disc-jockeys exhibit and did original research for the background-singers documentary *20 Feet from Stardom*, which won an Academy Award in 2014.

Come on, let's go…

THE SIXTIES

If the Sixties appear underrepresented here, the decade is nonetheless when and where the writing starts. It may be hard to believe today, when major-newspaper critics routinely analyze the intent, content and social impact of anything that reaches the upper reaches of the Billboard *charts, but serious coverage of rock 'n' roll simply did not exist before 1966, with one exception: Don Paulsen's* Hit Parader *magazine, whose bread and butter was reprinting lyrics to the day's Top-40 hits but whose pages also gave generous space to hip new acts (Paul Butterfield, the Charlatans, Magicians) and veteran blues and jazz cats. Underground papers like the* L.A. Free Press, Berkeley Barb *and* Village Voice *also heard the call, and by '68 and '69, dozens of music and 'new culture' mags crowded the news-stands:* Rolling Stone, Creem *and* Soul, Strobe *and* Circus *(originally* Hullabaloo), Eye *and* Cheetah *and more. At the start, though, in '66, there were just two dedicated rock periodicals. I was first published in Paul Williams'* Crawdaddy *and San Francisco's mimeographed weekly* The Mojo Navigator Rock & Roll News. *The latter was run by Greg Shaw and David Harris, two guys I met early that year on the Fillmore-Avalon scene. I contributed to the latter publication until it folded in 1967. A year later I wrote my first review for* Rolling Stone *—and knocked the publication in a piece for* Jazz & Pop; *"In Defense of the Beach Boys" was a rejoinder to Ralph Gleason and Jann Wenner's recurring putdowns of the band as unhip pretenders. (About the only part of the article I'd take back 48 years later is the unfair dismissal of Jan & Dean.)*

FEATURE:

San Francisco Bay Rock

Crawdaddy! magazine, Sept., 1966

The San Francisco rock scene is a complex one. It is a plentiful jumble of hard rock, folk-rock, blues-rock, bubble-gum, and adult bands that have given the city its title as "the Liverpool of the West" (aptly provided by jazz critic Ralph Gleason).

San Francisco has contributed its fair share of pop stars to the teen market. The ill-fated Beau Brummels, and the We Five, started in the Bay Area; but the city's current claim to fame rests in the strength of its performing underground bands. At present, the local rock scene revolves around weekend dance-concerts presented in renovated ballrooms and auditoriums. Few of the groups perform at clubs (The Matrix, a nightclub in San Francisco's Fillmore district, was the pioneer hip club when it began presenting Jefferson Airplane, and it continues spotlighting local rock acts today). Most activity is connected with the dance-concert performances which were started almost a year ago.

Last November, a group of "concerned" people in San Francisco banded together to form The Family Dog, an organization for the promotion of local hip groups in assorted halls throughout the city. The first Family Dog dances at Longshoreman's Hall featured The Lovin' Spoonful (just after they'd come from New York, and just before they'd hit with "Magic"), Jefferson Airplane, the Great Society, and a number of since disbanded aggregations (the Mystery Trend, the Family Tree, the Hedds, etc.). These initial productions were quite successful in creating a forum for the expression of the new music, grown-up rock 'n' roll.

The Family Dog continued to present their dances and moved to the more accommodating Fillmore Auditorium, where local groups shared the bill with Love, the Sons of Adam, the Grass Roots (all from Los Angeles), and the Butterfield Blues Band. In January of this year, the new dance-happening scene was advanced even further by Ken Kesey in his first "Trips Festivals" (gatherings attempting to duplicate the psychedelic experience without the use of drugs). Kesey's first three-day festival utilized liquid light projections, old movies, strobe lights, etc., to the thunderous accompaniment of top underground bands (particularly the Grateful Dead, who can be considered nothing short of fantastic). From here the dance-concert-happening idea was parlayed into an obvious commercial venture, and now covers the entire Bay Area. It is from these early experiments, however, that San Francisco's current adult rock scene evolved, encompassing most of the following groups.

Jefferson Airplane was the first of San Francisco's underground bands to attract national attention (even if Koppelman-Rubin had nothing to do with them). The Airplane still remains the area's most popular group. Their bag is folk-rock, mostly original material handled superbly by leader and male solo Marty Balin, female singer Signe Anderson, lead guitarist Jorma Kaukonen, rhythm Paul Kantner, bass Jack Casady, and drummer Spencer Dryden. The Airplane's sound is folk-based, with the creative contributions of six truly talented contemporary musicians. Their first single, "It's No Secret"/ "Runnin' Round This World," was a flop. It was too good. The bubble-gummers wouldn't buy it. Their second attempt, "Come Up the Years"/ "Blues from an Airplane," though not as original or stimulating as their first, hit big enough locally to signal an album, which should be available nationwide soon, *Jefferson Airplane Takes Off* (RCA-Victor LPM-3584). This is perhaps the best rock album ever produced; "Blues from an Airplane" is lightning and thunder, "Let Me In" (an original) rocks relentlessly. "Run Around" and "Don't Slip Away" (originals) shine, particularly the guitar-vocal blends and Jorma's soloes. "Chauffeur Blues" shouts as it awakens. "Tobacco Road" is a good song made into a masterpiece by the group. Its sway and vocal backing in the end make it the power machine of the album. There are eleven cuts, each one a great testimony, and collectively a pop prophecy: Jefferson Airplane is a beautiful accomplishment.

The Grateful Dead are rapidly gaining prominence and ascending from their underground status to a position close to the Airplane. Most local dance-concert attendees, when confronted with a question about the Dead, will mention "Midnight Hour." The Dead's closing number is usually Wilson Pickett's blockbuster, and it is transformed into a type of half-hour (sometimes longer) "Everybody Needs Somebody To Love" performed by the Dead's organist, Pig Pen. (A recent concert featured "Midnight Hour" performed by a joint "Grateful Airplane" with the assistance of Joan Baez and Mimi Farina.) "Midnight Hour" is not the

Dead at their best. They are a hard blues-rock band, a powerhouse unit of organ, drums, and three guitars. Their best accomplishments are Pig Pen's gutsy version of "Good Morning Little Schoolgirl" (with fantastic controlled harp work), "The Creeper," "Empty Heart," and "Smokestack Lightning" (both now performed only by special request), and an unbelievable grooving piece about "Born in Jackson" (supposedly written by rhythm player Bob Weir). "Sittin' on Top of the World" jumps, and "Dancing in the Streets" is a railroad trip. Jerry Garcia's lead working is exciting, sustained genius. Bill Sommers is the Bay Area's best drummer. Their repertoire is chiefly city blues, some old folk and early rock, with some strong originals. A single is to be issued shortly. A Grateful Dead album is being re-prepared (a first effort was discarded). The group has a $10,000 sound system. The Grateful Dead figure to be important movers in imparting San Francisco's message to the world.

The Great Society is one of the city's strongest, most original groups, but has remained underground for some time, and recording company recognition has been much too slow. The Great Society is carried by Grace Slick, the single most talented woman in San Francisco's performing rock scene. She sings lead, plays electric organ, flute, alternates on bass at times. Darby Slick plays an effective lead guitar, Gerry Slick is a strong drummer, and Peter Van Gelder is a heavy bassist. Van Gelder also uses an alto sax on a few jazz numbers whose effect can be described as nothing less than spectacular. The group shows a strong Indian influence and has for some time (re their North Beach single, no longer available, "Someone to Love"/"Free Advice"). Their material is penned by Grace and Darby. Particularly impressive are "Someone to Love," "Sally Go Round the Roses," and the few Dylan numbers ("Black Crow Blues" is great). The Great Society was reportedly planning a new single and an album, probably on Warner Brothers.

Koppelman-Rubin's big find in San Francisco was the Charlatans. The Charlatans are hard rock, specializing in John Hammond blues and original country & western numbers. They also utilize some real traditional frontier tunes as well. They have great strength in their ragtime piano with pickups, and their rhythm section is adequate. Lead is handled well too. George Hunter is leader and sings (occasionally) and plays percussion and autoharp. Drummer Dan Hicks pens the original stuff; his big claim, "How Can I Miss You If You Won't Go Away?" The group's best numbers are "Backdoor Man," "Sweet Lorraine," "Wabash Cannonball" and "Codeine" (which the group was dismayed at Kama Sutra for refusing to release as a single). While the disenchantment with

Kama-Sutra lingers, an album is in the works.

Other local groups deserve mention for their contributions as well as the aforementioned pop heroes. These people are all adults, and seriously intent on perfecting good rock as an art. Another of the more established units is Quicksilver Messenger Service. They are a good dance band. No recorded efforts have appeared yet, perhaps as the group has until recently been void of any substantial number of original compositions. Their best numbers are "Codeine," Hamilton Camp's "Pride of Man," "Mona," and "Smokestack Lightning."

The Sopwith Camel are another Koppelman-Rubin development, a strictly goodtime band patterned after John and Zal and the boys. Their blues numbers are ineffective, but on ragtime and happy stuff they excel. "Little Orphan Annie" is great. A single is to be released soon on Kama Sutra; they recently embarked for New York.

Country Joe & the Fish gained underground prominence with their version of psychedelic, new-mown grass music. Delicate interweaving of harp and organ over a solid rhythm line give them the correct emphasis...their music is lulling. A Rag Baby e.p. is available in Berkeley for $1.00 (Country Joe & the Fish, Box 2233, Berkeley, California).

Big Brother and the Holding Company do good hard blues and revised country music. They were supposed to have been signed with Mercury, but no records have appeared yet. The Wildflower are a powerful band when they are on. They have bad nights. Their lyrics are from poet Michael McClure and their music is Byrds. They are loud. A Mainstream single is being readied. The Blue Light Basement has appeared a few times, they rock fairly well, but all their harp rings of "Mojo." A female vocalist is quite good. P.H. Phactor and the Jug Band are as they sound, an electric country band which has interesting moments. Current underground attention is being given Freedom Highway, a supposedly unique group with fancy lead work. They have not appeared extensively as yet.

The San Francisco rock scene continues, churning out new sounds, capturing experiences and setting up new expression. The audiences have plenty of room to delight at the marvels at the Avalon Ballroom, the Fillmore, Straight Theatre, F.W. Kuh, the Matrix. Most of the bigger bands are now at the point where they have found their bags and it is just a matter of time before they will be given exposure and a chance at national recognition. In the meantime, countless new units are forming, analyzing, experimenting, perfecting their own sounds. "The City" continues to provide an open, receptive and progressive testing ground to assimilate and perpetuate the good new thing, Rock.

PAUL WILLIAMS

20 Mellen St.
Cambridge, Mass, 02138
Sept. 17, 1966

Gene Sculatti
1516 Graysen Ave.
St. Helena, Calif.
94574

Dear Mr. Sculatti,

I thank you very much for your report on the San Fransisco rock scene; it is an excellent piece of journalism which I shall be proud to use in the upcoming Crawdaddy (#6). I wish I had more articles as carefully and perceptively written. If you're at all interested in writing Crawdaddy-style reviews, by all means submit them. Ground rules are: a) insight counts; b) readability helps; c) you don't have to agree with me, by any means, but you will find oblique evidence of editorial slant (i.e., I don't mind if you like Yellow Submarine, but if you don't like Eight Miles High you'd better have a pretty good reason). Deadline for #6 is October 4; I'll let you know about the deadline after that (Oct 4 is sort of close, true). Any album that is pop and has appeared since about Aug 1, that we haven't already printed a review of, is fair game.

But I get sidetracked. I wrote to say how pleased I am by your article. You know, I hope, that we aren't paying contributers; we haven't any money--we scarcely pay the printer. This will change, I think. At any rate, we are influential; several Crawdaddy articles have already been picked up for reprinting elsewhere; and I just got a letter from the president of Chess Records, who wants to use last month's cover on the next Howlin' Wolf album. Impact.

I expect to have the next issue distributed in the Bay Area; Paul Schneider (a junior) and Bruce Merrill (freshman) at Stanford, Paul Gifford (freshman, Oldenberg Hall) at Berkeley, and Larry Mc-Combs (Science Research Associates, 165 University Ave, Palo Alto) are potential Bay Area staff members, whom you might be interested in contacting. Probably what I will do is send 500 Cd#6 (or more) to Schneider, and other volunteer distributers can get copies from him. Any promotion, seeking out of willing bookshops, etc, that you or anyone would be willing to do would be greatly appreciated. Approximate publication date of #6, by the way, is Oct 20. We work with bookshops on a consignment basis, offering 35% discount. And that's about all the useful information I can think of at the moment. Thanx again....

Sincerely,

Paul Williams

REVIEW:

Simon & Garfunkel
Parsley, Sage Rosemary and Thyme

Mojo-Navigator Rock & Roll News, Nov. 8, 1966

Simon and Garfunkel's third album is quite different from their second (their first all-folk album was produced before their first hit and is nowhere as interesting as their succeeding two). For one thing, their second album, *Sounds of Silence*, had a heavy predominance of rock, or at least amplified, material. This third album features mainly acoustic guitar work, although there are instances where accompaniment is employed (bass, drums, organ, strings, and the Indian sound) with mixed results.

The best thing here may be "Scarborough Fair/ Canticle," a remarkably crisp, clean sound. It is a very delicate melody with interesting interweaving of background voices in a manner quite resembling church choir music. The single acoustic guitar, chimes and delicate intricacy of the harpsichord all work to good effect. "The Big Bright Green Pleasure Machine" rolls along well with sturdy drum structure and changing guitar lines. More play should be given the organ, which merely bubbles in the background. The happiest cut on the album is "The 59th Street Bridge Song." Its strength is all in its vocal arrangement, a haunting, clean set-up balanced by good clean snare work. "Patterns" is S&G's first venture into the Eastern sound. It doesn't come off too well, because of overwhelmingly poor lyrics, but the instrumental track itself is interesting.

The only really rock thing on the album is "A Simple Desultory Philippic." It features a steady fuzz with a circus organ in the back, together with bass and drums. It is an amusing number but not musically of great achievement. "For Emily, Wherever I May Find Her" sounds vocally like Donovan. "A Poem on the Underground Wall" is terribly bland.

"Flowers Never Bend with the Rainfall" is third-rate Bob Lind (if that's possible). "7 O'clock News/ Silent Night" is "Silent Night" sung over a news broadcast about war, rape, murder, LBJ and other bad things; a nice effect but hardly of musical merit. "Cloudy" is a pleasant Cyrkle-type sound.

Parsley, Sage, Rosemary and Thyme doesn't come across as strong as *Sounds of Silence* did (not referring to the abominable single). *Silence* rocked heavy with "Somewhere They Can't Find Me," "Blessed," "We Got a Groovy Thing Goin.'" *Parsley* is content with lighter stuff.

REVIEW:

Kinks *Face to Face*

Mojo-Navigator Rock & Roll News Nov. 22, 1966

When the Kinks come up as a topic for conversation, the situation is always relatively uncomplicated. Either you've never cared for them, or you've dug them straight since "You Really Got Me and "It's All Right." If you have grooved the Kinks all along, you probably realize there's usually a problem in previewing a new Kinks album. At first play, the songs have a tendency to all sound alike. It therefore takes two or three runs through an LP to realize just what's there. In the case of *Face to Face*, there's plenty there.

Providing you understand the Kinks' music and acknowledge their talent, the obvious conclusion to be made about *Face to Face* is that it is the Kinks' *Rubber Soul*. It has he ingredients; it's right (structurally in content, and in performance), it has a theme (sunshine), it has variety (contrast "Party Line" with "Rainy Day in June"), and it has abundance—fourteen bands. The headliner single is here, "Sunny Afternoon." C&W is handled in "Party Line," (fairly Beatle-ish) goodtime in "Little Miss Queen of Darkness." Blues is the foundation for "You're Lookin' Fine." "Holiday in Waikiki" manages to successfully integrate sound effects with instrumentation, much in the manner of "Summer in the City." Even Ray's "Dandy" is palatable here. The most striking achievement, however, is "Rosy, Won't You Please Come Home," which, while definitely within the context of the Kinks, comes off as one of the most refreshing pieces in some time.

So the Kinks have reached *Rubber Soul* status with their sixth album. It's interesting to note that what formerly characterized the Kinks style is all but removed here. Pete Quaife's tough bass and Dave Davies' Chuck-Berry-derivative leads seem to have given way here to more subtle rhythms and a consistent, uniform sonority. The results provide for a new Kinks music which is softer, infinitely more textured and stylishly more sophisticated.

Review:

The Mason Williams
Phonograph Record

Rolling Stone, Sept. 14, 1968

The recording debut of Mason Williams is an intriguing affair. *The Mason Williams Phonograph Record* was released many months ago but only recently has it received any attention, primarily due to the fact that one of its cuts, "Classical Gas," is currently a top-selling single. The album is a collection of ideas from a cat who has written seven books and who was the head writer for *The Smothers Brothers Show*. Here he emerges as another in the growing number of non-mainstream composers; not so avant garde as Van Dyke Parks or Randy Newman, more like Nilsson or even Cat Stevens.

Williams' music is subliminal; one initially has the feeling that one really shouldn't be digging this stuff, but it nevertheless is captivating in a strange way. One reason why is that this music bears a very noticeable resemblance to schlock (Williams has written for such unnotables as Glenn Yarbrough and Claudine Longet). "Here Am I" and "Wanderlove" seem like genuine schlock, but the strongly stated sense of rhythmic constancy evidenced throughout the album, combined with the exceptional vocal maneuvering, disclose them as substantially textured folk ballads. "She's Gone Away," described by Williams as "my Rock Tune," comes on at first like the Turtles doing a Coke commercial, but then it begins to resemble something Nick the Greek might have written for Quicksilver—a simple ditty full of early rock vitality. A minor achievement is "Long Time Blues"; basically a country style piece, it affects the same kind of melancholy tone as "Mr. Bojangles" (dig the violins and piano interplay); a near perfect fusion of words and music. "The Prince's Panties" is Part One of a five-part "Dada Trilogy."

The remainder of the LP consists of three instrumentals. "Classical Gas" is the most ambitious of these, though "Sunflower" has its own acoustic-guitar-silence-whistling kind of beauty. In the album notes, explaining why he turned the three songs over to the orchestra and dispensed with vocals, Williams sums up his musical identity fairly well; "Most phonograph records are only what people can do. Singers sing. players play. Well, my problem is I can think up more things than I can do." In light of that, he manages to come up with plenty of good ideas. The result, in his first album, is that he displays a lot of potential—in composing and singing.

FEATURE:

Villains and Heroes:
In Defense of the Beach Boys

Jazz & Pop magazine, September 1968

Brian Wilson and company are currently at the center of an intense contemporary rock controversy, involving the academic "rock as art" critic-intellectuals, the AM-tuned teenies, and all the rest of us in between. As the California sextet is simultaneously hailed as genius incarnate and derided as the archetypical pop music copouts, one clear-cut and legitimate query is seen at the base of all the turmoil: how seriously can the 1968 rock audience consider the work of a group of artists who, just four years earlier, represented the epitome of the whole commercial-plastic "teenage music industry"?

The answer is a simple one. The Beach Boys' approach to their music is as valid now as it was in 1962 and vice versa. Brian Wilson owes no one any apologies for his music, present or past.

The most popular charge leveled at the Beach Boys is their apparently excessive immersion in and identification with mass culture and "commercialism." An association with mass culture was indeed a characteristic of the Beach Boys' music up until 1966. Moreover, it was an "honest" association.... Wilson's world circa 1962 was seriously involved with all the then dead serious/now ludicrous manifestations of adolescence: hot rods, surfing and making-out in the school parking lot really do exist. A fascination with popular culture has proven to be a significant part of the twentieth century artist's personality. It has served [Andy] Warhol and Chuck Berry (the Beach Boys' earliest influence) equally well.

Southern California teenage culture provided Brian Wilson with material for his art in "Surfin' Safari" and "Little Deuce Coupe," as did the drug experience in "Good Vibrations," as does whatever in *Wild*

Honey. The aforementioned charges would, however, have been valid (as certainly they are when applied to performers like Jan & Dean) if the Beach Boys' music had proven to be of no artistic merit, but such is not the case. Despite the oversaturation of the public with surf and drag argot, despite the fact that their recordings became somewhat anachronistic for a while, the Beach Boys have maintained a consistent impressive musical output....

In retrospect, the first Beach Boys music was a relatively crude product. In their initial LP effort, *Surfin' Safari*, the only talent evidenced is Brian Wilson's empathy, his ability to assimilate his environment and structure it into lyrical form. In their third LP, *Surfer Girl*, the Beach Boys emerged as the first authentic "rock 'n' roll group" in the modern sense; they were at once composers, singers and musicians, arrangers and producers, the first major self-sufficient rock band. In *Surfer Girl* Brian Wilson supervises the whole recording operation; still working with the formula, he is able to create a work of variety and subtlety.

By *Little Deuce Coupe* the formula has been polished to high gloss, directly working from Chuck Berry and Four Freshmen stylings. Brian's proficiency at composing intriguing melodies is displayed in "Car Crazy Cutie" and "Spirit of America." The formula works perfectly, for the last time.

What ensued after *Little Deuce Coupe* was a period of artistic transition which lasted roughly from 1964 to 1966. From *Shut Down Volume 2* through *Beach Boys Party Album* formula is necessarily discarded and the LPs become uneven collections, replete with boring bull-session fillers, displaying commendable experimentation and sophistication, moments of beauty amid dullness.

The most ambitious of the group's transition efforts was *The Beach Boys Today!* While it avoids contextual unity, *Today!* is remarkable in its embodiment of Brian's oft quoted "voices-as-instruments" philosophy. The perfect vocal intricacies of "She Knows Me Too Well" and "Please Let Me Wonder" originally elicited Jack Good's famous quote that "Beach Boys' records sound as if they were sung by eunuchs in the Sistine Choir." A precursor of *Pet Sounds* orchestration is found in the elaborate treatment given Spector's Ronettes' "I'm So Young." Perhaps more than any previous work, *Today!* substantiated Brian's stature as one of the all-time great composers of melody in rock (along with Lennon-McCartney, John Phillips and Smokey Robinson).

Two important singles mark the Beach Boys' final transition phase. "Sloop John B" early in 1966 was a partially effective attempt at erasing the band's youth-cult leaders image by adapting folk-rock to traditional Beach Boys' style. "God Only Knows," a truly distinctive 45, was the lead-off cut on the most fascinating and creative Beach Boys album to date, *Pet Sounds*. *Pet Sounds* was by no means a revolutionary work in that it inspired or influenced the rock scene in a big way. It was revolutionary only within the confines of the Beach Boys' music. The concept behind the album was part of a tradition established by *Rubber Soul*; *Rubber Soul* was the definitive "rock as art" album, revolutionary in that it was a completely successful creative endeavor integrating with precision all aspects of the creative (rock) process—composition of individual tracks done with extreme care, each track arranged appropriately to fit beside each other track, the symmetrical rock 'n' roll album.

Rubber Soul established itself as the necessary prototype that no major rock group has been able to ignore; *Rubber Soul*, *Aftermath* and *Pet Sounds* are of the same classic mold. Brian's omniscience is surely felt in *Pet Sounds*, the master hand collecting and selecting, shaping his musical expression to exhibit all of the parts of the whole; the Freshmen harmonizing, Spector's cavernous hollows of sound, lush 1940's movie music, adolescent romanticism. Like the prototype, *Pet Sounds* was a final statement of an era and a prophecy that sweeping changes lay ahead.

"Good Vibrations" may yet prove to be the most significantly revolutionary piece of the current rock renaissance; executed as it is in conventional Beach Boys manner, it is one of the few organically complete rock works; every audible note and every silence contributes to the whole three minutes, 35 seconds, of the song. It is the ultimate in-studio production trip, very much rock 'n' roll in the emotional sense and yet un-rocklike in its spacial, dimensional conceptions. In no minor way, "Good Vibrations" is a primary influential piece for all producing rock artists; everyone has felt its import to some degree, in such disparate things as the Yellow Balloon's "Yellow Balloon" and the Beatles' "A Day in the Life," in groups as far apart as (recent) Grateful Dead and the Association, as Van Dyke Parks and The Who....

Smiley Smile was an abrupt collection of comic vocal exercises. The most promising cuts, "Vegetables," "Gettin' Hungry" and "She's Goin' Bald," act as illustrations of the voice-as-instrument thing (they're mainly freaky-hip vocal diversions, not even songs), but *Smiley Smile* was predominantly a downer.

As if enough fuel hadn't been added to the fire, shortly after the radical (it is nothing if not experimental) *Smiley Smile*, an astonishingly conventional album, *Wild Honey*, made its appearance; the Beach

Boys come on really schizoid now. In *Wild Honey* they have the audacity to fool around with R&B, a territory indeed alien to them. Surprisingly, *Wild Honey* works well. It isn't the least bit pretentious; it's honest, and convincing. A whole lot of soul is used up on "Wild Honey" and "Darlin'," as well as the re-make of Stevie Wonder's "I Was Made to Love Her." "Aren't You Glad" achieves a Miracles style smoothness via a Bobby Goldsboro-type song, and Brian's weird ear for melody is again evidenced in "Let the Wind Blow" and "Country Air." *Wild Honey* is ambitious but not obnoxious. It's where the Beach Boys presently are at, in many ways it is where they have been all along (a kind of lyrical romance rock); and it is precisely where they belong, doing their thing uniquely like no one else can.

The Beach Boys' most recent work, *Friends*, may actually be their best. This album represents the culmination of the efforts and the results of their last three LPs. Demonstrating their highly distinctive approach and their own sense of organicism, *Friends* derives primarily from *Pet Sounds, Smiley Smile, Wild Honey*, and little else. The characteristic innocence and somewhat childlike visions imparted to their music are applied directly to the theme of the album: friendships. As usual, the lyrics tend to be basic, yet as expressive as they need to be; words, like individual voices or instruments, are all part of the larger whole of music; the sole qualifications for Beach Boys' lyrics is that they partake of, and don't visibly harm, melody.

Friends is certainly less "complex," as regards harmonic intricacies, than much recent Beach Boys work. Compared to *Pet Sounds* and *Smiley Smile, Friends* seems to be vocally thin. The emphasis is on very strong melodies and it is here that Brian Wilson scores again.... In "When a Man Needs a Woman" Wilson again treats sex as he did in "Gettin' Hungry" (*Smiley Smile*), with a stunning directness and surprisingly effective simplicity. *Friends* differs little in effect from most other Beach Boys albums. It is another showcase for what is the most original and perhaps the most consistently satisfying rock music being created today.

11-30-73
R&R

R&R INTERVIEW, PART ONE

JOHN LENNON

ON "MIND GAMES," OLDIES, SPECTOR, BEATLES, AND AMERICAN RADIO.

(Like they say, John Lennon "needs no introduction." While in Los Angeles cutting his next album, he recently held a two-hour conversation with Bob Wilson, Mark Shipper and myself. He covered a lot of ground, and rather than reprint the interview in full, we've excerpted the most pertinent questions and John's answers and comments. — G.S.)

R&R: Over how long a period did you write the material for Mind Games?

John: I didn't do them in a bunch, actually, though a few I completed just before I went into the studio. I've found that once you book the time, the product comes. The stuff I wrote just prior to recording was "Intuition," "Meat City," "Tight A$." I wrote the middle eight of "I Know" just before we went in.

I'd had the sound of "Mind Games" in my head for awhile, but the words didn't come till about two weeks before we cut it. Lyrically, I think "Mind Games" might be similar to "Imagine," though I don't think they resemble each other but it has a think "Imagine" perhaps said it better, but it has more conventional structure, where "Mind Games" sort of rumbles out. It doesn't behave itself.

R&R: It's a powerful song in the way it comes on surging, and proceeds to build from there.

John: Yes, I like that feeling. Where the song comes on and sounds as if it's been going on for a long time. You say "I must have missed something." It's the feeling you usually get on the fadeout.

R&R: Did "Mind Games" sound like a single to you?

John: It sounded like one, although when I went into the studio, I thought "Only People" would be the single. In the end, "Only" didn't get me off as much as "Mind Games."

R&R: Do you formulate your writing for hit, Top 40, AM singles?

John: No, I just sort of think in terms of single always. The bestones are the songs that you know are singles even when you're playing them to yourself, with no one to back you.

R&R: There seems to be a certain touch of Elvis in

Lennon: Gimme some airplay

THE SEVENTIES

The Seventies was rock journalism's real heyday, as depicted in the movie Almost Famous *and the recent documentary* Ticket to Write. *It's when rock criticism 'grew up,' expanding both the range of venues in which it appeared (by mid-decade, it seemed that every major magazine and daily paper ran a pop-music column) and the depth of its coverage. The* Rolling Stone Illustrated History of Rock & Roll *and Greil Marcus'* Mystery Train *lent the music firm historical perspective (record-company reissue programs start here), Lester Bangs famously sparred with Lou Reed on rock-press pages, and later luminaries like Patti Smith and James Wolcott first made names for themselves, in, respectively,* Creem *and* The Village Voice. *Writing about rock and roll, and pop music in general, back then was especially gratifying for a couple of reasons. There was still good new music arriving (I got to review the first Ramones album!); the editorial freedom and irreverence allowed, if not encouraged, in such publications as* Creem, Fusion *and* Phonograph Record Magazine; *and the fact that you could actually make a living in music journalism. My 1973-74 tenure with* Radio & Records *found me interviewing John Lennon, and my 1975-1981 stretch as Editorial Director of Warner Bros. Records had me overseeing the label's promotional magazines* Circular *and* Waxpaper, *a great gig.*

FEATURE:

Gary Usher Interview

January 1971 (published in *Scram* magazine, 2002)

The following interview has never been published. Granted, much of what Usher revealed then is now common knowledge in pop-fandom circles; still, his comments—about trends, corporatism and his prolific '60s work—say a lot about him and the time in which he made them.

Interviewing Gary Usher was something I just had to do. His credits graced too many wonderful/silly/inspired records. Who was this relentless Superhack who churned out boss knock-off albums like Hot Rod Rally *and* Dracula's Deuce *while co-authoring the twin peaks of early Bri-Fi emotionalism ("The Lonely Sea" and "In My Room"), who produced the sublime* Notorious Byrd Brothers, *soft-rock gems by Sagittarius and Millennium—and wrote both "School Is A Gas" and "School Is A Drag"? After much rescheduling, I flew down from Frisco, tape recorder in hand, to meet the man at his Coldwater Canyon home—the afternoon he'd been fired by RCA Records.*

How did you get into the business in the first place?
I was working at a bank, working my way through college. The City National Bank in Beverly Hills. I was at my uncle's house. He was like a father to me, 'cause my parents had moved to Lake Tahoe. One night I was over at his house, and there was a bunch of loud music going on across the street. He said some kids there had started a band. So I was just curious and took a walk across the street and introduced myself. And the kids were the Wilson family, and I met the guys. The older of the brothers was Brian. He and I hit off a pretty good friendship and decided that night to become songwriters. We'd been plunking around on the piano; I'd learned some chords on a guitar very crudely and basically...
How old were you then?

I was 24. Brian was about 18, 19. And I think that night we wrote a song called "The Lonely Sea," which was eventually on one of the Beach Boys' albums. And we wrote about 30 songs, over the next two or three months, out of which about 15 were recorded by the Beach Boys. The more successful ones were "409," which was a gold record, "In My Room," which was a gold record...

Plus a lot of the songs on the first Capitol album: 'Chug-A-Lug', 'Heads You Win—Tails I Lose'.

Yeah, I think six on the first album, probably two on the second, and one on a couple of albums thereafter. I'm not sure how it was broken down. We'd written some that they hadn't recorded.

Would they still be in the can now?

No, I don't know if they ever recorded them. It got to a point where I lost track of Brian. I don't know what was recorded, what was not. I think the last song we wrote was "Let's Run Away." That was probably 1965.

That was on the *All Summer Long* album.

Right...Brian had a little temporary office up in Sunset Towers, which he went to once a month. He tried playing businessman for a while, and that fell through. He had a piano up there. One night I was up there, we were messing around, and we wrote it in about 20 minutes. That was about the time that the Hondells scene happened.

The Hondells featuring Ritchie Burns?

Dick Burns, yeah. Brian and I had just written a thing called "Buddy Seat." It was a follow-up to "Little Honda." We were over at the office talking about that song and we just happened to write another one...But, in answer to your question, I got into the business through that. I got to know the group. They were called the Pendletons at the time.

Had they been contracted to anybody yet?

Candix Records. They had done a record with Candix as the Beach Boys which stiffed out nationally but was a top-5 record in Los Angeles. And then they cut some miscellaneous things which never did anything. Then we went in together and cut four masters over at Western Recorders and took them to Capitol. Capitol bought the masters. That was Murry Wilson, Brian and myself. 'Course, the first one they put out was "Surfin' Safari"/ "409," which was top 5 nationally, and that launched my own personal career as well as the Beach Boys. And as Brian started going out on the road I had excess amounts of time, so I began writing myself and producing. I didn't like the way my songs were being cut by other people, so I started producing, back in '62, those days.

You worked in a group for Capitol, Gary Usher and the Super

Stocks, that did several LPs: *Shut Down, Thunder Road, School Is A Gas*. One 45 you did was called "R.P.M"/ "Stingray" by the Four Speeds on Challenge. You're credited with co-authoring the songs with Mike Borchetta.

Yeah. How'd you know about that? That was all bullshit. The whole scene was a money scam.

What about the Super Stocks? Were they a legitimate group?

It wasn't a group. Just me, and I hired Hal Blaine to play drums, Dennis McCarthy playing piano, Dick Burns on bass, Glenn Campbell on guitar, myself on rhythm or percussion or inside producing. The business at that point was in a very sickening, very undeveloped state. It's easy to look back now and say that, but at the time, that's what was happening. So we all did it, and it was a means for a living.

Did all those records sell?

Yep, they all sold. Ironically, the *Shut Down* album [a hot-rod anthology featuring the title track by the Beach Boys, and various old masters by Robert Mitchum, the Cheers and the Piltdown Men] sold a million copies, which would be like a double gold record. *Hot Rod Rally* did about 100,000. The others decreased accordingly. It got to be a scam. It got to where we were doing about one hot-rod album a week for different companies. It tended to be an abortion, the whole scene.

So, did any of your groups ever gig at all?

We gigged. The Four Speeds record was Dennis Wilson and I. Dennis once lived with me when I had my apartment. We went to Tijuana and I took some benzedrine. We were in the car on the way and we wrote those two songs, "R.P.M" and "Stingray." We came back and worked out the music and went in and cut them. Mike Borchetta put up the money, so he demanded to have his name on everything. That shit only happened once and I said, "No more of that crap." Funnily enough, though, the record was a hit, and that led to the whole Capitol scene with Nick Venet. We sat down and dreamed up the *Shut Down* album. Got the old masters, put a flashy hot-rod cover on it, and the rest is history. It was at the time a trend, but business nowadays has moved away from massive trends, into just personalized pockets of statements.

Do you think that whole scene, even if it was somewhat artificial, was the wellspring of the first music indigenous to California, because it was mainly a California phenomenon?

Yeah. I think the Beach Boys were the first true California group, really representative of a so-called West Coast Sound. There were a lot of things coming out of the West Coast, such as the Lettermen and so on, many other acts. The Beach Boys really started a whole scene roll-ing. Phil Spector had split for New York, and of course Brian turned out something like 21 or 22 top-10 records, which has gotta be some kind of record outside of the Beatles. And he kicked off a lot of the people into the business. As you know, Glenn Campbell toured with the Beach Boys, Bruce Johnston too. Terry Melcher and I worked with them. Jan Berry and Dean Torrence were an offspring of the Beach Boys. Terry was inspired by them.

Bruce & Terry. "Summer Means Fun."

I was over at Terry's house all afternoon before you came. Terry's go-ing to sign with Warner Brothers as a recording artist. But the Beach Boys probably had more influence on the industry because nobody could fig-ure them out. They were a trend in and of themselves. Trends weren't really that obvious in those days, before '62. It was mainly music coming from different parts of the country, but we kicked off the hot-rod trend, our surfing trend, a motorcycle trend, a school trend...

Skateboard trend.

Skateboards. Anything that was unique that kids to relate to.

How about the things that came out of the East via the soul trip—the various dance crazes?

No. It all influenced us, though. I remember, Brian and I, our fa-vorite records when we started out were "Locomotion" by Little Eva, "Mashed Potatoes" we loved. The 4 Seasons' "Sherry" was a big influ-ence on Brian. The Cascades. That whole Cameo-Parkway East Coast sound. "The Twist." We didn't understand it, but we liked it, like any young consumer. We were very impressed with what Goffin and King were doing. We followed them very closely, and Barry [Mann] and Cyn-thia [Weil].

Barry and Cynthia were writing for Spector, about that time?

Right. That was a little bit later. I know that Spector with the Crys-tals' "He's a Rebel" really hit Brian hard. I think the Spector influence is obvious in productions like "Be True to Your School."

You co-wrote "In My Room" with Brian. At the time, that seemed like a real progression for the Beach Boys. Their earlier work was ob-servations of external, social phenomenon, but that was their first in-trospective, personal piece. How did you and Brian work together?

Well, when we wrote that one, we actually wrote another similar ballad at the same time. The other one wasn't recorded. I can't think of the name. We wrote them about two in the morning. I was on bass, Brian on organ. I started that one off, Brian picked it up. The chords were a combination of both our thoughts and the melody was totally Brian's. We used to write mostly like that. We'd get an idea, one of us would hop on piano, one on guitar, and we'd figure out the chords. Almost all the lyrics we wrote together. We'd sit and pick apart each other's lyrics, trying to get them tight and as good as we could. I never bothered with Brian's melodies, because, well, he's one of the most prolific melody writers of all time. Once in a while I'd object to chords or certain patterns. With Brian it was the same way. From that point on, anybody who wrote with Brian never got involved musically: Roger Christian, Asher [lyricist for *Pet Sounds*].

Van Dyke Parks...

Maybe Van Dyke. I don't even know if he got involved, because Brian become so strong and authoritative it was hard to wrestle any kind of control from him. Van Dyke affected his piano playing. That was around "Good Vibrations" and that scene.

Did the whole surf music scene begin with Dick Dale, in '62?

Yeah. Dick Dale started it. His sound was considered "surf." For example, his "Peppermint Man." Dennis Wilson was the first Beach Boy to pick up on surfing. He was aware of Dick Dale, the Pendleton jackets and that whole shot. It just rubbed off. I never surfed. I was a hot-rod freak. I had a 409. One day we were driving up to Los Angeles looking for a part for my car, and I said, "Let's write a song called '409'. We'll do a thing 'Giddy up, giddy up,' meaning horses for horsepower," just kidding around. We came back and put it to three simple chords in five minutes, and it developed into a million-dollar car craze.

It was one of the first songs that California kids could identify with as being a mirror image of them. Maybe before that everything in music was East-Coast oriented.

Another thing. California has always been the leader in car trends: raked, lowered, moons. So when you think about it, when someone came out with a song about those things, the kids glommed onto it.

The surf mania phenomenon that Dale was a part of was especially indigenous to California at first. Didn't Capitol spend about $1,000,000 to push him nationwide, and he only sold in Southern California?

That's incorrect. Capitol paid $100,000 to get him, two albums a year. The reason he didn't happen was that they put him with Jimmy Economides, who didn't know what he was doing. And you know, Dick went down the tubes. I didn't call any shots on that. I don't know where Nick Venet was; Voyle Gilmore produced Dick's first album. He was a good producer for standard pop, but he didn't understand contemporary stuff. He had done the Kingston Trio. Nobody really understood rock music of this particular vein. It's what we used to call straight eights with the accent on the fourth beat that was the basic premise. It was a feel thing. Maybe a few guys had that feel. Brian had it. I had it. Terry Melcher and Jan Berry had it. Terry and Bruce Johnston put out "Little Cobra," called themselves the Rip Chords. Brian and I sang on a lot of Jan & Dean records. Jan couldn't sing for beans, but he had good production ideas. He was with Lou Adler. Lou didn't understand it, but he knew Brian had talent and he went after him. That's one of Lou's fortes.

What happened to Dick Dale and Jan & Dean?

Dick made about four albums for Capitol which stiffed out. It was all a big merchandising scam and it didn't work. They took Dick out of his environment and put him in a manufactured one. He got discouraged and around 1965 he split for Hawaii. He started gigging there and built up a following for two years. Somebody suggested he try to come back to the States, so he pooled his funds and bought a club in Riverside, the Dick Dale Club. He plays every weekend now to a full house. I was going to sign him to RCA and cut him. It was like, bring back a living legend! Jan & Dean. Ironically, in '64 or '65, about six months after he did "Dead Man's Curve" (which Brian and I sang on), Jan got in a wreck. He had a Corvette, used to whip around town. He was on Sunset Blvd. and he turned off some street and hit a parked car. Had a very bad head injury. They didn't expect him to survive the operation. He survived, but he came out not exactly normal in the sense that we might recognize it. So that now, in January 1971, he's maybe 80% normal, but there was a time when he was only 40% normal. He's into producing still, and in three or four years he'll be back to normal. Now Dean...Dean never sang on any of those records. He was kind of left out, never got a chance to develop his talents. He has a company called Kittyhawk Graphics, and he's done a lot of artwork for me, a lot of album covers. He's a very simple, quiet, very together guy.

The next scene after hot rods was what might be called folk-rock. The L.A. scene with the Byrds, Adler's people like Barry McGuire and P.F. Sloan, the Mamas and Papas.

The Byrds were the first, then the Grass Roots through Sloan and Lou Adler, then the Mamas and Papas, the second wave of California music. Later, another "longhaired" group was the Peanut Butter Conspiracy at Columbia, which I produced. First one of those groups I recall was called the Sons of Adam. I signed them in '65 when I was working at Decca.

Did you do their single cover of the Yardbirds' "Mister, You're A Better Man Than I"?

Right.

The Peanut Butter Conspiracy seemed to me at the time to be an L.A. version of the Airplane.

No, absolutely not. They were just a group I saw at the Troubadour one night. I dug the chick's voice, signed them. We cut two albums for Columbia; one single hit, "Twice is Life."

Were you on Columbia's staff as a producer or independent?

On the staff. I came over there, did an album with Gene Clark, then the four albums with the Byrds. Did two with Chad & Jeremy. Cut a couple of chart records with the Spiral Staircase. Worked on four cuts on [Simon & Garfunkel's] *Bookends* with Paul and Roy Halee. That's when Sagittarius started, in my free time. Are you familiar with that scene?

Yeah. The Sagittarius and then the Millennium LP with Curt Boettcher. What kind of market were those records aimed at? Sort of an intellectual Association-type thing? At the time, '68, they were labeled "art rock."

They were both done right after the Byrds. I don't know if it was an ego trip or what. I just wanted to have something of my own to experiment with. I had a song called "My World Fell Down" that I wanted to cut with Chad & Jeremy. They said no. I knew it was a hit, so I went down and cut a track. And it was the first 16-track recording in the industry, to my knowledge. I synched up two eight -tracks, put marks on the tape, put them on one drive train. It worked. Glenn Campbell sang on it. I was afraid he'd have contractual problems as he was signed to Capitol, so he said, "I'll disguise my voice" and he did. Bruce Johnston came in, 'cause they were cutting "Heroes and Villains" in the next studio. He put a few tracks on. Contrary to what some people thought, that record was not a spin-off of the Beach Boys. Brian had nothing to do with it.

Did either Sagittarius or Millennium sell?

Yeah, Millennium did about 26,000 when I left there. Sagittarius still gets ordered. It was the first metaphysical trip.

It was one of the first albums to used tasteful segueing, from track to track.

That's one of my pet scenes. And I must give Brian Wilson credit for that, from "Heroes and Villains." But you don't have to have a story to segue; you can segue from song to song. Just overlap a little track. Curt Boettcher produced Millennium. He had a group called The Ballroom that did a fantastic album that was never released. It was cut in '65. At the time, it made *Sgt. Pepper* look pathetic.

How'd you get with the Byrds?

I didn't. I had very short hair; I'm coming off "Younger Girl" by the Hondells. The Byrds were ultra hip and longhaired. They kind of reject-ed me because of the way I looked and was. It was a long hassle, win-ning their respect. It took me about four months and the *Younger Than Yesterday* album to get to the point where we had good mutual respect. Winning Crosby's respect is no easy job, believe me. He's very sharp in every right. So's McGuinn. Finally ended up hitting it off very well. Did *Notorious Byrd Brothers*, which is still a favorite of many people, like Jac Holzman. When I met Mick Jagger that was the first thing he said: "You produced my all-time favorite album." And I think *Notorious* would be placed among the top 100 albums of the decade.

You did a great single with the Byrds that never made it: "Lady Friend."

Well, that was a creation by Crosby and myself. Everybody else, in-cluding Columbia, was against it. The record didn't happen. Went to No. 1 in Hawaii, though. Then we did *Sweetheart of the Rodeo* in Nash-ville. The first rock group to cut a pure country album.

There's a void between that and when you went to RCA. Was that when you formed Together Records?

Yeah, Together Transcon Records. We did *Preflyte* with Jim Dickson, bought a bunch of Byrds masters, which I knew were lying around some-place. We put out a good package with the Byrds' consent. There was an archives thing, *Early LA.* It was mostly pickup stuff, tapes of Crosby, Dino Valente. It didn't chart. Some people enjoy that stuff. I get a kick out of exposing developmental stages. I think that's good, to see your mistakes, and laugh at them, and grow.

***Vintage Dead* has proven that theory.**

That was me. I bought those tapes from Bob Cohen of the Family Dog.

Together folded shortly after those two albums, didn't it?

We got about nine months into it, then Transcon's stock went from 32 to 7 ¼ in about two months, so all money was frozen. The entire en-tertainment scene under Mike Curb folded. We froze too. I got out of it OK. I have a way of doing that. A lot of people are concerned about me since I left RCA, but give me a call a year from now and I think things'll be going smooth as hell. Part of it might relate to Dr. Malthus' Psychocy-bernetics: a nice positive power approach to positive thinking.

Were there any further archives projects planned at Together?

Yeah, a whole series. A [Lord] Buckley album, a bunch of early San Francisco bands.

Is there any chance those albums will get out?

No. Because Bobby Cohen, Peter Abrams and those paranoid pricks from San Francisco don't know what the hell's going on and they just cause a lot of problems. They're afraid to let go of those tapes. That Dead album has done 100,000 copies already. I did two of those for Columbia, the Grace Slick and the Great Society albums. They sold over 150,000 with Grace's permission. They were crude, you know, but I admire people like the Dead. Jerry Garcia, Grace, who can stand up and say, "OK, I was crude. That was a worse side of us and now there's a better side. We're not ashamed." I think it's a good attempt at opening up yourself in a different way. I'm sure Barbra Streisand would never go along with it.

What about RCA? You were West Coast vice president in charge of rock. Why did you leave?

Well, I'm not really into the linear approach that corporate politics has to offer. "RCA" is only three letters, and there's always a wall behind them to hold them up. "RCA" does not breathe, it doesn't vote, it doesn't perform. It's personalities involved. RCA's most detrimental aspect is corporate management. It's run by accountants engaged in a "business" who only put out good records as an occasional sideline. Look at their treatment of Nilsson. RCA is the kind of company that will give up on somebody if he doesn't hit big right away. Harry worked on his new album for several months. It's called [The] Point and it's going to be one of the best albums you'll hear. But RCA wanted me to go in there with him and do it in four weeks. You just can't do that. Warner Brothers or Elektra spend time with their acts, stand behind them until they make it. Look how long it took them to hit with the Dead, James Taylor. The list goes on forever.

Have you ever cut any soul?

No, I guess I've never dug R&B. The only R&B I like is Otis and Motown. I'm just doing what I do straight ahead. I do best what I like. I like to have fun, that's a way of being creative. Otherwise I could kiss ass at RCA for 20 years. Hell, I'd rather go out screaming now than walk out smiling. I owe music a lot. I've hung out with some very talented people and I'm grateful.

Whither rock 'n' roll? You mentioned you thought trends have given way to personalized statements. Now it seems to be moving toward solo performers: Elton John, Van Morrison.

What's going on now is a reaction to the over-saturation of the audience with amplified brash music. It goes in cycles. Tom Jones is filling Sinatra's spot. Glenn Campbell is replacing Dean Martin. The Beach Boys replaced the Four Freshmen.

There's a great cut on the Super Stocks' album, "Draggin' Deuce." It has these fantastic cascading Leon Russell type piano rolls, castanets all over.

Yeah! My Phil Spector period. That was Leon; he played all those dates, with Hal Blaine, Tommy Tedesco, Glenn. The fad records. Well, Capitol would say, "Can you do us a skateboard album for $10,000?" Sure, finish it up in a couple of days. Jimmy Economides got the idea that hot-rod albums were the coming thing. Somebody said slot cars were going to happen, so Roger Christian and I did the Revells' album for Reprise. And they sold!

What about Detroit? Isn't there an indigenous scene there, like the early LA days? The music is homogenous: hard, loud, simplistic, but vital in a way to those people. Where does your work with Sky (RCA) come in? Are they a typical Detroit band to you?

No. I signed Sky and worked with them a little on the album. That was Jimmy Miller's baby, and he does everything great. I prefer to call them 'Suburban Rock.' Their parents are bankers and doctors. They're a diverse band, really a lot of variety for kids 18 and 19. A lot ahead of them. *[Note: Good call, Gary. Sky was future Knack leader Doug Fieger's first band. —ed.]*

It seems the Beach Boys have lost their commercial appeal. Maybe their potential audience is yet to be fully realized...

Maybe. They haven't had a chart hit in a long time. Brian just doesn't care anymore.

What might happen in future rock worth noting?

I think the next thing to happen will be a religious group, people with a leaning toward the occult and able to reach a mass audience deeply.

Like early Doors or *Wild in the Streets*?

The rock kid who becomes president? No, a real cult thing which is able to affect masses. One last thing. Progress in the industry will come about from new people working together, contributing to improve the industry from within. New acts need to be nurtured and there have to be people with the power to do that, to confront the old corporate consciousness attitude.

REVIEW:

The Sonics *Boom*

Fusion magazine, Nov. 12, 1971

She's got long black hair and a big black car
I know what you're thinkin,' but you won't get far
She's gonna make you itch
'Cause she's a witch!

The Sonics, of 1965 "Witch" fame. They're not "back," but they did leave a few artifacts laying around, one of which I picked up at a second-hand store in Santa Rosa last week. Depending, this album will run you anywhere from forty-four cents to seventy-five cents, and it's worth every penny.

In the rock archives they're listed I guess under "Pacific Northwest Scene, Early Sixties." Apparently, they were just clean young kids decked out in 3/4 length 1964 trench-coats, hooded wool-lined jackets and hard shoes, digging the Wailers, Frantics, Kingsmen and Viceroys, maybe at the Spanish Castle just south of Seattle. Rainy weather gear. Vox organ and burping sax, they had the right combination. But The Sonics weren't another in the long line of in-bred Northwest groups. They drew just as heavily back then from Ray Davies and his brood, and that's what makes their music such a kick in the ass even now. In fact, they make even more noise than the Kinks did and they're total punks! The two post-"Witch" blasters here are "Cinderella" and "He's Waitin'" (on which the rest of the group bunches up behind lead vocalist Gerry Roslie and apes Davies & Co.'s phrasing to a T). These two songs are thunder and lightning, and the Sonics' "Louie Louie" is hands-down the brashest version I've ever heard.

It's out of hand, how they could rev up so hard on such primitive nuggets as "Jenny Jenny" and "Let the Good Times Roll." The old Lenny Welch "Since I Fell for You" is given a great late Fifties ballad feel of its very own, and it's truly fine. You also get a really sloppy 2:45 of "Hitch Hike" and just over two minutes of Adam Faith's stateside non-hit "It's Alright." The latter is a nonstop special with Roslie's screaming, a fuzzy Fender solo through a tube amp and Mick Avory-type drumming roughing it up better than Faith ever did.

And since those soggy Seattlelites put a lot of stock by Freddie King, Roslie conveniently penned "Shot Down," a hardcore King-sized guitar/ sax romp. Machine-gun snare, Rufus Thomas guitar breaks and James Brown are in there too.

Wow!

REVIEW:

Eggs Over Easy Good 'N' Cheap

Creem magazine, January 1973

Sometimes it gets downright hard to remain cynical. Witness this latest destined-for-obscurity near-masterpiece (produced by Link Wray) from three former Berkeley folkies who pulled out for the Big Apple, thence to England where they turned into ace rock & rollers thanx in part to Chas Chandler.

Make no mistake. Eggs Over Easy is America's closest answer to Brinsley Schwarz, who were England's answer to America's answer to England's answer to America's... and they also have something to do with the long dead Lovin' Spoonful and legitimate "goodtime music."

It must have been about 1969 when I stopped listening to *Daydream*, *Hums* and *Do You Believe in Magic*. By then the Spoonful canon of innocent love songs and sweet post-teen ditties to sunlight, new mowed lawns and jug band music, their humor—all seemed suddenly distant, as if the shadows of "You Didn't Have To Be So Nice," "Good Day Sunshine" and the Sopwith Camel peaked with the bright Pop optimism of the '65-'66 season and would never flicker past us again. Then, I reasoned, Times Had Changed, apocalyptic visions crowded every head, and the light focused on every scene, music included, became a little darker, a shade more resolute and serious.

Times do change, I guess. 'Cause in *Good 'N' Cheap* there's a plentitude of good-feeling, good-sounding American rock music once again, and it's rather delicious. For some idea of the flavor, start with the deja vu jacket; it invites scrutiny if only for its depiction of a scene so oft repeated (comic books, movies, oil illustrations in *Esquire* and *Playboy*), so deliberately American in conception and execution, as to have attained legit mythic status years ago. You can't escape it, or the premise of every square inch of music it packages. Love it or leave it. This is plastic salt

& pepper shaker, stainless-steel creamer, magenta-trim restaurant cof-
fee-cup music, short order U.S.A. stuff, no more and no less.

Did they garner their firm roots vision from that trip to Merry Olde,
from hanging out with Link Wray, from California or Ohio or Wisconsin
Sixties kidhood? I don't know, but Austin de Lone's voice is as arch-state-
side as Jackson Browne's or that guy in Earthquake and it's the first one
you hear, on "Party Party," a perky tune with a familiar yet untraceable
ring. "The Factory" comes on strutting a little J.Geils/Contours spunk
with de Lone's dandy phrasing and somebody's (his, or Jack O'Hara's)
quick cut guitar. On the soft side, "Song Is Born of Riff and Tongue"
sports a readymade 'Spanish' melody lilt and a vocal that eases into territory somewhere between Art Garfunkel and Little Feat's Lowell George,
Silvertone ether pretty.

They've got a solid synthetic aesthetic too, Eggs. "Don't Let Nobody" and the great "Henry Morgan" prime themselves on bass figures
on loan from the Soul Survivors and the Capitols ("Cool Jerk"), and
yet, with "Runnin' Down to Memphis," display equal affection for Floyd
Cramer pianistics.

And the best comes last: "Night Flight," a taut rocker with lines strung
to both C. Berry and Grand Funk's "Upsetter" that finds the whole band
sounding their strongest and noticeably digging every second. Perfectly
placed, simple guitar frames the song around the same kind of full-chord
flame that made Link Wray's recent "God Out West" such a mover.

When groups like this show up with records like this one, it's casino
odds that something's in the air. It's almost enough to push those apocalyptic visions right outa your head, for a while at least.

REVIEW:

America *Homecoming*

Creem magazine, February 1973

Come on. You didn't think "Horse with No Name" and "Ventura Highway" would get these guys voted into the pantheon of CSN&Y Springalopoco second-liners where such as the redoubtable Guess Who ("These Eyes") and Stampeders ("Sweet City Woman") resided for a while before packing off to greener pastures, did you?

That was just initial surface scratch. Where this lukewarm expatriate combo belongs is at the absolute head of seventy-two-ish Blandrock, that ignominious contemporary subgenre whose ascent has been torched by stalwarts like Bread, Gallery, Jonathan Edwards, the new Neil Diamond and the ever-glossy T of P, Al Green and, only by indirect taint, James Taylor, Neil Young and those everlovin' Carpenters.

Never mind that it's mediocrity *en excelsis*, gutless and indulgent, vacuous and acoustic. This bass- and drumless trio of simpering Seventies rollos decorating the cover, with their upswept three-part croon, off-balance leads and mournful ego-sobs, represent the smiling countenance of what is so far the single most pervasive radio trend of the new decade. Their transparent half-melodies and almost maddening thinness and lack of imagination cover both dials and have been known to drive intolerant rock 'n' roll motorists just a little insane on numerous occasions. But they do connect to the main body of rock stuff, somewhere around where the forlorn Bee Gees and the winsome Lobo hang out, and hell, their naiveté and the insolent stupidity of their lyrics are too good to pass up!

With squeaking frets, chandelier piano, a persistent wimp melody and oblique scraps of California Myth scattered throughout, "Ventura Highway" is the group's stupidest hit yet and a real contender for this month's Blandrock crown; white, glassy, colorless space maneuvers, that's all, and absolute verbal outrage; phrases like "wind blowing through your hair," "nights stronger than moonshine," "purple rain" riding around that idiotic guitar figure. They don't even try to disguise the fact that the singer's heavy two-line conversation with free spirit Joe is an idle means of filling up unused musical space. This is great!

What else? Nothing you'd remember me telling you. "Don't Cross That River" timidly approaches Thunderclap Newman on a rundown night, "Cornwall Blank" redoes "Wooden Ships," and "Saturn Nights" breaks into a one-riff-factored-to-infinity scheme like most of *After the Goldrush*.

But that's all peripheral, just like America's music. What we have here is the perfect imperfection of a major Seventies strain seen up close. No opaque tones, depth or gross appendages left hanging out, just well-polished surface gloss, shining aural accompaniment to four more years, the Rise of Vapidity and the global enshrinement of Blandrock.

Put on either side of *Homecoming*, sit back and if you try, visions of the embittered P.F. Sloan of 1965 and the arms-folded Standells will materialize. After all, part of what made those two greats so much fun was their total naiveté and lack of 'integrity' in the face of the musical identities they parlayed into quickflash immortality. Shameless teen wimps caught by public favor in the midst of performing gross imitations of their very own pop idols under the hot lights, they prospered in a disarming, funny sort of way that once again proved the existence of the undecipherable magic ethos of this parallel rock & roll world. It isn't that far between "Sins of The Family," "Mainline" and "Horse with No Name." Enjoy it now and later too.

FEATURE:

The Beach Boys: A California Saga

The Revival of Coastal Consciousness featuring The Beach Boys, Dean Torrence, California, American Spring

Written with Greg Shaw, Ken Barnes, *Phonograph Record Magazine*, May 1973

One of the perks of running a record company's in-house publication in the Seventies was that, for the most part, as long as he or she hyped the label's product, an editor was free to fill up the pages with whatever else seemed worthwhile. I enjoyed this benefit editing Warner Bros. Records' Circular *and* Waxpaper, *and Marty Cerf enjoyed it at United Artists'* Phonograph Record Magazine. *It's no secret that at PRM Cerf and Greg Shaw and contributors had an agenda: promoting classic pop and basic rock 'n' roll, genres that, by 1973, were in much disrepair, thanks to the self-conscious progressivism that grew out of psychedelia. The following cover story, while it hardly threatened the preeminence of the Golden State studies of Carey McWilliams, attempted a socio-musicological analysis of California teen culture. We'd write some version of this piece every year, on premises as slim as rumors of the Beach Boys planning a recording session, or a new single by Sunrays singer Rick Henn (I think one year it might've even have been the Wombles' "Wombling Summer Party"). That's all it took and we were off, predicting the return of good times and great records.*

It's summer once again in California. While much of the country is still buried in snow, early April has brought the first heat wave. Air conditioners are being dusted off, stores are stocking up on t-shirts, and kids are counting the days till the end of school. The beaches are starting to fill up, and observers are quick to point out that they haven't seen this many surfboards in years.

California summers have always had the potential for something greater than mere summer anywhere else. That old truism about "the land of milk and money" begins seeping out of the collective unconscious as people, especially the young, throw themselves into the roles of pleasure-seeking mobility that are theirs by birthright.

You don't have to prowl the beaches to know that it's becoming less unconscious all the time, nothing like it was in '64, but rapidly approaching the same level of self-assertion. The air is full of car radios blasting out the Beach Boys' latest single, *"water, water, get yourself in that cool clear water..."* To a lot of us, it's the most agreeable invitation we've heard in a long time...

MILLION DOLLAR BABIES

In a time when most Americans between the ages of twelve and twenty spend their golden days basking in the reflected radiance of a widely acknowledged Youth Culture (constructed and maintained by people pushing thirty and beyond), when most adults daily preen before that same light, ever conscious that it is their concern as well to honor the integrity of that precious flame in times like these, it's hard to conceive of 1963, of that age of the last big kidhood wingding before the generational shift, when contented kids and contented parents weren't one and the same.

Though it's hard to believe, there actually was a time when Youth simply signified non-adult status. Adults and youth each held to their own preferences, standards and models. Unlike Fifties folks, early Sixties moms & pops weren't vigilant in their efforts to destroy an incipient youth revolt. Nor were they preoccupied with trying to participate in it. They simply didn't care. The economic situation of the period afforded them the luxury of reveling in their own liberation. Toward the activities of the young they remained mildly disdainful, yet tolerant. There was—particularly in California—enough space, time and currency for everyone to indulge themselves. *"Have a good time, kids."*

And they did. If the violent upheavals of rockers, radio and the Big Beat ignited the initial spark in '58 and set kids to thinking of themselves as outcasts from the privileged world of adults, the cash and tolerance of '61-'65 torched the even more profound second flash: the realization by growing numbers of teenagers that their collective strength possessed a power that could reckon with anything in the adults' arsenal. On the

West Coast, a combination of factors stoked this point of view, and the resultant teen group stance, to bonfire proportions.

Surf and hot-rod music simply furnished the images for the articulation of certain widely held teenage attitudes and assumptions of the day. Kids spoke to other kids about matters indigenous to their world. This exclusivity precluded the participation of anyone other than those whose age qualified them for membership in that world. The music itself didn't translate; Ralph Gleason, Andy Warhol and the editors of *Newsweek* had no way to comprehend it, and it carried its power with a confidence and cool grace totally unlike the sounds of the frantic Fifties. One was a fist through a plate glass window and the other was riding comfortable shotgun on a downtown cruise run. As anthem and background score, the splash and pit blast of surf/drag accompanied what was essentially the first of a series of solidified moves toward the building of authentic generation-consciousness.

THE KOOKIE LITTLE PARADISE

California was long ago assigned its role as Paradise West and it's never quite managed to shake it. Early landscape painters charted the baked-in surreality of the land and spoke of *"the mocking brilliancy of the sky,"* while everybody from the Mamas and Papas to the Trade Winds ("New York's a Lonely Town When You're The Only Surfer Boy") lamented their temporary absence from utopia.

Whether California's claims are valid belittles the point. Somewhere beneath the splayed fascha-lights of the corner Jack in the Box are hidden the terms of the shotgun marriage of ambition and imagination that has always defined the reality of the Golden State. To have been a teenager in California from 1961 to 1966 was to have been the ace-high end product of the most affluent, leisure-oriented consumer society in the history of the planet, and from the enviable situation proceeded *Surf*, the music and the style.

That particular California, that blazing daylight and floodlit nighttime printed circuit of a place overrun with long clean boulevards, beaches and billboards, where hamburgers sizzled on an open grill night and day, where the pursuit of fun was practically the duty of everyone under twenty-one — that was the everyday utopia inhabited by the people like Dick Dale, Jan Berry and Dean Torrence, and the original Wilson brothers.

There was no special reason for surfing or hot-rodding to command the central role in all of this. The crucial component was the teenage impulse, the fun drive, the precise element that's been gingerly removed from the lives of today's teens by a multitude of devious older brothers intent on leaving their mark behind them. Miniature golf, slot cars, snow-skiing or trampolines could have functioned equally well, since the basic process was the linking up of visible, reinforced images from adolescent experience with that single prime impulse. Together they would lick the world.

Surf Route

"From Balboa to Anaheim, San Bernardino to Riverside/All the kids in all L.A. come to hear Dick Dale play..."

The genesis of a distinctly California rock style can be traced to the Lettermen's super casual, harmony-laden "Come Back Silly Girl" (1962) or the Four Preps' "Down By The Station" (1960), whose clean-cut white vocals prefigured standard surf music maneuvers. But the real antecedents in the specific sense were of course the two West L.A. blonds with the two-track and the empty garage. Jan & Dean's "Baby Talk" (1959) and "Heart and Soul" (1961) once and for all set the standards for California rock and roll; brisk, lightweight, sparse or Spectorian, always white and pop. With friends like Bruce Johnston, Sandy Nelson, Terry Melcher and Lou Adler they forged the prototype, even if they had to wait a few years for the potential market to reveal itself.

The potency of the surf and dragging metaphor should be fairly obvious; an obsession with speed and performance, one part sport challenge, one part adolescent crazy, all of it pertaining directly to the concept of *"coolness"* as perfected in the Fifties and handed down even to the present day. Dick Dale, the Marketts and the Duals had already placed surf-labeled instrumentals on California charts in 1961.

The Beach Boys, ne Pendletons, hit with "Surfin'" in February of '62, followed with "Surfin' Safari"/ "409" five months later, hit top ten nationally the following March with "Surfin' USA" / "Shut Down." By August and "Surfer Girl" / "Little Deuce Coupe" it was unarguable: a major phenomenon was taking place. West Coast youth culture had actually, through the brothers from Hawthorne, asserted itself and shouted back at both the Eastern pop establishment and the non-rock world at large.

To Jan & Dean, already established stars since 1958, "Surfin'" sounded familiar and not especially innovative. It was, after all, built around a reworking of the bass vocal riff from "Baby Talk." Things changed considerably, though, when the duo played a South Bay hop and were backed up by the Wilson kids. "We did a couple of their songs with them as an encore and the crowd response was very enthusiastic," recalls Dean. "On the way back from the show Jan and I agreed that something pretty strong was starting to happen around this style."

Soon enough, the nucleus of the premier California-rock family began forming, around the Beach Boys; Jan & Dean and with them writers Phil (P.F.) Sloan and Steve Barri and Don Altfeld, disc jockey Roger Christian as lyricist on 90% of all surf/drag records, writer-singers Bruce Johnston, Terry Melcher and Gary Usher, session men like Glen Campbell and Leon Russell.

With the music's generally enthusiastic reception across the country ("even in places where the nearest thing to surf is maybe the froth on a chocolate shake," Nick Venet's notes to *Surfin' USA*) came the demise of New York as the absolute stronghold of teenage music. For the first time in California, kids turned on radios and heard other kids who sounded just like them, singing about how great it was to be living on the West Coast. Now an alternative to the pomaded, thin-tie & sport-coat regalia pushed by Clark's *American Bandstand*. No more the reedy accordion pipes of the Brooklyn Italians. Hell, KFWB's playin' this record and the guy's singing about La Jolla, Manhattan Beach and Santa Cruz. Walk proud.

The ultimo tuff riff, home-grown, surfin,' man. The exhilaration of Chuck Berry's "Almost Grown" and "Back in the USA" coupled with the Malibu breeze, provided the mirror image. Identification. And the whole scene was hustled into a bigger and better sense of participation for all involved, through the combined efforts of a) the folk poet-historians themselves, singing about experiences close to their audience, and b) the merchandisers who merely followed the crest of the wave. "Surf City" and "Catch a Wave" supplied the idyllic vision. It was only up to Janzen, Hang Ten, John Severson and Rick Griffin, Levis (immortalized in the Majorettes' classic surf costume anthem, "White Levis") and Vita-pakt (skateboards) to lend an assist.

> *"It was hard to know exactly how much what we were doing was affecting the teenage music audience in general. We'd go into auditoriums across the county and there'd be kids dressed exactly like us, but we never knew how widespread it was, if the phenomenon extended beyond what we ourselves could see. Until it was all over the cover of Time.*

*"We came to look at it like we were piloting a boat. We'd pull all
these maneuvers and then slow down and wait for our following to come
around. It was strange to think, that at one time, you could go out to
Malibu and there'd be nobody out there. Then, one day—whoosh!—So
crowded you couldn't even get in the water. And in some way we all were
the cause of that whole situation."*
—Dean Torrence

"Fun Fun Fun" and "Summer Means Fun" roiled up the tunedecks, doing Scott McKenzie-type chamber of commerce honors. What
they synthesized was a perfectly cut, organized world view, emanating
from Los Angeles, California. The custom raunch and ritual of surf/drag
explained both motivation and the means to success in the sunburnt paradise. Records like "Our Car Club" and "All Summer Long" supplied
the foundations of an extensive value system that offered participants
(any kid with the money to buy a 45) advice on automotive aesthetics,
boy-girl relationships, slang glossaries and informal tips on cool and uncool behavior. Rather like knowing whether or not to like Carly's new
album or sew patches on your perfectly new jeans.

School's Out Forever

So complete was the idealized California portrait as sung by the
Beach Boys, Jan & Dean, Hondells, etc., everybody wanted in. Surf
bands sprang up in Colorado (the Astronauts), Minnesota (the Trashmen of "Surfin' Bird" fame) and Michigan (the Rivieras with "California
Sun"). In California, the influx of teenagers eager to join the in-crowd
overcrowded the public beaches and kicked sand over the once noble
surfer image.

John Severson's *Surfer* had been a bi-monthly sheet for genuine en-
thusiasts of the sport. With the rise of Surfmania in '63, the magazine's
circulation spiraled, the format slickened, and old line readers filled
the letter column with denunciations of the irresponsible new breed of
surfers and their music, citing the image-tarnishing activities of hodads,
greasers and assorted surf vandals; Iron Cross-wearing punks breaking
into beachfront homes, beer orgies, looting, girl surf packs terrorizing
beachgoers. Clearly, rock 'n' roll had begun to demonstrate its awesome
powers of triumph through trivialization. Rock can literally take the puff
out of anything's sails, and when enough mindless teenage numbers
amass behind it, it can rub the seriousness and respect off any polished

surface. Hawaii and Haight-Ashbury will never be the same again.

If Surf, in its brief three-year reign, furnished the focal point for the channeling of youthful energy, it gave testimony that such energy had always existed and indeed always will. Mid-50's teenagers rioted in theatres around the globe with the premier of *Rock Around The Clock.* By 1964, there were dozens of unexplainable outbreaks in Ft. Lauderdale (cf. Bob Seger's "Florida Time") and along the Oregon seacoast, where thousands of high-school and college kids would gather and brazenly attack outnumbered police in a drunken frenzy. Officials nervously wrote the events off to the influence of alcohol alone, but something stronger was plainly beginning to assert itself. These were the first the visible displays of those feelings of mass youth solidarity that have, until recently, provided the substance for all talk about the existence of a genuine youth culture. We now recognize that sense of community as having worldwide dimensions.

In actuality, the perspective that surf music lent to the members of its group was less hostile and more gently assertive, as in the lyrics to the Trashmen's "New Generation":

> There's a brand new generation lookin' for a lot of room
> Ninety-nine days' vacation, everybody's outa school
> They all got somethin' goin,' their plans have all been made
> And when they get loose this summer, nothin's gonna stand in their way
> They're gonna go dancin' every Friday night, swim when the song comes
> on
> You couldn't wake 'em Sunday with a hydrogen bomb
> Shakin,' surfin,' flyin' high, there's gonna be a party tonight
> Grab your baby and your guitar too
> We can't get started any too soon
> Well, this brand new generation is movin' at a terrible pace
> That'[s a good indication they ain't got time to waste

Brian Wilson, Roger Christian, Jan Berry & Co. left an incredible canon of work celebrating their version of the land of fun & sun. "The feelings you get from going to school, being in love, winning and losing in sports" gave Brian his inspiration. The legendary 409 Chevy belonged to Gary Usher, who recalls driving around L.A. with the Wilsons when the idea to write a song about his car struck. "We'll do a thing 'Giddyup' meaning horses for horsepower," said Usher. "We were just kidding around. We came back and put it to three simple chords and it developed into a million-dollar car craze"

Christian drew largely on his recollections of high-school hot rod-
ding back East. Someone suggested he write a song about a gutless car
with sharp looks, so he fitted his pitstop poetics to Brian's melody "No-
Go Showboat." An ad for Lyons dragstrip he heard over the air one day
suggested a novelty line to Christian: *"The dee-jay is sayin' on my favorite
Station/Drag City races are the fastest in the nation."* While clocking in
high speeds along Sunset Blvd. in an effort to straighten the sequence
of street names for "Dead Man's Curve" he was stopped by a cop who
released him on the strength of his unusual yet valid explanation.

Various family members sang on each other's records, and most of
Jan & Dean's hits bore the co-authorship of B. Wilson, including "The
New Girl in School," "Surf City" and the production opus "Ride The
Wild Surf." Sloan and Barri, songwriting for Jan & Dean, managed a
brief stint as the Fantastic Baggys and one special summer hit "Tell 'Em
I'm Surfin,'" while also penning Bruce & Terry's super "Summer Means
Fun."

Johnston and Melcher in turn commandeered an existing group,
the Rip Chords, restyling their sound and in fact performing in place of
the group on some records. "Hey Little Cobra" went top five in late '63,
followed by "Three Window Coupe."

Christian and Gary Usher acted as a writing stable for anyone who
required their talents. Their output graced three Super Stocks albums
and dozens more by Dick Dale, the Hondells, Astronauts, Wheel Men
and Surfaris (whose instrumental "Wipe-Out" remains classic and
whose flip "Surfer Joe" is proto-punk). Bobby Darin wrote songs for the
Catalinas ("Hot Rod USA"), as did Jim McGuinn ("Beach Ball"), and
a multi-instrumentalist from Nashville dubbed himself into Ronnie &
The Daytonas and took honors with the acoustic-flavored "G.T.O." Usher and Dennis Wilson became the Four Speeds to do the rare "R.P.M."
single, while Brian revamped his own "Country Fair" as "I Do" for the
Castells. Also-rans include the Surftones, hundreds of Central Valley instrumental combos, the Chantays and their ghostly "Pipeline" and the
bald-headed Pyramids with "Penetration." East Coast counterfeiters included the Tokens and the Trade Winds.

The last loud notes of surf music were blown in 1965 and 1966,
but they were sweet. Murry Wilson had appropriated songwriter Rick
Henn from the Renegades and fashioned a group, the Sun Rays. Their
excellent "I Live for the Sun" and "Andrea" were speedy sunlit hits, but
mismanagement killed the group's hope for growth. They later surfaced
as the Rangers and the Snowmen for a couple of Kim Fowley fad sides.

Henn still scores bonafide surf films and still surfs with Dennis Wilson.

As genre pioneers, the Beach Boys quickly outgrew their competition, and their peak period can be discerned as commencing with the demise of their specifically surf-oriented material. "Fun Fun Fun," "I Get Around," "Dance Dance Dance" and "California Girls" provided their finest moments. In many ways these records capture the essence of California much better than the earlier, higher profile stuff.

SURFERS RULE

Almost from out of the blue the music appeared, owing totally to the interaction of the core California-rock family of writers and artists. Unlike subsequent surprise turns, these people all managed to propel themselves with an ineffable teenage grace for quite a while before fashion abandoned them. In the long run, they remained what they were at the outset: kids having a good time. They wound up grabbing the record industry by the balls long enough to insure that the presence of youth would never again be underestimated. You can trace the process. Take a look at either the covers of *Surfin' Safari* or *Surfin' USA* (1963) and you see the polite teenagers, rock 'n' roll aspirations tempered by the humility their youth enforces upon them. By *Shut Down Volume Two* (mid-'64), that reserve has vanished, replaced not by mean punk bravado, but by the epitome of casual suburban cool. There's the implicit acknowledgment that, yeah, they are the top dogs now. Y'know. Surfers rule.

But the surfers' reign was quickly swamped by the wave of British groups who took full command of the 1964 charts. The first outstandingly successful new American counterassault, the Byrds' "Mr. Tambourine Man" and folk-rock, combined a basically British instrumental/vocal sound with elliptical Dylanistic imagery; folk-rock's borrowings from the surf sound were chiefly restricted to a strong emphasis on production craftsmanship, stemming from the Beach Boys and Jan & Dean records, and a preoccupation with topicality. Bob Dylan followed in the Byrds' wake with "Like a Rolling Stone," and the boom was on, once again centered mainly in L.A.

FOLK CITY

Where hundreds of surf bands had flourished, folk-rockers in droves now sprang up. One such surfing group, the Crossfires, changed their name to the Turtles, recorded a Dylan song, and achieved national stardom virtually overnight. Even more successful was ex-Fantastic Baggy Flip Sloan; he and his partner Steve Barri, even while immersed in the surf, had been writing commercial tunes on the side for the likes of Betty Everett and Round Robin. Thus, being quite sharp and working closely with Lou Adler, who was probably quite sharper, Sloan found it very easy to adjust his handle to an enigmatic "P.F." and dash off an apocalyptic polemic called "Eve of Destruction." Sloan parlayed that hit into a national reputation as a folk poet (with two albums in that vein), and extensive songwriting assignments for the Turtles, Grass Roots, Johnny Rivers, and even Herman's Hermits.

The Beach Boys continued to sail along relatively unaffected by all the commotion, both British and folk-rock-induced. Having foresightedly abandoned explicitly surf/car-oriented records as far back as November 1963 ("Little Deuce Coupe" was the last), they moved to broaden their base of appeal with anthemic celebrations of teenage solidarity and good times ("Be True To Your School," "Fun Fun Fun," "I Get Around"). Brian Wilson, heavily influenced by Phil Spector's colossal production extravaganzas, honed his already impressive skills in that direction to the point where records like "Don't Worry Baby" achieved breathtaking heights of harmonic mastery. In an introspective moment, the Beach Boys wondered if they'd feel the same when they grew up (a disturbingly perceptive inquiry, as it turned out, both for them and the audience), then shook off the mood with two urgent invitations to dance, and roared back to No. 1 with a direct appeal to Rhonda.

Then, in the turbulent summer of '65, while McGuire ranted, the Byrds jangled, and Dylan wheezed out his vengeance, the Beach Boys struck a welcome note of normalcy with their epic tribute to West Coast feminity, which (despite generous and tolerant compliments to the rest of the country) left no doubt as to their essential ethnocentricity. Propelled by its unbeatable production, "California Girls" was another mythologizing monster, but a follow-up fling in a sophisticated style, "The Little Girl I Once Knew," was a relative failure; and it took the sheer sloppy exuberance of "Barbara Ann" (Dean Torrence taking lead vocal), a record which managed to capture the essential California spirit because it was strictly for *fun*, to bring them back to the top. Next came the group's first overt acknowledgment of folk-rock (not counting the perhaps unintentionally satirical version of "The Times They Are A-Changin'" on the *Party* LP), "Sloop John B." Characteristically, the Beach Boys steered away from controversial Dylan/protest-type numbers, preferring to dig up an old chestnut (previously recorded by Dick Dale back in '62) and create a brilliantly polished arrangement from worn-out folkie dross.

Other surf-era notables also prospered. Session men present on many a surfing hit (Hal Blaine, Leon Russell, etc.) played on "Mr. Tambourine Man" and other folk-rockers. Terry Melcher produced the first two Byrds albums and the hugely popular Raiders as well; while Bruce Johnston produced the first Columbia Raiders LP, did numerous sessions, and wound up joining the Beach Boys in '66, replacing temporary member Glen Campbell as Brian's touring surrogate, becoming a full-fledged B.B. and remaining with the group until 1972. Steve Barri continued to write with P.F. Sloan for a time, then became a hugely successful pop-schlock producer. Lou Adler, Jan & Dean's long-time producer, managed to keep his finger on the pulse all along, masterminding such successes as Johnny Rivers, Barry McGuire, the Mamas & Papas, Scott McKenzie, the Monterey Pop Festival, Spirit, Carole King, and Cheech & Chong.

Jan & Dean themselves had a rockier time of it. Where the Beach Boys had quickly jettisoned cars and surfing for singles topics, Jan & Dean persevered, satirizing the subjects half to death with "Dead Man's Curve," "Little Old Lady from Pasadena" and others; and had their final hit in the genre with "Sidewalk Surfin'" in November '64. Their plum M.C. role in the sensational *T.A.M.I. Show* was their last mass fling, but the theme song, "From All Over the World," was only a minor hit. Subsequently, they flirted with neo-Spectorianism ("You Really Know How to Hurt a Guy"), Sloan-Barri pop ("I Found a Girl") and folk-rock. Just as they had mocked the car craze, Jan & Dean demolished the self-consciously serious folk-rock phase in their devastatingly satirical *Folk 'N' Roll* LP, with numbers like "Folk City," "A Beginning From an End"—a sendup of their own satirical "Dead Man's Curve"; convolutions upon convolutions—and the right-wing parody "Universal Coward" (at least it sounded like a parody, until you considered Jan's subsequent WB effort, "Only a Boy," an apparently dead-serious musical attempt to justify the Vietnam War). Even Batman was a Jan & Dean target, but save for a fluke late '66 revival of the novelty "Popsicle," from their *Drag City* LP, they had no more real hits. They even lost a chart battle with the Yellow Balloon on the latter group's namesake song; and after Jan's accident, from which he is still slowly recovering, they faded out.

THE PROGRESSIVE ROCK EXPERIMENT

Folk-rock, particularly protest, enjoyed only a brief vogue, but strong new influences were coming to the fore as 1966 dawned. A novel concept of musical progression, pushing back the boundaries of pop music, was in evidence, spearheaded by the Beatles' *Rubber Soul* and *Revolver* albums. The Byrds, too, left Dylan behind, and soared off into new areas of instrumental improvisation and lyrical obscurantism ("Eight Miles High," "5D"). Simon & Garfunkel brought in a new, arty seriousness in lyrical approach, while the Mamas & Papas did the same for vocal arrangements. In England the Yardbirds were exploring guitar technology while the Kinks toned down their raucous blasts and turned to witty sociological essays, and the Rolling Stones smashed the three-minute barrier once and for all with their 11-minute vocal jam, "Goin' Home." Butterfield disseminated the blues, and up in San Francisco a loose-knit community of new bands began to explore uncharted musical regions. The pop press came into prominence, mostly on a tabloid level *(Beat, Go, Record Beat,* etc.), but also with the '66 debut of *Crawdaddy* on the East Coast and *Mojo Navigator* in San Francisco, along with continued coverage from the pioneers at *Hit Parader.* Drugs made their presence known increasingly, there were riots on the Strip, and a growing alienation among youth from "straight" society was in the air.

In other words, it was a time of flux and widespread, enthusiastic experimentation. Often the resultant music was brilliant, and it was an undeniably exciting era. The Beach Boys were right in the thick of it, as Brian, stung by the Beatles' advances, retired from the road and devoted endless studio hours to the crafting of complex new creations, masterpieces of moods. Besides "Sloop John B," more attuned to the folk-rock epoch, four superb singles ("Caroline No," "Wouldn't It Be Nice"/"God Only Knows" and "Good Vibrations") came out of 1966, along with the group's most revered album, *Pet Sounds.* Admirable as these new songs were, however, there was a lack of primal vitality evident quite often, with a correspondingly dreamy ambience dominating and a newly personal lyrical development in many of the tracks, which was a far cry from the generational solidarity promulgated in their '63-'65 records.

On a more general level, the bewildering welter of trends, signs in the wind, and changes worked together and separately to affect pop music drastically—with California mythologizations still wielding a profound influence. From "Fun Fun Fun" the Beach Boys had gone on to eulogize "California Girls"; and the Mamas & Papas generalized further with "California Dreamin.'" Scott McKenzie's "San Francisco (Wear Some Flowers in Your Hair)" provided a new geographic focal point; and, with the national breakout of the Jefferson Airplane and the

Monterey Pop Festival (organized by envious Southern Californians attempting to capture the San Francisco spirit, which was already past its idealistic peak as '67 began), the Bay Area became the new center. With its huge ballroom scenes, soon importing a wide spectrum of musicians (jazz, blues, Indian, etc.) along with the experimental local groups, it was an ideal melting pot of cultural and musical influences, with frequent opportunities for diverse styles to come together, play together and influence each other. It was also thus partially responsible for the decline of the simple, enthusiastic Californian teenage music which had started with the surfing songs of '62.

There were manifold other contributing factors, of course. 1967 saw the birth of *Sgt. Pepper*-influenced concept records, of widespread drug consciousness with its built-in elitism ("acid aristocracies" and ironclad freak/straight divisions), of the pseudo-poetic psychodramas of the Doors; and, probably most significant musically, the ascendancy of Cream and Jimi Hendrix, with the resultant guitar-worship syndromes and emphasis on improvisational jams and instrumental virtuosity (as opposed to the concise craftsmanship of the pop single).

The San Franciscan musical ideals of improvisatory exploration dovetailed neatly with this last development, and helped to spur it along, with homegrown concepts in the areas of lyrical abstraction, vibrations, and a preoccupation with introspective investigations of the mysteries of the mind. More significantly, San Francisco had become the new repository for that peculiarly cocky Californian self-confidence which the surf/rodders had earned by successfully creating a sound and a stance back in '63, supervising every musical detail of its realization (in contrast to previous middle-aged musical media manipulators) and selling it in vast quantities. The brash ultimatums of the youthful folk-rockers were an outgrowth of the same assurance, and the contagion spread to San Francisco, where the nascent counterculture proposed to build, with music, dope, and spiritual enlightenment, a new reality. The word got around, and kids flocked to The City, emulated the prevailing life style, and spent hours huddled on hardwood floors, stoked on speed and acid and digging the sounds. The rock publications and underground press whooped it up, the new progressivism became the international musical ideal (as a facet of the more general San Franciscan cultural model), and the bandwagon was rolling once and for all.

INTO THE POP WASTELAND

The next few years served to sharpen various polarizations and in-tensify the trends. Pure musical complexity dropped off after extremes like *Satanic Majesties* and *The United States of America* proved to be unpalatable commercially or critically. But omnivorous eclecticism con-tinued unchecked (with strong infusions from blues, soul, jazz, folk and country), as did the pervasive intellectualization of the music furthered by the rock press. Lyrical introspection increased apace, with Maharishis and other bizarre religious sects (including Jesus) emerging; and then with the current navel-based singer-songwriter vogue. The worship of virtuosity reached new heights, as 20-minute drum solos were greeted with rabid audience frenzy. Production concerns shifted from the all-out assault impact of Spector records and surf epics to a preoccupation with technique, clarity, and musicianship.

In opposition to prevailing trends, a pop music form designated as "bubblegum" returned to the accessible three-minute single model, but was so lyrically mindless and musically simplistic as to alienate all but the 15-and-under population (although much of it sounds excellent to-day, especially compared with current degenerate soft-rock radio fodder). FM Underground radio sprang up, playing the "advanced" progressive music; it attracted a hefty proportion of older teenagers and former teen-agers, and AM radio was accordingly left as a desert preserve for pim-ple-rockers. Not content with such a limited audience, radio moguls launched a drive to attract wider demographics, and by the '70s were gar-nering substantial 18-34 bracket listeners by purveying a mushy mélange of moronic pop material and singer-songwriter soft-rock. Harsh political realities of the late '60s and early '70s rendered the conceptions of fun and hedonism even more remote; and, with few exceptions, the general musical situation worsened dramatically.

The Beach Boys, whose *Pet Sounds*-era production explorations had a profound influence on latter-day musical trends, ironically fell victim to the cultural pretensions fostered by the progressives. They lost their commercial momentum when an unprecedented seven months elapsed between "Good Vibrations'" chart drop-off and the eventual debut of "Heroes and Villains" in August '67; in addition, the new single was so complex and elliptical that it confused many and inaugurated a popu-larity decline which simpler singles like "Wild Honey," "Darlin'" and "Friends" were unable to stem. The group's name conjured up hopeless-ly antiquated images, affiliation with the Maharishi hardly helped, and only a hard core took their music seriously. Many of these boosters were avid disseminators of the Brian Wilson Genius myth, reveling in untrammeled progressivism (as Bruce Johnston hyperbolically remarked, the Beach Boys at, one point seemed to be recording material because "four guys at *Crawdaddy* are going to love it").

Actually, though, such hyper-intellectual devotees were doomed to disappointment, as after a brief flirtation with the outer limits on *Smiley Smile* (even then a much more humorous approach than any other avant-garde exploration), the Beach Boys promptly returned to a simple, uncluttered sound which dominated the *Wild Honey, Friends* and *20/20* LPs. Despite superb exceptions like "Do It Again" and "I Can Hear Music" (both quite reminiscent of mid-'60s hits and ironically their biggest singles of the last six years), however, most of their material was rather too diffuse lyrically and suffered from over-sparse production; fine records in general but not as inspiring or impressive as, say, *Beach Boys Today, Summer Days and Summer Nights* or *All Summer Long*.

Their 1970 LP, *Sunflower*, was in the same league as the aforementioned classics, however, chiefly because of a stunning production job and a number of complex but melodically enchanting songs. The album slipped by without sales or significant attention; but *Surf's Up*, with the legendary title track rescued from the ashes of the never-released *Smile* album, received a huge, laudatory press reception. Unfortunately, the album was very spotty, with the bulk of the material either over-trivial ("Take a Load Off Your Feet") or pretentious ("Long Promised Road," "A Day in the Life of Tree"). 1972's *Carl & the Passions—So Tough* suffered even more drastically from the same problem despite a pair of lush romantic Dennis Wilson numbers and the amazing summer song "Marcella."

Let's Do It Again

"Marcella," a joyous tribute to a nimble masseuse, was one of the first beacons of a resurgence of that California pop spirit, an apparently widespread and extensive movement with the potential to shake the radio and music scene in general out of its depressive and diffuse doldrums. Other songs include, on the sympathetic periphery, the return to flash-rocking singles consciousness in England, led by Slade, Sweet, and (for a while there) T. Rex. Then there is a quiet revival of interest in the Phil Spector songbook and other classic high-spirited girl group songs— notably Dave Edmunds' brilliant recreation of "Baby I Love You"; also the British Seashells' last two singles, "Maybe I Know" and "Best Part Of Breaking Up" (also cut by Flo & Eddie); the Pearls' "You Came, You Saw, You Conquered"; Ellie Greenwich's new album, on which she sings ten of her great girl-group songs; and even the Ronettes' return to live performances.

It all points toward a monumental resurgence of pop consciousness. Not a "Sixties rock & roll revival" to follow in the wake of the "Fifties revival" fiasco, although that too will happen. More like a belated acknowledgement that there's no substitute for the basics in pop music — simple structure, catchy melody, background harmonies, and an emphasis on production. There is nothing better than a good pop-rock single, except perhaps a good rock & roll single, but we seem to have blown the chance of re-integrating fifties rock & roll into our musical culture (where it certainly belongs), for the present at least.

But with that brilliant stuff of the early and mid-'60s as a model, not copied but used as a foundation for the advances in production, studio technique, and hard rock technology that the last decade has brought, we are clearly in for some great things. Surf music, in these terms, is only a convenient, pre-mythologized focal point for the whole thing.

Mind you, we're far past the point of prediction. Two years ago, we were predicting the return of surf music and sixties pop. Now it's happening all around us, although most observers don't seem to have noticed yet.

"Marcella" might have been a call to arms in the summer of '72, the way fun records seemed to erupt out of nowhere in the ensuing months. Three brilliant new American groups debuted around then with hugely enjoyable lightweight pop-rock records — Stories, Big Star, and the Raspberries (who even broke the AM barrier with two of the best Top Ten records in years); the second Stories and Raspberries albums were better still (note also the latter group's well-executed Beach Boys/Emmit Rhodes tribute, "Drivin' Around"). And the Wackers, who were one of the first, continued to be one of the best, along with fellow Canadian residents Pagliaro and Thundermug.

In England, a similar process has been shaping up, as chronicled in these pages over the past year. Slade poured forth a stream of energy-jolt singles reminiscent of the early Stones, the Easybeats returned as Marcus Hook Roll Band with a taste of early Who/Velvet Underground, and lesser examples are legion. The best new English pop group may well be the Sweet, who are still scorned at home as "bubblegum" but are actually far superior, on a hard-hitting, flash singles level, to almost everyone. They are more than anything a Mod group, very close in effect to the early Who, Small Faces, Stones sound.

CALIFORNIA REVISITED

It's great to see these things happening, but the best sign of all is the fact that good ol' California once again is becoming a real hotbed of fun music. Curt Boettcher and Mike Fennelly (ex-Crabby Appleton), both of whom once worked with Gary Usher (on some intriguing late-'60s Beach Boys-derived pop experiments with Sagittarius and Millennium), have gone solo. Fennelly's soon-to-be-released Epic album is a fine collection of light pop morsels, and Boettcher's recent Elektra album was one of early 1973's biggest delights, featuring the unforgettable "Love You More Each Day." Boettcher's roots reach, through his partner Gary Usher, back to 1964 hotrod music—and another circle closes.

With or without direct surf linkages, however, the type of music we're discussing (which has no label yet but might well be called "summer music") is about to have its best summer since '66. Not the least contributing factor is Johnny Rivers, who in the last year has returned to his 1964 discotheque rock sound, but with a tremendous new band and much improved vocal technique. "Blue Suede Shoes," like ELO's "Roll Over Beethoven" a 1956 hit, is nonetheless a perfect summer song for 1973. And his latest album, which includes such timeless fun songs as "Searchin'," "Hang On Sloopy," "Solitary Man" and a killer remake of the Byrds' "Feel a Whole Lot Better," is as perfect for parties and beach bashes as *The Beach Boys Today* was in its time.

But what about surf music itself? Surfing today is not only still a part of youth culture, but reports from surfing beaches as far away as Florida and Texas, plus of course along the Malibu-Hermosa run, indicate that a new beach scene is breaking out big. Kids are being seen in greater numbers, cruising around, making the beach scene, hanging out and looking for action. The newly-legalized pinball parlors have become an instant rage in Southern California, featuring jukeboxes with solid rock & roll songs. If some sort of nascent teen summer culture is indeed in the offing, all that's needed now is a musical soundtrack. And as you might have expected, there are strong signs of this.

Last spring a number of surf patriarchs went into the studio to record new vocals over an old Jan & Dean track. These notables included Brian Wilson, Bruce Johnston, Terry Melcher, and Dean Torrence. They had no intention of engendering a surf revival, they were just itching to have some fun. The record, "Gonna Hustle You" / "Summertime, Summertime" came out (by the Legendary Masked Surfers), but because its release was held until September it had little summer impact. Now, however, it is being reissued both here and in England, and who knows? It sounds great, in a nostalgic novelty sort of vein.

Beyond that however, the record signaled an interest on the part of these guys to try and recapture some of the spirit that went out of California rock after their heyday. Plans were drawn up for a group to be called California, who would attempt to revive that spirit without the use of overt surfing and car symbols. As Dean put it, "glancing back is okay" but the new group will offer a contemporary approach to the paramount goal of making music that is, above all, fun to make and fun to listen to, full of the timeless images, of sun, beaches, the ocean, freedom and young love. While waiting for the perfect recording deal (two large offers have already been declined as "not quite right"), California's ideas are being tried out via Terry Melcher's forthcoming solo album.

Another vastly encouraging development is that of Spring (now American Spring), the duo consisting of Brian Wilson's wife Marilyn and her sister Dianne Rovell. Formerly two-thirds of the Honeys, who made a handful of prized Wilson-produced surf/girl group records through the '60s (as well as singing backgrounds on Beach Boys albums and cutting demos for the Shangri-La's, among others), Marilyn and Diane made a perfectly delightful album in '72, with uptempo natural single hits like "Good Time" (thwarted only by endemic cretinism among radio program directors). The album also included such enchanting, elaborate mood pieces as "Sweet Mountain" and the Beach Boys' "This Whole World" and "Everybody" among other excellent tracks. Now with Columbia, their new single, "Shyin' Away" (recorded in a small studio in Fort Dodge, Iowa), is an ultracommercial, immediately infectious summer record with all the enthusiastic elements of the early '60s surf era and girl group sounds and none of the "oldies" stigma which usually surround such material. The flip, "Falling in Love," is a beautiful slower-paced number, with an absolutely breathtaking string arrangement. Spring's second album is not yet finished, but the other two completed tracks also sound spectacular, and there is no doubt that Spring has the potential to be a very big part of what's about to happen in music.

The Beach Boys themselves, on their successful *Holland* album, show signs of a return in spirit to what Rick Henn of the Sunrays calls "Coastal Consciousness"—demonstrated most clearly, of course, on their new single "On My Way to Sunny California," part of the *Cal-*

ifornia Saga trilogy. Despite some of the most jarring lyrics yet to hit the radio and a pervasive bass line reminiscent of nothing so much as "Canadian Sunset," it's nearly impossible to avoid becoming captivated with the record. The harmonies and instrumental track are very similar to the feeling of numbers like "California Girls" and "Help Me Rhonda," closer than anything in years. The lyrical content, though shifting its unwieldly emphasis to dwell on the natural glories of Northern California, marks a return to a general California orientation for the group, an orientation which hopefully will come to dominate more of their music.

In one sense, the Beach Boys always had that orientation. There was never a time when their excesses in other directions weren't made up for by a "Marcella" or a "Do It Again." But now it appears those excesses themselves might be giving way to popular pressure. The Beach Boys have come to terms with the fact that their fans want only summer songs and hits from their golden age, in concert at least, and now would be an appropriate time for that to spill over onto their records.

A recent appearance at the Hollywood Palladium, in Los Angeles was a powerful remainder of how much life the Beach Boys' classic songs still have in them. The place was sold out far in advance and packed to the rafters with kids, much younger than the usual Palladium audience—predominantly under 18, I'd say. When the Beach Boys came on, the place erupted in a roar not unlike that which once greeted appearances by the Beatles. People were going crazy, jumping into the air, lapsing into religious ecstasy on all sides.

For this show, the Beach Boys bowed to the crowd's unspoken desire and played all old songs, with the exception of recent fun-slanted songs like "California Saga," "Marcella" and "Do It Again," No Van Dyke Parks songs, nothing else from *Holland* except "Sail On Sailor." As they ran through "Surfin' USA," "Surfer Girl," "Fun Fun Fun," "Darlin'," "Don't Worry Baby," "I Get Around," "Help Me Rhonda," "Wouldn't It Be Nice," "Sloop John B," "Caroline No," "Wild Honey" and "Barbara Ann," the crowd became more and more hysterical. When they left the stage, the sound of the audience screaming and stomping and shouting in unison "We want more!" was almost unbearable. It went on for over five minutes.

Finally the Beach Boys returned, augmented by Bruce Johnston and Billy Hinsche (of Dino & Desi fame) and took the energy level even higher. As the last song ended, Brian wandered onstage and was embraced by everyone, his first public appearance in what must be years.

In all truth, I've rarely seen an audience as turned on as this one was.

It was as though they were responding and paying tribute to the fact that the Beach Boys had written the supreme tributes to them, their homeland and their way of life; as if they instinctively felt all of what we've been trying to explain. It was a sublime moment.

Yeah, it'll come around again all right. The time is so right for light-hearted, exuberant, high-spirited music that I can feel it, straining and aching to come out from behind the bricks of you-know-what that have stopped up the wellsprings of youth spirit for so long. Thanks to the eternally magnificent Beach Boys and others, it looks like if we're lucky, we'll never hear psychedelic music again.

REVIEW:

The Wailers *Catch a Fire*

Fusion, May 1973

After all these veers, a new Wailers LP! But wait, *Catch a Fire* doesn't have anything to do with those soggy Seattle-ites who rocked hot and cool in the days of old. These Wailers hail from Jamaica in the Caribbean, home of rum, brown sugar, crumbling colonial forts, white duck togs, blacks with goofy English accents and this kind of music they call reggae.

I'm no expert on reggae at all, but I know what I like (Jimmy Cliff, Johnny Nash and Desmond Dekker's boffo *Israelites* album) and a passable amount of history; i.e., the Kingston Sound came north in the mid-'50s on the shoulders of the deep-staring Harry Belafonte, failed to insinuate itself into the national consciousness via the Ska craze of the early '60s (at which point these here Wailers under Bob Marley commenced to function), poked through again in '64 on the wings of Millie Small's confectionery triumph, has been going great guns across the pond for years and most recently has tugged the coattails of AM addicts with "Mother and Child Reunion" and "I Can See Clearly Now."

What can I say about reggae and the Wailers that'll sell you on 'em? 'Many parts are edible!'? How about: This music knocks me out in a manner not that different from the way those first Beatle discs did back in 1964. Which is not intended as a pronouncement, but rather as an intimation of the base potency this music possesses. Since there haven't been all that many completely unique rock & roll musics—flukes, hybrids, readymades, whatever—each time you do come across a distinctly different one for the first time, it tends to be a rather delicious experience.

There's these foreigners, Western Hemisphere black dudes singing movie English, oohing and wee-oohing in that odd distanced manner, bouncing around chunks of very pliable yet almost frictionless instrumental sound that, for all its alien tongue traits, is unquestionably rock 'n' roll of the purest universal strain. It has earmarks of American soul, New Orleans rock, the corner crooners of the '50s, bubblegum in big doses, even gentle touches of pop psychedelia, and parents, teachers and church leaders are probably jacked up over it somewhere already.

Nor is the appeal sheer novelty. Marley's Wailers are consistently refreshing in the way successful, enduring groups used to be. Johnny Nash is making "Stir It Up" a hit, but the Marley original sounds even better, its combination of sinewy mechanical (Moog/ organ?) calisthenics, primitive sing-song lyricism (the closest radio referent I can find is 1971's faster, yet similarly nursery-rhymed "Chirpy Chirpy Cheep Cheep"; see also the ace pronunciation of "bay-bee"), and that hopscotch rhythm make it hard to dispel, fluid yet insistent. Sort of like Mel Torme trying to be sexy.

"Slave Driver" balances itself on a light airy vocal repetition of the title phrase (kind of like the start of some typically obscure New York R&B group side, where pregnant pauses and their regular punctuation by keynote choral assaults carry the entire performance) over the buckboard jostle of the bass and drums.

Marley's vocal on "Kinky Reggae" is absolutely elastic, riding the music's sandy rhythm with sheer R&R finesse, and there's more than a trace of smooth Sam Cooke inflection laced through "Stop That Train." If there were adventurous radio programmers, "Baby We've Got a Date," the current single from the LP, would certainly be a smash, thanks to its fashionable Teenage quotes, the superb soft-shoe rhythm and electric doorbell guitar.

There is a lack of tension and high-strung volume dynamics at work in this music, but you don't even have to try to overcome the barriers such unfamiliar conditions set up. It's downright seductive, if you wanna know the truth; you'll be addicted before you know it and then it'll be too late.

I can't speak for the bulk of the potential audience this reggae stuff stands ready to command, but if it's gonna take simple infectious recipes to provide the cure to a perennially ailing American pop scene, reggae and the services of the Wailers particularly oughta be enlisted pronto. We can always use a few good men.

INTERVIEW:

John Lennon,
on "Mind Games," Oldies, Spector,
Beatles and American Radio

Radio & Records, Nov. 30, 1973

In 1973, I became editor of the trade paper Radio & Records. *That November, a month after John Lennon's* Mind Games *had been released, publisher Bob Wilson, production manager Mark Shipper and I drove to Lou Adler's house in Bel-Air to conduct a two-hour interview with Lennon. Lennon may have commenced a formidable solo career, but, as with any act, each new album needed airplay, which meant 'the intellectual Beatle' was obliged to perform the same dance as any other artist: visit stations, schmooze with programmers and promo men, make nice in hopes of winning some spins. At the time, R&R was the must-read paper for the radio industry, so this was an important stop for Lennon. My main memories of the interview: how cordial, and casual, Lennon was, how animated he became talking about records and American top-40, and how abashed Mark and I were when Bob Wilson, in the midst of it all, blurted out, "Why did you marry Yoko?" A pause as we waited to be kicked out of the place, then Lennon quietly answered, "Because I love her." The interview ran in two or three parts; the first is all I could find.*

R&R: *Over how long a period did you write the material for* Mind Games?

John: I didn't do them in a bunch, actually, though a few I completed just before I went into the studio. I've found that once you book the time, the product comes. The stuff I wrote just prior to recording was "Intuition," "Meat City," "Tight A$." I wrote the middle eight of "I

Know" just before we went in. I'd had the sound of "Mind Games" in my head for a while, but the words didn't come till about two weeks before we cut it. Lyrically, I think "Mind Games" might be similar to "Imagine," though I don't think they resemble each other musically. I think "Imagine" perhaps said it better, but it has a more conventional structure, where "Mind Games" sort of rambles out. It doesn't behave itself.

R&R: *It's a powerful song in the way it comes on surging, and proceeds to build from there.*

John: Yes. I like that feeling. Where the song comes on and sounds as if it's been going on for a long time. You say, "I must have missed something." It's the feeling you usually get on the fadeout.

R&R: *Did "Mind Games" sound like a single to you?*

John: It sounded like one, although when I went into the studio, I thought "Only People" would be the single. In the end, "Only" didn't get me off as much as "Mind Games."

R&R: *Do you formulate your writing for hit, Top-40, AM singles?*

John: No, I just sort of think in terms of singles always. The best ones are the songs that you know are singles even when you're playing them to yourself, with no one to back you.

R&R: *There seems to be a certain touch of Elvis In your singing on "Tight A$." Has the influence of the "oldies" crept in more and more as you progress toward your oldies album?*

John: Well, the Elvis is certainly there. It was there in "Crippled Inside" on the last album. We always threw a bit of it into things, even with the Beatles. Every time I've been making an album, whether alone or with the Beatles, when it comes time to take a break, I always play 12-bars or oldies, 'cause they're the ones you knew when you were starting out. When I'd relax or get drunk, I'd start singing Little Richard stuff, you know. There's so many reels of tape, in London and New York, which have me singing the oldies. Most of the time I'd never finish them because I couldn't remember the words. So, finally, I thought, "Now's the time!"

R&R: *How wide a period will the songs on the new ·album cover?'*

John: Fifties and Sixties. And I can't resist throwing in some of my own stuff; so it'll really be Fifties, Sixties and Seventies. There's the two of us, Phil and I, working on the album, and we really get down with it. I wanted it to be Phil Spector, his sound and all, with me singing. Because both of us have the same sort of dream, you know, of a symphony of guitars. We've got like five rhythm guitars, two basses and two drummers. People have come and gone on the session, but there's a hard core of survivors. Steve Cropper came in and played guitar. Leon Russell did keyboards. Hal Blaine and Jim Keltner played drums, Nino Tempo and Jim Horn played saxes. Jeff Barry showed up, and today Jose Feliciano came in.

R&R: *The proverbial question: Will the Beatles ever get back together?*

John: There's always a chance. That's the answer. There's certainly no rift between us. I talked with George yesterday. I talk with him and Ringo more often than with Paul, but that's only because Paul is on the road right now. As far as our differences, it's like Paul said in *Newsweek*; "It's just a matter of moving the decimal points now."

R&R: *Even if you did get back together, wouldn't it be next to impossible to live up to the audience's expectations of you?*

John: Right. No matter what we'd do, it wouldn't be good enough for the old Beatle maniacs. We'd have to make records that would convert people anew, something that could stand on its own. People would tend to say, "It's not as good as .... " But that wouldn't stop us, if we felt like doing it. We'd try it. But there's nothing in the cards, you know. "Anything's possible."

R&R: *You said recently that you found a certain appeal to "meaningless" type oldies songs. Has the kind of naive charm that made those songs so appealing vanished, or do you think the musicians, like yourself, who've grown and aged, can make lighthearted music anymore?*

John: I don't know. I find it harder, especially, to keep from messing around with the words of my songs now. If the lyric, "Oh baby, I love you" came to me now, I'd tend to say, "Wait, I can't say that!" I'd try to change it, say the same thing 'better.' But that's my own problem. Led Zeppelin's done it, gone with the simple, basic approach, on that new reggae single, haven't they? ["D'Yer Maker"]

R&R: *Are you aware of the current AM radio situation here, the move toward tighter playlists and less exposure of new material?*

John: I know FM has somewhat vanished, from what people tell me. Top 40 forever, is it?

R&R: *Records tend to stay around longer now. Lots of people are saying that the early '70s are looking like the early '60s. Because most of the hits are "produced" records, as opposed to the middle '60s, when the hits came from groups and bands.*

John: Yeah. I feel that too. And it's probably like everyone's saying: '74 is going to be the year for something new, wherever it's coming from. I think it all does go ten year cycles. It was ten years between Sinatra and Presley, and ten years between Presley and the Beatles. I reckon next year is the year, not that I know anything.

R&R: Are you aware that the group which we're in, 18-34, Is the largest proportionate group of consumers, of music and goods In general? There aren't that many teenagers left to provide an audience for rock 'n' roll.

John: We're the majority, then? I had no idea of that. Then what do the teenagers listen to? Perhaps Cassidy and the DeFranco's. My boy Julian, who's ten, told me he's buying Gilbert O'Sullivan and Gary Glitter, stuff like that.

R&R: What do you like among some of the current records?

John: My favorite record right now is the Ann Peebles ["I Can't Stand the Rain"]. I like Al Green too. I liked Todd Rundgren's thing, "I See the Light." I like Charlie Rich, and country-and- western (Hank Williams was one of my earliest influences; "Honky Tonk Blues" was my big number at the church socials, you know.) I like the C&W influence in pop, but groups like the Allmans I find a bit too "musician-y." I love singles. The idea of trying to put your message across on TV or on record in under three minutes, or thirty seconds, appeals to me, because there's no time for anything else, really. Singles have become important once again, I think. We can't all be going on those long, twenty-minute trips on the air. It's as if now, things are speeding up once again. We went through the downer bit, and things are getting fast again. I'm glad. I prefer it that way. I don't mind Top 40, especially if I'm in it! When you're not in it, it can get boring. I haven't been in Britain for three years, but I understand they're getting into commercial radio there. It was good when they had the pirate stations over there, because it was done a Ia American radio. I like American radio. It was everywhere.

R&R: Do you foresee doing any live performances?

John: Yeah. I was all for it, whenever it was, when I was with Elephant's Memory, a year ago. But then when I announced I'd like to do it, they suddenly didn't want to. I had them on standby for it, you know, and finally I got fed up trying to get it off the ground in the midst of going to court and P .R.-ing and all. We haven't done any vocals, outside of my leads. We've done about half of the instrumental tracks and we're taking a break now. There's guitarists with their arms in plaster, you know!

R&R: How do you and Phil work out the arrangements?

John: We sit around with the proverbial bottle, and play the hell out of a couple of cassettes we have. We play the hell out of one song till dawn, and we'll suggest where we think a guitar lick could go, ideas for the horns, etc. If we're still alive the next day, we go into the studio.

R&R: What prompted you to get Phil to re-mix Let It Be?

John: Well, he'd been an Influence on us, as he was on everybody, for a long time. I mean, since the days of "Spanish Harlem" and "Save the Last Dance for Me," you know. At the time of *Let It Be*, we were going through a bad period. Nobody had their heart in the recording of that album. We didn't even want to hear the playback, and once we finished it, we didn't want to have to mix it or deal with it in any way. Phil just sort of came along, not knowing about all that, and I asked him to deal with it, and he did. He came in and saved *Let It Be*.

NEXT WEEK: *"My reaction when I first heard her stuff was 'What is this?' It sounded like she was having an orgasm." In Part II, John Lennon talks about relationship with Yoko Ono, songwriting, "the price of fame," criticism and the future.*

Review:

The Righteous Brothers
Give It to The People

Zoo World magazine, October 10, 1974

They did it in Las Vegas and they sure do it here. Recombine their talents, hop into the saddle with strong material and take hold of the reins like they'd never left. Like Buck and Susan Raye, like April and Nino, Billy and Bobby are together again, bathed in blue and teamed up with yet another catalytic duo, producers-writers Lambert & Potter (Four Tops, Gene Redding lately).

The Brothers being solidly together in sound and spirit, it's to Lambert-Potter's credit that they've faced the task of fashioning a new Righteous model without casting too many backward glances; there's none of that Moonglow monkey-hips-and-rice soul coaxin' and no towering Spector architecture. Just lots of good songs, sharp arranging, crisp but spacious production and those voices.

The Brothers themselves took "Rock And Roll Heaven" from popular non-hit status (Climax and Flash Cad had already done it) to the Top Five, and it remains a brilliant frontispiece on this LP. It's less a generation-galvanizing statement, more a '74 "American Pie," gingerly sifting a handful of pleasing Recent Past images through an 'accessible' pop screen. How could anyone not respond to it?

Second honors have to go to the title track, more pop myth and dashtop din revolving around that devastating hook line, "I made a deal with the angel of music..." The tune itself is reminiscent of Mann-Weil's "It's Not Easy" (Medley soloed on it for A&M a year ago), and the chorus packs a hell of a wallop.

"Dr. Rock And Roll" sticks close to the theme; everybody's saying "music is love." Bobby pulls slick Curtis Mayfield moves on the Mann-

Weil "You Turn Me Around." "Dream On" is smooth and tough, a magnificent job by all parties involved. Sounds like a Bert Berns arrangement
of a Drifters song. If Medley's talent seems wasted once, on the inferior
"Lines" (a labored wordplay tune *a la* Alex Harvey's "Rings" but not half
as clever), there's plenty to make up for it. Both bro's work out to the
fullest on LP's "Love Is Not a Dirty Word" and "Together Again" (great
appropriation of that Main Ingredient flute figure on this one).

      If you liked the single, *blah blah*. Forget it. If you've got any appre-
ciation of blue-eyed soul, radio-records craftsmanship or fine singing,
you'd be a chump not to spring for this set. And rest assured there'll be
more; these guys are trigger-happy for hits and loaded for bear. Nobody's
gonna shake 'em.

REVIEW:

David Cassidy *Live*

Creem magazine, December 1974

Here's a guy with some claim to status. His dad's distinguished himself, right alongside Claude Akins, as one of the slimiest heavies ever to grace the TV cop shows, and his mom runs a tight musical ship nightly, riding over a rowdy herd that includes Danny Bonaducci and Dave Madden.

Where Cass Jr. shines is up onstage, out in front of maybe six or eight thousand screaming Briton boppers. He's got a lot of what pre-rock 'n' roll audiences used to clamor for—polish, showbiz spunk, and that trouper stamina occasioned by plenty of public pratfalls on the boards. Davy's thoroughly pro: slick and choreographed, well versed even in intra-song patter and convivial coyness. Since these qualities are generally associated with another, older brand of performer, and since his vocal skills, while impressive, are hardly commensurate with that kind of bravado and slickness, he comes off beautifully—as a precocious star-kid having way too good a time to worry about credibility or critics or anything. He's a natural ham, takes to smalltime Bigtime like Anka or Darin did.

Who's to say this isn't the best live "rock" album of the year? I'll take this Dave over that downhill skidding other one [Bowie] any day. Coiffed and spangled, this one sounds like a cross between a 38-year-old karate-chopping Presley and the grinning, apple-cheeked Wayne Newton. He picks killer material, strokes it with a gentle show biz hand ("Some Kind of Summer" and the slowed-down "Breaking Up Is Hard to Do" sound like companion pieces to sloppy El Pres glut like the live "Suspicious Minds," all over-recorded rhythm and trashy tambourine-on-high-hat), and walks away a winner every time. His versions of oldies by the kiddo Beatles ("Please Please Me") and Rascals ("How Can I Be Sure") are double-sided xerox, his rock medley (a gruntoid "C.C. Rider," "Jailhouse Rock," etc.) irreverent, and his job on Stills' hoary "For What

It's Worth" the best that song's ever had; the band goes crazy once Cass burps up his helium vocal, running amok like G. Dead turned loose on 12,000 Haight St. regulars on a 1967 Sunday. "Mae" is classic Dennis Yost, and "Delta Dawn" out bludgeons Cocker and Russell's well-known assaults on subtlety. Slicker than the once-blissful Bonos, almost as powerful as Rory Gallagher, twice as hammy as the Hudsons, Jack and Shirley's firstborn has distinguished himself this time. Are you ready, brothers & sisters?

As some of the preceding LP reviews show, I could occasionally get pretty hyperbolic in my praise or putdowns. My good friend Ken Barnes (still the most knowledgeable writer/music historian around) nailed me with this 1974 parody review of a nonexistent Cat Stevens album.

Cat Stevens
Scalawag and the Mongoose

A question. What's bouncier than a double bubble barrelful of beardless Buddah pests, rocks harder than a rubber bullet and lays down a grits-ain't-groceries groove smooth as the fab moptops themselves? Not those supersonic Southern cats sporting the two-time motorbike highjinx, or even that lad insane who runs the freak rock riffs up the flag poll to see who'll salute. Which is to say, it's that tubercular Catman, Stevens by name; and before all you guys 'n' gals out there in teen fantasyland haul off and reach for the flip-flop-'n'-flyswatter, give a listen hereabouts.

Try "The Comet Fairies" for starters—bass line throb no less earthshaking than the Spiral Staircase, swampgrass harmonica a la John Fred's disguised Judy, and a bridge from across the Bay where the yodelin' Youngbloods used to play. Or "Gingerbread Cookie," a delectable morsel compounded of equal parts pre-Garcia Grateful Dead, the fatso from Sweathog, and the palpitating pop-cycle shtick of those hard-riding Hondells. All reet petite and a mile wide, as the streetwise bopper punks down in San Clemente say.

Piano player's got all the leonine one's Gary Lewis session savvy, and that anonymous axeman's prefabricated the cool, crisp Golden Gate guitar snap-crackle-'n'-pop of Quicksilvery Cipollina's bag of electrics. Hand-clappin' and bass-slappin' from some savage bopcat Sun worshipper; strings 'n' things from the Philly Soul kitchen of Gamble 'n' Huff; and horns that cook with East Bay Grease from the Tower of Power bowery-boy bastion of Southwestern Oakland.

Which means the Cat's thrown his hat into the ring-a-ding raucous caucus of teens 'n' twenties stalwarts like Purple, Sabbath and P. Harum. Cat charges those lyric lines like that goat's head souperstar or the Manassas Mauler, more pounce to the ounce than a fistful of Felicianos or the wimp-rocker with the flowers in his hair from '67 pop heaven.

Here's a hip tip. Grab a slab o' long green, make the local discoteen scene, and flash the cash for this brisk disc; and you'll be toppin' the boppin' at the high-school hop in no time flat. The Cat's got a platter that matters, and when you hear "Hard-hatted Mermaid" you're sure to say, like those 1910 Fruitgummers from the summer of '69, "Goody Gumdrops! Have mercy! Yabba Dabba Do!" Get your cat clothes on, let's rock awhile! Hoo hah!

FEATURE:

The Guess Who

Creem magazine, February 1975

> "*I'll kill your kid sister, I'll murder your dad, I'll rip the lashes off your eyes*
> *I'll slaughter all your cattle and I'll burn your crops if you're dancing with another guy*"

If you happened into a Macon diner one night, do you suppose you could pick Butch Trucks out of the assembled suppers and slurpers? Would you recognize Ken Hensley or Ritchie Blackmore in a London bookstall? Lori Lieberman's face in a subway train, Chris Jagger's speaking voice? What's the name of the Sha Na Na fatso who looks like Victor Buono?

The problem is the proliferation of trained rock personnel. Attached to groups or floating solo, there are so many singers, writers, percussionists, synthesizers and slide players, you can't tell 'em apart.

Like this one group. They've sold millions round the globe, charted close to twenty single hits and are on their fourteenth album this very minute, yet they trek about in their Mapleleaf showbiz shoes virtually unrecognized. High sales and low profile. Raise your hand if you know who wrote "These Eyes," who handled the speaking part in "Rain Dance" or who grafted that steely solo onto the midsection of "Share the Land." It ain't easy.

"I was like 20 years old and every time I'd turn around I was getting a gold record, and that really didn't sink in until about a year ago. We'd be flying all over the country, hearing our stuff as flashbacks everywhere. And it started dawning on me that, 'Wait a minute, those were pretty big records.' But it seemed very easy to us at the time."

Not John Fogerty. Not Danny Hutton. But Burton Cummings, 26 in 1974, trim at 165, laying on the bed in his Sacramento motel room, nine hours before he takes the stage in front of 15,000 Guess Who fans at the California State Fair. By then it'll be 10 o'clock, the temperature will have dropped to 85 dry heat degrees and he'll front his group through 100 minutes, giving the tanned, t-shirt crowd what he's got to show for nine years' playin' in the band: "Hand Me Down World," "Undun," "Star Baby," "American Woman," "Glamour Boy."

Everybody's in the room, checking out the Gucci traveling bags, compliments of booking agent Jerry Heller, sniffing cologne in dark-glass guitar bottles, courtesy of some longtime female fans from Cleveland. Bill Wallace picks at his cordless bass in a striped surfer shirt, new guitarist Dom Troiano adjusts his beret, accepts a joint and worries about the band having to back up Wolfman Jack for his two numbers during the show.

Drummer Garry Peterson has probably seen it all. "Next year," he laughs, "I'll have spent half of my 28 years in this band." The pay's good and it's fun. Cummings coughs up his last toke: "We'll have to get you a gold watch, Peterson," he sputters. "May the next 14 be as good as the first 14!"

> *"Maybe I'll be there to shake your hand, maybe I'll be there to share*
> *the land*
> *That they'll be giving away when we all live together"*

Don Hunter, the portly manager who swears he discovered Cummings when the Winnipeg lad delivered his evening paper, strolls in, beaming. "Clap for The Wolfman" has just jumped from 18 to Number One at KIMN, Portland. It's all frosting. An hour earlier Cummings was notified that he's set, for sure, to score and star in *A Fool, A Fool, I Met A Fool*, a full-length feature. Hunter's been busy all afternoon, trying to get the fire marshal and fair officials to make more tickets available for tonight's concert.

It wasn't always like this. There'd been a slight slump, about two years ago, after "Rain Dance," when the hit stream slowed to a trickle, when co-writer/guitarist Randy Bachman quit after hurling a couple of well-publicized brickbats at Cummings.

("Sure, I said that," Cummings later tells a kid backstage who's inquired if he meant what he said about the B.T.O. leader in *Rolling Stone*. "I hate the guy. He was down on the rest of us 'cause he thought we were blowing it with dope and all this ridiculous shit. He was like some kind of Mormon or something." And the dismissal of guitarists Kurt Winter and Don McDougal? "They were drunks. We got tired of babysitting them.")

The turnaround came with the success last year of the dynamite "Star Baby" single and "Clap For The Wolfman," together with a couple of strategically placed *Midnight Special* appearances. People, suddenly, were ready to take the band seriously once again. And they looked and sounded better than most people had remembered; hungry for hits, with Burt in short hair, Hawaiian sport shirt and hush puppies, pounding out certified gold at a white baby grand like an amped-up Brian Wilson. They were visible again, even hard to dismiss.

> *"Anybody here seen the fuzzy-wuzzy lovin'- cup explosion? I think we missed it…"*

If the recent uphill climb has been long and hard, it wasn't accomplished without the help of the legion of Guess Who freaks, the hardcore fans whose persistence and tenacity have thrust the band (like Grand Funk first time out or the recently re-arrived Beach Boys) through some unguarded backdoor into the pop limelight. Cummings once explained them to me as "about 200,000 loyal fans who buy everything we do." Everybody knows one and they're as dissimilar in costume and attitude from one another as they are in musical taste from the Allman, Bowie, Cooper or Tull crowds. All over the world they congregate, listening over and over to *Artificial Paradise, No. 10*, to *Greatest Hits Vol. I* and worn singles of "American Woman"/ "No Sugar Tonight." Their ears perk up to those weirdo lines in both versions of "Don't You Want Me," to the goofy alliteration in "Attila's Blues," to the chords and Cummings' insanely beautiful singing on "Glamour Boy."

And they pack air-conditioned concert halls on the West Coast and sweaty hockey arenas back East, insuring pre-show fever pitch and fulfilling the promise of hysteric encores. They generate pandemonium in Detroit, Chicago and Long Beach; juvenile, rowdy, racially mixed, college couples, hip-tailored longhairs and greaser chicks with cro-mag foreheads and frowns, the perfectly crossbred AM-FM audience, earnest-eyed guitar and piano kids who've just gotta ask Cummings what he was talking about in "Orly" with that line, "Better get to Rome and have a look at younger sister of my Dad."

Cummings, one gets the idea, used to protest, but it seemed inevitable he'd carry the weight himself of *being* the Guess Who. At 17, he auditioned for Chad Allen and Bachman and the rest with an organ xerox of a Manfred Mann hit; six months later Allen, envious of the Winnipeg whiz kid's class and style, split. When Bachman left it became Burton's show, an unstated but definitely pre-existent state of affairs regardless of Bachman's presence.

It's Cummings' unique and incredibly varied professional persona the Guess Who freaks have come to know. It's a curious character blend that can stand with equal grace and balance on all the bases. He can compose and perform everything from classic love songs to dorko political tracts, from genuine sentimentality to labored attempts at drawing a given response. And, so complete is the fans' identification with him, his occasional excesses—the Jim Morrison phase and its effects onstage several years back—are received more with affection than resentment. And he sings, all the time, like a mother.

> *"Well, have you ever seen a Madras monkey, have you ever seen an*
>   *orlon eel?*
> *I had a pet pitiful penguin and I taught him how to pick and choose*
>   *and drink my booze*
> *I got the help-preserve-'em, don't-deserve-'em, try-and-serve-'em-all*
>   *blues."*

"Our audience is growing up with us," Burton admits, "and that will happen with anybody who develops some real staunch fans. They read the lyrics. Like last week: some guy calls me up at 3 am. He and his friends had been sitting around all night listening to all of the albums and he wanted to know what I meant in the fourth line of such-and-such. That's great.

"There's this kid in Virginia who's been a fan since the beginning. He calls himself Mark Mars and he's always writing to me. So I put this line in 'Road Food' about 'Old Mark Mars is alive and well, sir.' You know he must've dug hearing that. Stuff like that is just fun to do."

Mark Mars probably didn't make it out to the California State Fair, but 15,000 Guess Who freaks did. They've sat through Elvin Bishop and Montrose, about 2,000 of them have scaled the cyclone fence circling the racetrack grandstand and they're ready.

At the barbeque thrown backstage by the promoter, Bill Wallace is antsy to get going, ready to do it again like in Chicago and Minneapolis. Peterson, decked out in t-shirt and tennis shorts, looks like Bobby Riggs

Jr. He taps his drumsticks on his plate. Troiano's in good spirits, though he's still suffering from the identity crisis of being *the new Guess Who guitarist.*

"One reviewer in Milwaukee thought I was Kurt Winter," he explains. "He said I played well and looked good after losing all that weight. That's almost as good as when I was in the James Gang. People'd ask me, 'Where's your Les Paul, Joe?'"

After a roaring welcome, they walk onstage, receive a Wolfman Jack intro ("How ya doin', Sacramenna?! Here de are: da Guess Who!!"), plug in and fire away. The sound onstage, Wallace and Troiano will later complain, is terrible, but it goes unnoticed.

Wise set programming or killer performance, the audience goes crazy. After four songs, half a dozen joints hit the stage and roll toward Cummings' penny loafers. He talks to the crowd for the first time, stretches back and announces "Glamour Boy," the anti- Bowie song. "This next one is dedicated to the kind of people who've made the record industry the stinking pile of shit it is today!"

Much later, after the round of back seat congratulations is over inside the departing Caddie, Cummings falls back, contemplates dozing off, then starts singing to himself. First, a languid verse from the Beach Boys' "Warmth of the Sun," then oldies from the Cookies and Ray Charles. The car reaches the freeway, en route to the party the promoter's throwing. Wide awake, Cummings laughs and breaks into one more selection: in a nasally tenor:

> *"You get us every mornin' from the alarm clock's warnin,' take the 8:15*
> *into the city...*
> *We been takin' are of business..."*

REVIEW:

The Ramones *Ramones*

Creem magazine, August 1976

"I don't wanna walk around with you
I don't wanna walk around with you
I don't wanna walk around with you
So why you wanna walk around with me?
I don't wanna walk around with you."

The most radical album of the past six years isn't Bowie's, isn't Ferry's, isn't Eno's or Reed's. Kraftwerk couldn't have conceived of such Teutonic conquest in a dozen light years and it's doubtful Bob Marley could've ingested enough ganja to perceive its decidedly non-Rasta dimensions. Oddest of all, it's an album that probably would have stood a 99% chance of being dismissed as archaic, or at best an anachronism, had it been released four or even three years ago. Even if it turns out not to be the clarion squawk of a raw new age, the Ramones' *Ramones* is so strikingly different, so brazenly out of touch with prevailing modes as to constitute a bold swipe at the status quo.

As such, *Ramones* threatens hard rock's current ruling caste (Bad Co., Zep, Frampton, et al.) with a razor sharp E-string to the throat. (Most 'progressive' programmers will assuredly turn away from this album, toke up and thumb-cue that new StillsStonesQueenWakeman onto turntable A.)

Ramones: four guys, 14 great two-minute songs, three great chords. Proficiency, poetry, taste, Art have nothing to do with the Ramones. Nor do blues, improvisatory solos or pedal steel. White, American rock 'n' roll is what they practice and in this sense the Ramones are the latest speed-crazed cruisers to drive chicken down that white line that extends straight from Eddie Cochran to Iggy to their own Bowery loft.

Ramones reads like a rock 'n' roll reactionary's manifesto. The kind of driven, primal, mindblasting r&r that fueled Stooges fanclubs and formed the editorial backbone of fanzines from *Who Put the Bomp* to *Punk* comes alive in "Blitzkrieg Bop," "I Wanna Be Your Boyfriend" and "Chain Saw." The infusion of the Kinks, Herman's Hermits, fake Mersey accents, DC5, MC5 and BCR into the Ramones' music is all the more crucial, vital to the survival of rock 'n' roll. Once the whole ballgame, r&r has been reduced to a less than flourishing subgenre whose '70s mutation from 'hard' to 'heavy' has crowned ponderous middle-aged labor unions like Zep, Bad Co. and Foghat giants in the field. Serving its radical function, the Ramones' debut drives a sharp wedge between the stale ends of a contemporary music scene bloated with graying superstars and overripe for takeover. Right now, the Ramones have their hands on the wheel.

Can the first 'New York band' to record survive? Should we expect Joey, Dee Dee, Tommy and Johnny Ramone to 'grow musically'; to do their first sensitive ballad backed by the London Festival Orch on Album # Five, or collaborate with Ken Russell on their tenth anniversary? Who cares? The rambunctious speed & noise equation outlined by "Today Your Love, Tomorrow the World" or "Loudmouth" will do just fine for right now. If their successors are one third as good as the Ramones, we'll be fixed for life. Right fucking on.

Editorial:

Free the Agent Noun!

Waxpaper magazine, Warner Bros. Records, Sept. 1978

It has come to the attention of the ever-observant editors of WAXPA-PER that significant musical changes are now taking place. Changes so sweeping, so profound, that the English language itself (to say nothing of the culture which surrounds it) is being forced to evolve to meet the challenge of this startling phenomenon. We're talking about 1978's most salient trend: the proliferation of Agent Nouns! Verbs left and right are being pressed into service, forced to bear the added responsibility of the cumbersome -ER suffix as rock groups seek the all-important handle on fame.

If you're observant, you've already noticed Agent Nouns creeping into the musical lexicon: groups like Piper, Striker, Trooper. Rock history is rife with similar syntactic assaults; the psychedelic '60s carelessly conscripted pronouns (Who, Them, We Five, Guess Who, Just Us), but nothing compares with the wanton forced surgery that today is transforming hundreds of helpless verbs into mutant (and meaningless) nouns, making these predicates the subject of much misery! Even a casual look reveals the grand scope of this infamy...

Badger
Boxer
Crawler
Cryer
Dancer
Derringer
Driver
Fever
Flyer

Foreigner
Fotomaker
Glider
Kracker
Merger
Piper
Player
Quiver
Ripper
Roadmaster
Runner
Sailor
Shiver
Silver
Sister
Splinter
Strider
Striker
Strutter
Teazer

The benefits derived from agent nouns are obvious. Primarily their use connotes action in the extreme, the kind of movement and aggression that only the most expressive verb can convey.

Clearly, Piper have exercised their option well; strapping on the –ER, this quartet moved from the realm of the passive puffer to broad-lunged stem-toters literally choking on their own smoke. Likewise, had they forsaken the -ER, Striker would have merely demonstrated an awareness of the *method* of political redress. With the –ER added, they lay their bodies on the picket line.

Personalization plays a key part in the appeal of agent nouns; by adopting the –ER suffix, soft-rock kings Player move closer to the listener's heart, suggesting a variety of pleasant associations—your favorite shortstop or goalie, your new turntable or those imported cigs you've been brandishing lately. Boxer calls up your favorite Far East rebellion, that drip-nosed canine down the block or your preferred mode of briefs.

The power of agent nouns lies also in their economy. They are almost exclusively two-syllables, the brevity insuring maximum bombast and drama. Widowmaker's expansionist four-syllable moniker diluted the -ER form (and the group's career). Badger, who shrewdly chose a verb with -ER suffix built in, missed their chance for the Agent Noun

Hall of Fame by not adding the apocalyptic, more orthodox second-ER (making them Badgerer). Needless to say, Badger are no more.

Clearly things are getting out of hand. To escape being left behind by the trend, many of today's established superacts are preparing for the switch to agent nouns. Certain East Coast ABBA fans are already calling Bjorn, Benny & co. ABBER, while it's rumored the Bee Gees will resurface as Geezer before year end, with Meatloaf planning a new MOR career as Loafer and Olivia pursuing androgyny as Newter. Even now agent noun ranks are swelling with Segers, Tylers, Summers, Palmers, Sayers, Saygers and Klemmers. Where will it lead?

For the sake of language and music, *WAX PAPER* would like to inject a little common sense into the fray. Our plea: some discretion, for pete's sake! *WAXPAPER* thus announces the establishment of the Agent Noun Review Board, by whose authority all recording artists would be enjoined from unlicensed use of such linguistic forms, and which would review all applications, awarding or denying usage permits accordingly. In the interest of preventing further agent noun depletion, *WAXPAPER* is pleased to print the following word list, which comprises remaining nouns available for licensing in 1978. Rock group rights to these -ER forms may be secured:

Plumber
Badgerer
Broker
Bugger
Liver
Lather
Logger
Sucker
Wanker
Stapler

(Already awarded by the Board: rights to Trawler—founded by remnants of Crawler and Trooper--, athletic splinter bands Jogger, Sprinter and Biker, and infant punksters Slobber and Diaper.) We hope you will join us in our common cause. Free the agent noun!

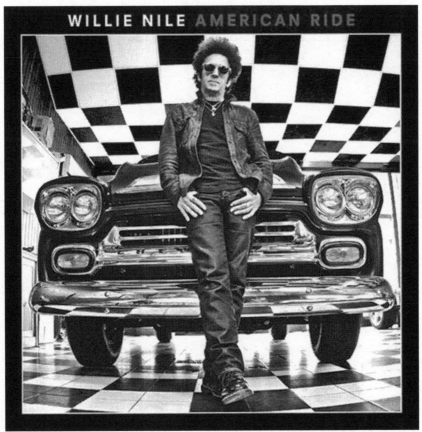

Blinded by the Boss: Willie Nile

THE EIGHTIES AND NINETIES

Other than the rise of New Wave, rap, grunge and ever more ludicrous strains of heavy metal, I'm not sure if the music of the Eighties and Nineties is generally classifiable. On the critics front, we sure didn't get the minimum $25-per-review wage that had topped our demands list at the 1973 Rock Writers Convention in Memphis (cited in the Big Star documentary Nothing Can Hurt Me), *but there was still plenty of work. These were decades when the music business got busier and bigger, and at least twice I got gigs writing about the biggest name artists: Sinatra (liners for a themed compilation issued by Vegas' New York New York casino) and Madonna. The former assignment I approached as an homage to classic Sixties-style sleeve notes. The latter was strictly one from the heart, since I heard much of that early Madonna music—and of the period's effervescent female freestylers (Cover Girls, Expose, et. al.)—as naturally descended from the Spector-era girl-groups. The Eighties yielded two books,* The Catalog of Cool *(my, and my contributors,' response to the practical-hippie toolbox* The Whole Earth Catalog) *and* San Francisco Nights: The Psychedelic Music Trip); *the Nineties a return to writing for fanzines and specialist publications (Kim Cooper's* Scram *and WFMU-FM's L.C.D.).*

Born To Run Also-Rans Hit The Road

Los Angeles Times, Dec. 7, 1980

"Hey, kids! If you're like me, you just can't get enough of Bruce Springsteen. You sat through his four-hour concert and still wanted more, right? You've worn out three copies of the 20-song *The River* already and you're getting panicky because it'll probably be another two years before his next album, right?

"Well, we at K-Boss Records have the answer. Now, for the first time on TV! One hundred songs in the Bruce Springsteen tradition! Road songs! Night songs! Anthems! Soul-searching serenades! All sung almost as you remember them by the original—*original?*—artist!"

Such a TV commercial is unthinkable. Or is it? No rock figure in recent years has been as imitated as Bruce Springsteen. His songs have been covered and re-covered, his vision borrowed by legions of would-be Bruces. He has, in fact, spawned a growing market in Xeroxes of himself.

It started in 1976. Following the enormous impact of Springsteen's *Born to Run* LP, dozens of then-normal young Americans took to the streets of fire, in the hope of duplicating the success of 'The Boss.' As a growth industry, however, Springsteen mimicry didn't really get rolling until 1979. In the lull between *Darkness on the Edge of Town* in 1978 and the new *The River*, untold numbers of pretenders rushed to answer-the audience's calls for "Bruuuuuuuce!" Among them are John Cougar, Billy Falcon, D.L. Byron, Arlyn Gale, to name just a few.

Some of Springsteen's imitators have made two, even three LPs already, and you begin to get a sense many of them are making careers out of being overparked at the Cadillac Ranch. The following is a by-no-means-comprehensive list of Born to Run Also-Rans. Whether or not you know their names, you've heard them all before…

There was a time, it seems, when almost every new singer was accused of sounding like Bruce Springsteen. Elvis Costello, Graham Parker and even Thin Lizzy were among those thus charged, but most of them went on to dispel such notions quickly. All except for Meat Loaf. As the most successful of Springsteen-inspired artists, this heavyweight rocker made his debut album (*Bat Out of Hell*, Cleveland International, 1977) sound like *Born to Run, Take* 2. His song "All Revved Up With No Place to Go" pretty well sums up Meat Loaf's approach, though you might want to add "verbose" and "bombastic."

Mr. Loaf recites the familiar litany of Springsteen images (sandy beaches, broken promises and "bloodshot streets") and tries to go his hero one better; for every crescendo on "Born to Run," Meat Loaf adds three or four more to his own songs. The result is a histrionic meeting across the river of street poetry and heavy-metal overkill. Titles: "Bat Out of Hell," "You Took the Words Right Out of My Mouth (Hot Summer Nights)" and "Paradise by the Dashboard Light," the latter featuring E Street Band pianist Roy Bittan and vocalist Ellen Foley.

Foley kicks off her 1979 album (*Night Out*, Cleveland International) with "We Belong to the Night," a Boss-styled stab at the anthemic whose piano introduction is cribbed from Springsteen's "Jungleland." Despite its overall Spector-style production, Foley's LP steers clear of aping too many other Springsteen mannerisms, which is considerably more than can be said for *Billy Falcon's Burning Rose* (Manhattan Island Records, 1977). Ventriloquism is not at work here. Nor is ESP. This earnest New Yorker literally composes and phrases with the mind and mouth of Springsteen—no mean feat.

With its melody grafted from "Thunder Road" stock and its cataloguing lifted off B.S.'s *Greetings from Asbury Park* LP, Falcon's opus, "Friday Night," sounds more like the Boss than the Boss. Hoarse vocals, triumphant saxes, they're all here, along with a generous helping of bright lights, fire bombs, "mystery" and "romance." "Friday Night" also is memorable for the inspirational verse: *"Without you I'm drivin' lost in a stare/Since you're I gone haven't bothered to comb my hair."*

Falcon overloads his album with references to neon, docks, dreams and Sam Cooke (also see John Cougar). But, while his mentor stays shore-bound, Falcon displays a strong aquatic bent, hanging around under piers ("Another Lonely Night"), singing of shipwrecks ("To Be Alone With You") and seas ("Sail Away," "Sailor Boy").

Falcon's water-brothers include Arlyn Gale and Desmond Child, both of whom underscore their urban guerrilla stances by posing beneath New York City bridges on their LP covers. That's Arlyn over there under the arching Manhattan span on *Back to the Midwest Night* (ABC, 1978), and Desmond searching for stories under the 59th Street Bridge on *Runners in the Night* (Capitol, 1979). Gale was ex-Springsteen manager Mike Appel's first signing upon parting with Bruce, and it's easy to see what Appel saw in Arlyn—lots of edgy darkness and sound-alike vocals.

Naming his LP from a line in Springsteen's "Blinded by the Light," Desmond Child works the bland middle of Thunder Road, conjuring melodrama from such titles as "Tumble in the Night," "The Night Was Not" and "Runners in the Night."

And then there's John Cougar. If you've liked Bruce's blue-collar blues ("Promised Land," "Factory," "Out in the Street," "The River"), you'll flip for Johnny's *Chestnut St. Incident* (MCA, 1976). Indiana-born John roars down Chestnut Street on his way out of a "dream killin' town" only to sample a Springsteenish "American Dream" which informs:

> *Some of the girls are out teachin' high school biology*
> *And all of my boyfriends they work down at Cummins' factory*
> *But me I'm still out on the street*
> *Trying to locate my destiny*

Despite his heavy-reliance on Springsteen as a model, Cougar eventually located his own destiny last year with a hit single, "I Need a Lover," from his *John Cougar* LP (Riva). Dead-end jobs, tattooed love girls, hot cars, backstreets and pool sharks populate Cougar's Badlands.

But the album, and his current "Nothin' Matters and What If It Did" (Riva), at least find Cougar straining against the saxophones-and-Chevy's limitations of the genre. He still apes Springsteen's vocal mannerisms, chases unwinnable women with names like Angelina and hears Sam Cooke coming out of every radio he passes, but Cougar's better songs reveal something real and original beating beneath the hood.

This is more than you can say for such Golden State opportunists as D. B. Cooper. The characters who fill his *Buy American* (Warner Bros., 1980) all seem to pump gas, "live for a thrill" or spend summers "Chasin' Rainbows in the Night," often to the tune of "Born to Run" or "Tenth Avenue Freeze-Out.'"

Space really doesn't permit more than a passing mention of such would-be Jersey Devils as Sumner, Willie Nile, Bill C. Blue, Carolyn Mas or discofied Tony Sciutto, but no discussion of the subject at hand would be complete without including D. L. Byron. Produced by *Born to*

Run engineer Jimmy Iovine, Byron's *This Day and Age* (Arista, 1980) is a 10-track Boss tribute that reveals Meat Loaf, Falcon and Gale as the rank amateurs they are. Byron uncannily apes Springsteen's vocals right down to the midsong "Hey! Hey! Hey!" interjections, and outdoes Springsteen at erotic auto imagery. If you enjoyed the "Strap your hands across my engines" line from "Born to Run," Byron figures you'll flip for "Tell me are your headlights real/Do you mind if I have a feel?"

Poor D.L. In "Today," he addresses the angels of "Oh holy nite" (sic), "laying my love on the line." In "Listen to the Heartbeat," his "Bowery girl" bites his tongue and is "real handy with a rubber glove," but, D.L. assures, he "never gets tired of stiletto love." Elsewhere, he studies his pain, throws roses in the rain and brandishes his sincerity. But it's finally up to the closing lines of "Backstage Girl" to sum up the dilemma of D.L., D.B., Foley, Falcon and the rest:

> *Backstage girl, all we do is smoke and toot*
> *But I'm just a substitute*
> *A superman in a rented suit*
> *But I've been waiting for you.*

FEATURE:

Today's Teens on Yesterday's Rock Classics

Los Angeles Times May 31, 1981

"I don't care what people say, rock 'n' roll is here to stay"
—Danny & the Juniors, 1958

Rock looks as if it *is* here to stay. But are today's teens able to appreciate the records that thrilled their counterparts 10, 15 or 20 years ago? Does the rock of ages past communicate beyond its time? Surely, a classic record is a classic record, regardless of who's listening. Or is it?

For an answer, we gathered 15 teenagers for a blindfold test. We played them 10 records, acknowledged as classics by critics and fans, and asked the teens to rate each record. Each participant wrote down his or her comments, then took part in a general discussion at the end of the session.

Based on these kids' preferences, Buddy Holly deserves to be a rock legend, Phil Spector might be advised to seek a new line of work, and innovators such as Dylan and Jimi Hendrix would likely find it tough going impressing today's audiences with their bravely experimental early work.

The test group was comprised of 14-to-17-year-olds from the San Fernando Valley. They represented a variety of schools, including Taft, Birmingham and Granada Hills high schools, Portola Junior High, Montclair and Egremont private schools and Pierce Junior College. A pre-test disclosed the following: The students' favorite radio stations included KRTH, KMET, KHTZ and KROQ. They averaged 3.2 album purchases a month, buying everything from the latest Styx and REO Speedwagon to the Dead Kennedys.

(Curiously, the area of most agreement was "first records ever owned." Here, the Monkees and Partridge Family easily outscored all others.)

The methodology: Records were rated on a 1 to 10 scale, making 150 points the highest total any one record could receive. While we've listed the records chronologically below, they were not played in this order for the test. Three contemporary were mixed in with the 10 "classics" to broaden the sample.

1—ELVIS PRESLEY's "Baby Let's Play House" (Total points, 84). Part of his 1955 repertoire that inspired riots and enabled Presley to buy his first Cadillacs, this jumpy rocker drew strong ratings but inspired some odd comments. Most participants recognized the singer, but many younger listeners were thrown by the rockabilly style and sparse production. "It sounded like he was singing under water," said Bobby Wagner, 15. The record made Alaina Shapiro, 15, "really nervous," while Scott Hulett, 14, found it "too country." Presley's accomplishments were universally praised, but some listeners likened the rock king's vocals to a bad case of hiccups, gobbling or "a sudden speech impediment."

2—BUDDY HOLLY's "Rave On" (Total points, 105). The late Texas legend outscored all the competition with this 1958 single, a rousing anthem now frequently performed by Bruce Springsteen in concert. Holly, whose last hit charted five years before the oldest of our listeners was even born, won praise as a timeless artist. "I only wish he didn't die," noted Eric Troop, 14, while Bobby Wagner honored Holly as "a true punker." Most of the group saw Holly's film biography and have heard his records played on the radio.

3—THE DRIFTERS' "There Goes My Bay" (Total points, 72). This 1959 vocal-group hit—long hailed as revolutionary for its successful marriage of rock with orchestral backing—was outranked by a Jimi Hendrix record but significantly beat out a Bob Dylan selection. The Drifters sparked much controversy. Allister Watson, 16, "couldn't really hear it because "it sounded too slow." Melissa Belland, 14, called Ben E. King's lead vocal "powerful and clear." Paul Rhoden, 17, found a lot of soul in the record and felt it "got its point across, not like lots of the crap today." Scott Hulett likened the Drifters to hardcore punks Black Flag as "the singer yells instead of signing."

4—GARY U.S. BONDS' "Quarter to Three" (Total points, 89). Widespread agreement on this boisterous No. 1 record from 1961: It appears to remain one of the all-time party records. It made Debbie Davis, 14, "just want to get up and dance." "If I were in a bad mood, I'd play that record to put me in a good mood," explained Lysa Nalin, 15. "When songs are too long, you want to hear them once, but when they're short like that you want to keep playing them over and over." Robyn Taube, 16, thought the record was marred by too much clapping. (Bond has just returned to the charts with the Bruce Springsteen-produced "This Little Girl" single.)

5 — ROLLING STONES' "Last Time" (Total points, 95). Outscored only by Buddy Holly's "Rave On," the Stones' biggest pre-"Satisfaction" rock hit (1965) drew praise. When asked if the record resembled present-day Rolling Stones records, a unanimous response of "No! This is better" went up. "I think the Rolling Stones are trying to be like Rod Stewart now," observed Scott Hulett.

6 — BOB DYLAN's "Subterranean Homesick Blues" (Total points, 61). Few records came in for as much abuse as Dylan's first electric hit, this rambunctious rocker from 1965. His reputation as a poet was questioned (and defended by some), as was his controversial conversion to Christianity. "He was a brilliant songwriter before God took over," declared Robbie Rist, 15. Debbie Davis wondered if the song was recorded "before or after his Christianity phase." Lysa Nalin envisioned the singer as "chosen from a band of farmers just standing around, asked to sing with one of those old-fashioned bands. Like the Country Jamboree bears at Disneyland." Coincidental conclusion of two different listeners: The song's rhyming catalogue reminded them of Sugar Hill's "Rappers' Delight."

·7 — IKE & TINA TURNER's "River Deep — Mountain High" (Total points 45). A rolling, thunderous wall of sound, Phil Spector's 1966 swan song to the American record business has always incited strong reactions. When it was originally released, radio refused to air it and Spector accused the industry of conspiring to ruin him. The genius producer was vindicated when the single went to the top of the British charts. Among our listening group, several objected to the record's pronounced gospel feel and dense production. Bobby Wagner was reminded of Oral Roberts, Eric Troop of Ernest Angley, and Debbie Davis thought Tina Turner's vocal resembled the Mormon Tabernacle Choir. Robyn Taube thought the singer "didn't know how to use her voice." Ron Pivo, 14, disliked the "Broadway show" overtones. Lowest rated record of the day.

8 — THE DOORS' "Soul Kitchen" (Total points, 92). While it placed third overall, this track from the Doors' 1967 debut album took criticism for its speed. "X sings the same song faster and it's twice as good," remarked Scott Hulett. "They sound like they're dead," Melissa Belland observed. The music reminded Todd Gindy, 16, of "when everybody was

going to Vietnam and burning their draft cards. The Doors were back then, weren't they?" Doors defenders Lenny Sage, 15, and Allister Watson found meaning in the lyrics. "Jim Morrison was *the* songwriter and the Doors were *the* L.A. band!" declared Robbie Rist. "Without them, the L.A. band scene wouldn't exist."

9—JIMI HENDRIX's "Purple Haze" (Total points, 82). A staple of early FM programming, this psychedelic 1967 cut by the guitar hero appears not to have aged particularly well. Most common charge: that Hendrix's music was drug-oriented and an artifact of flower-power days. "I can just picture everybody sitting on the grass," said Jackie Pivo, 16, parodying the hippie 'V' peace sign, "all on acid and saying Hendrix was so 'into it, man.'" Paul Rhoden suggested Hendrix walked the wrong side of the "fine line between music and noise." When two female fans claimed Hendrix's music served the same purpose as punk rock does today, Eric Troop answered, "No way. I'll bet the Iranians tortured the hostages with that record."

10—CREEDENCE CLEARWATER REVIVAL's "Tombstone Shadow" (Total points, 50). This four-minute single, from the band's current *Albert Hall* LP (recorded a decade ago), did not appear to be "hit-bound" with the group. Scott Hulett couldn't see "how anyone could put out a record like that and expect to sell it. I think they sounded like hillbillies with corncob pipes." Debbie Davis thought John Fogerty and group "sounded like a combination of Jimi Hendrix and the Rubber City Rebels," while Melissa Belland felt one had to be "in a kicked-back, lazy mood to get into it." Several listeners allowed that the band might be better represented by other records.

As mentioned, three contemporary records were mixed in with our 10 rock classics. One of the more fascinating aspects of the test was the fact that one of these records—"White Girl" by Los Angeles' X—outscored the other records by a wide margin. Scoring a total of 133 points, "White Girl" was applauded by punk advocates and mainstream listeners alike, perhaps indicating X's ultimate commercial viability. Its companion contemporary entries were "Real Love" by the Doobie Bros. (total points, 98) and Billy Joel's "It's Still Rock and Roll to Me" (total points, 73). For the record, the Doobies were acknowledged as master musicians while Joel was chided as "an old man trying to be new wave."

Everybody Needs Somebody to Hate: A History of L.A. Punk Rock

Creem magazine, October 1981

"For God's sake, is that all you people in L.A. want to hear: aggressive lyrics and a raging guitar?!"
—*Chris Stein*
"Thriving on self-pity, racism, hippie-baiting, and an abhorrence of sex and the cheesiest sort of nihilism, L.A. punk is The Scene That Will Not Die."
—*Village Voice*
"A shallow imitation of British punk, a cheap fake."
—*New Musical Express*
"We don't need the English/ tellin' us what to do/ We don't need the English/ Their boring songs of anarchy/ Sayin' our scene's a fake/ Their brains are all half-baked."
—*the Bags, "We Don't Need the English"*

But of course Alice Bag doesn't need the Brits. Nor does she or any of the tens of thousands of punkin' Angelenos need the French, the Dutch, the plot-hatching Corsicans or teenage millionaires from New York like Mr. Blondie to tell them how to behave. Los Angeles doesn't need approval or advice, whether it's coming from a record biz on its bleeding knees or from rock crits coaxing their Selectrics into unspeakable acts in praise of Johnny Rotten's latest hippie music.

But L.A. punk keeps getting this abuse. How would one, er, go about dealing with this abuse on a, um, regular basis?

L.A. punk's answer to its detractors is exactly what it should be: a rigid little digit aimed faceward. After all, the burg has been undisputed Boss City of screaming R&R for what? Three or four years. It proclaimed itself capital the night the Weirdos first sang "I'm a mole/I dig your hole," the day the Alleycats cut "Nothing Means Nothing Anymore," when a hundred punks got their heads vibed by the LAPD at the Elks Lodge. And the town is likely to stay busy, until Keith Morris disbands the Circle Jerks to go study animal husbandry or Black Flag go down in flames over Omaha.

All of which may account for the bad opinion of L.A. held by the noisemakers of the former music capitals. El Lay merely accepted the challenge: to deliver on the promises New York and England wouldn't keep.

In 1976, after parenting the Ramones, New York quickly washed its hands of pogo and moved on to more serious concerns: art-rock, revivalism and fusing together the split ends of fagdom (what city invented 'rock disco'?). *[Ed. Note: Regrettable remark, yes.]*

And the English? They birthed the Pistols-Damned litter, then marched right off to power pop, ska, neo-R&B, all the way to gutless, guitar-less New Romanticism. 'Punk rock' was left up to Southern California (and Frisco with its Avengers, and Vancouver with DOA and the Young Canadians). L.A. accepted the challenge.

It wasn't easy.

Aug.24, 1976: 150 curious spectators and pre-trendies flock to the Radio Free Hollywood dance at Trouper's Hall, to catch what smells like the arrival of the new underground (Motels, Pop, Dogs). It isn't.

March 25, 1977: 100 people drift into the subterranean 'Hollywood Punk Palace' to hear the just formed Nerves, Dils and a handful of teen metal combos. Only the metal combos can play their instruments.

June 20, 1977: The Whisky a Go Go inaugurates 'New Wave Weekends': DJ Rodney Bingenheimer, a close personal friend of Chris Stein and rumored to be Truman Capote's illegit son, hosts an uneasy mix of old guard and punk acts. A big drag.

Then it happens! Overnight, Hollywood punk arrives in one roaring Big Blast that threatens to wipe the mellow smile off L.A.'s public face like an air gun stuffed with hydrochloric. *Friday, Aug. 12, 1977.* Myron's, a hoary old downtown ballroom. Packed with punks: pink-haired, dog-collared, in homemade "Pretty Vacant" and "Please Kill Me" t-shirts. It resembles a bad B-flick, a portrait of Youth Gone Stark Raving Psycho. Who let these crazies out? More importantly, *why have they come here?!*

They came to look at one another. And to see Devo, a concept band that looks like it hung too long in Bowie's closet, and the Weirdos. The Weirdos! L.A.'s 'answer' to the Sex Pistols, firing rounds of rage and silliness with the fury of a caged Bengal: bug-eyed John Denney prowling the stage, chainsawing the pogo-struck dancefloor with "Destroy All Music" and "Why Do You Exist." The Weirdos! Op art and Saran Wrap, leopardskin and paisley, fad glasses and decibels. The crowd goes berserk.

At 4 a.m. everyone drives home. In the morning, Hollywood has a punk-rock scene. History starts falling into place with the precision of dominos. Punks start growing like wild vetch—college kids, precocious high school brats, dropouts from the whole Eagles-Hawaiian-shirt world of SoCal '77. And bands, delirious, anarchic, each putting its own spit and spin on this bad new international lick: Deadbeats, Skulls, Eyes, Plugz, Controllers, Dickies, Bags, Spastics, Alleycats, F-Word, the infamous Germs and the underground's deepest dig, the Screamers. Fueled by appearances by the Ramones and the Damned, its first gobbing glimpse of the real thing, Hollywood goes gloriously batshit, breaking into new venues weekly (Orpheum, Larchmont Hall), looking for that elusive home base, some low rent nest that'll cohabit with the new r'n'r on a regular basis.

> "A cabaret of the macabre... a spectacle of simulated London street desperation in the promised land filtered through a rock 'n' roll sensibility of carbonated freeway fury and terminal swimming pool despair"
> —ad for Brendan Mullen's Masque, 12/77

Lodged in the basement of a Hollywood porn theatre, the Masque is just what L.A. punkdom is looking for: a sleazy subterranean headquarters. It's also what LAPD, the health dept. and an unsympathetic landlord are looking for: a walking bust. The Masque hosts Hollywood punk's wildest nights, then closes in January '78, forever seeking a new location.

But nothing can stop p-rock now. It's growing. Everywhere there are Mau Maus, Metrosquads, Flesheaters, Wildcats. There are hot one-off singles, a Slash label, and Dangerhouse is readying its *Yes L.A.* sampler LP. But there's this nagging question.

It doesn't really bother anyone, you know, but people are starting to ask it and back East they're already bad-rapping this loony beaut of a scene that Geza X and Craig Lee and Trudie and Kid Spike have mothered here. It's that old question: just how Serious is this thing you're doing anyway?

Well... The Weirdos had publicly admitted "We're very g-o-d-d-a-m-n serious," and the *L.A. Times* poured out tons of supportive print, and in *Slash* Kickboy Face was making the scene out to be at least the equal of the Renaissance or the Russian Revolution. But that question nagged. You've got lotsa speed & crazy revved up here with your wacky Dickies and double-strength wailing Bags, guys, but, um, what about... Art?

Enter X. Legend has it John Doe and Exene met at a poetry reading and decided to form a band. Why not? Guitarist Billy Zoom and drummer Don Bonebrake joined and X put out a Dangerhouse 45, "We're Desperate" / "Adult Books" ('77). In a year they were L.A's hottest band. Why?

Good riffs, melody, a hard attack. But where X really connected with crowds was lyrics. X turned the standard *progressive rock* trick, just like the Doors, like Procol Harum or Yes: they attempted the marriage of r'n'r and 'poetry'.

It's a coupling that won't work. Nature won't allow it. But rock audiences often will, and X's brand of pretentious nonsense ("Friends warehouse pain/Attack their own kind/A thousand kids bury their parents") is what sold them to the world.

X brought L.A. punk 'serious' attention from the outside world. What X does is perceived as more than mere 'punk rock'. Their first LP (*Los Angeles*, 1980) transcends genre. Like maybe *Sgt. Pepper*, it proved—along with the arrival of such Hollywood art packs as Human Hands, Wall of Voodoo, Nervous Gender—that Something Serious was shaking out there under the sun. And who's to argue?

Enter Black Flag and Fear. Boy! Hollywood's punk establishment wanted nothing to do with these two bands. I mean, here we are in '78/'79 and we've become legit and our little scene here is clearly maturing and here come these two aggro squads—screaming slabs of primitive pogo/slam, kicking crowds' chops in with songs like "(I Was So) Wasted," "Let's Have A War (So You Can All Die)," "Waiting for the Gas" (lines *and* ovens). I mean, really retro. What's going on here now?!

Slash couldn't bring itself to cover Lee Ving and his gross Fear crew. The paper would, you know, attend a gig and review all the other, in-crowd acts on the bill but somehow, well, *miss* Lee railing (tongue deep in cheek) about homos, whores and sluts. And *Slash* only brought up the subject of Black Flag after the Redondo batch got busted for inciting a rock riot at Polliwog Park. Somehow, the Flag qualified as victims of political discrimination. Hollywood punk establishment to punk audience: listen, kids, we know what's best for you. You won't like these bands, honest.

1980 punk audience to Hollywood punk establishment: Up yours, Gramps! Not only did the new kids dig the hardcore Fear 'n' Flag style, their appetite created a whole whomping second wave of blistering, rage-fueled crude that has yet to subside. The past year and a half has seen an eruption of first-class punk bands (many from the South Bay and Orange County): Circle Jerks, Crowd, Adolescents, Agent Orange, China White, the late great Klan and Redd Kross. Even Hollywood itself is rejuvenated, with the Cheifs (sic) and Mad Society (fronted by 12-year-old Stevie Metz).

"Our message is mental psychosis, basic hatred." So say the Angry Samoans, tireless campaigners for restoring contempt and abuse to the vocabulary of L.A. p-rock.

In 1981, things are going swimmingly: bigger audiences than ever, the music being exported out of state. There are, however, shortcomings. Maybe they come with success. Like the dwindling of good venues, and the intrusion of a few fresh-minted Mohawk clods with no grasp of ironic distance.

And there are the usual roadblocks; lack of airplay, except Rodney's pathetic continuing saga on KROQ-FM and the unwillingness of mainstream music consumers to try anything new. It can wear on you; Darby Crash did the wild brave Germs thing for four years without breaking beyond L.A. If he were here now, would he be playing Antmusic?

And where's Rik L. Rik, and whatever happened to The Last's noble experiment? And scene genius Geza X? At the very least, he's the new Todd Rundgren (i.e., he could write and produce *hits* for anybody), but his *Mommymen* LP languishes, uncompleted, for lack of rec co. interest. And the Gears, once sure bets for pro stardom. After overtures from Rolling Stone Records, they talk permanent splitsville. And the woefully underappreciated: Greg Burk's incredible, ignored Dred Scott or ex-Controller Stingray's KAOS...

But now there's a new tumult in East L.A. (the Brat, a feisty, gal-led quartet; the Undertakers, Los Illegals). There's talk of a Fear album, a second rockabilly set by the Blasters, a posthumous Germs live LP. The Go-Go's and Holly & The Italians seem set with what look like solid major label deals, and you can go see yourself in the 90-minute movie *Decline Of Western Civilization* and have you seen TSOL/the Minutemen/the Rim Pests/Saccharine Trust? Now what was it Chris Stein was saying anyway...

FEATURE:

'Home Runs, No Bunts'— Solar Power on the Rise

Does the Stones' latest album fail to start you up? Has your affair cooled with the New Romantics? You say you didn't grow up to be a cowboy? It's OK. Something of value is happening. It's the new black pop. It's growing in the street, right up through the concrete, right here in Surf City.

Los Angeles Times, Dec. 6, 1981

Melrose Avenue. In the crowded hallways of a West Hollywood office building, musicians come and go—a lean songwriter hustling his latest wares, a vocal group rehearsing dance steps. In a nearby conference room, guitarists and trumpeters plot a concert tour with the precision of military tacticians. At her desk, a receptionist informs a caller that "Mr. Griffey is very busy."

When is Dick Griffey, 40-year-old president of Solar Records, not busy? Behind his door, Griffey previews the Whispers' new album, confirms rumors he's signed Muhammad Ali ("to do a spoken-word record"), and talks, on the phone, to the stable master who tends his 17 thoroughbreds.

A perpetual-motion machine, Griffey is always making moves—and music. Among the moves: the steady advance of four Solar albums up this week's 'Soul LPs' chart in *Billboard* magazine, and the label's relocation early next year to a $6-million studio complex on Cahuenga Boulevard. Among the music: a dozen invigorating hits by Shalamar, Lakeside and the Whispers that may well earn Solar its own niche in pop history.

*

IF ROCK IN THE '70s lost much of its vitality to thundering heavy-metal hordes and simpering singer-songwriters, rhythm & blues was ravaged by equally destructive forces. Tuneless funk has robbed the music of its melody. Slushy ballads have stolen its heart and removed its guts.

While Solar hasn't singlehandedly spearheaded the revival of spirited 'black pop' (Chic, Sister Sledge and even Rick James deserve some credit), the label is impossible to ignore. Solar's best singles snap and crackle with an energy long missing from either Top 40 or FM play lists.

These records most recall the spirit of the early '60s—when daring writers and producers artfully arranged the pop-soul marriages that resulted in the Drifters' "Up on the Roof," Phil Spector's classics and the Temptations, Supremes and Four Tops hits that made Motown.

"Berry Gordy's a bright person. If it weren't for him, there probably wouldn't be a Dick Griffey," says Solar's boss about Motown's master builder. "We're like Motown, I think, in that we're one big creative family. We work together and we socialize together."

As proof, Griffey cites the secretary whose composition is being recorded by Klymaxx on its next album. There's also William Shelby, the former mail boy who's co-authored two gold Whispers singles, and Dynasty's Kevin Spence, who's written for Shalamar and Steve Shockley, and Otis Stokes of Lakeside who produced Klymaxx's debut LP. And then there's Leon Sylvers III.

POP FANCIERS SHOULD easily recall Sylvers' pedigree. His mid-'70s hits with brother and sister Sylver ("Boogie Fever" "Hot Line") were almost a prototype of the brisk Solar style. The soft-spoken 28-year-old seems eminently qualified for his role as Griffey's "Number One creative partner" and the label's chief arranger-producer-songwriter. The temptation to view him as a young Smokey Robinson is hard to resist.

"I should really take a vacation," Sylvers laughs. "I don't know how long it's been since I had one. But I can't really leave; all the groups have been hitting. They all require attention." Sylvers is actually less the workaholic, more the creative craftsman who happens to be, well, driven. He makes no attempt to conceal the joy he derives from making records that connect.

"My ideal is to have the whole record *sing*, to work on the music tracks so they take on the same character as the vocals." To that end, he oversees a stable of songwriters, rehearses musicians and, by his own admission, pushes artists to their limits in the studio. "Sometimes I'm too critical, but I have to be; I know how much they're capable of."

As if producing and writing for Shalamar, the Whispers, Carrie Lucas and Midnight Star weren't enough, Sylvers last year created Dynasty, a two-gals-one-guy trio that's scored with "I Don't Wanna Be a Freak" and "I've Just Begun to Love You." This year, Sylvers expanded Dynasty to a quartet and joined the group.

"I started with the idea of making a funkier Chic," he explains. "Now they're much rawer, more of a Sly & the Family Stone affair." Sylvers is currently rehearsing for the band's next tour (he'll sing and play bass). That overdue vacation grows ever more distant. "When I go out on a tour, I try to spend my time off looking for new acts," he says. "When I get back, I'll start working with some new groups."

Griffey insists it is artists, not merely records, that make Solar's pop sizzle. "I could go into the studio and cut a hit record with a chicken, but that's not what we're after. We're trying to build acts that will have staying power."

Good grooming helps. Griffey proudly lists the main prerequisite for being a Solar artist: "It's not that you have talent, but that you be ladies and gentlemen first." Most of Griffey's ladies and gents compliment their music with clean-cut good looks. Dick Clark would be proud.

Would the image requirement allow Solar to sign an artist like Prince, whose punkish demeanor and sexually frank lyrics make him one of black music's most controversial figures?

"I can't comment on Prince," answers Griffey. "But I won't deal with self-destructive artists. There's enough negativity going around, and I don't want to perpetuate it."

As 1981 draws to a close, Solar Records approaches a crucial juncture. Some observers think the label's spell cooled earlier this year when Solar left RCA for a lucrative distribution deal with Elektra Records; some recent releases, most by new acts, haven't fared as well as might be anticipated. Worse, long-awaited LPs by the company's big guns—Shalamar, Lakeside, Whispers—are due out shortly and will be forced to battle in the Christmas marketplace with the Shalamar, Lakeside and Whispers albums RCA has just released as part of its final Solar commitment.

"It's all Solar product, no matter who distributes it," is how Griffey sees it. He maintains that the RCA and Elektra discs can peacefully coexist. Griffey's more immediate concern is keeping the hit machine running. On the boards for '82: Solar's first movie soundtrack, the tentative start of a gospel subsidiary and a book division and more records. Dynasty could break big. And there's Muhammad Ali, comic Vaughn West and others.

He's also keeping his eyes peeled for a romantic new singing star. "But he'd have to sing like Teddy Pendergrass and dance like Astaire. I'm looking for home runs, no bunts."

Some have suggested Solar's sultan of pop might take a swing at politics.

"I'm friends with (Gov.) Jerry Brown, and with (Assembly Speaker) Willie Brown. But I have absolutely no interest in entering politics myself. My real secret love is horses. I've got a stable. Eventually I'd like to have a breeding operation with a couple of Triple Crown winners."

Business does have a way of intruding, though. "The last time I went to the track," says Griffey, "I walked to the betting window and this security guard stopped me. I thought, 'What now?' The guy pulled out a cassette. 'Here,' he said, 'would you listen to this? It's demo of my group'."

REVIEW:

Foreigner 4

Creem magazine, October 1981

This is what? These guys' second or third LP since Mick Jones publicly declared F'gner ain't dinosaurs and that they were really starting to get, er involved with "the new music scene." Not that the fabled yob squad behind "Hot Blooded" had gone "punk," mind you, but the guys didn't want to be left holding the dry ice in case New Wave did happen to seize the day.

But now it's 1981 and everybody, I mean everybody — "ESP Management" and the guys at *Billboard* and Warner Communications and everyone who knows — knows punk didn't happen. So what's old M.J. to do with his endorsement for the New Age? Stuff it like Chicago, who dedicated one whole album "to the Revolution" back in '69? Hell no! Foreigner acts as if '77-'79 NEVER EVEN HAPPENED! The primo Retro move of all time! The boot-wearing fairies of the New Romanticism have revamped disco, V. Halen and Judas P. have reinvigorated H-Metal, so all's right again out in the broad gutland of this great nation! Mick joins his compatriots in proclaiming the eternal, unbending Forever of AOR! Mid-70's music, long may its flag wave o'er the hunky home of the bland.

To celebrate, Foreigner give out with *Four*, a tidy program that literally breeds familiarity: recycled Stones ("Night Life") reforged Deep Purple ("Don't Let Go"), obligatory balladry ("Waiting for a Girl like You"), even vintage F'gner itself ("I'm Gonna Win").

There is a refreshing change of pace piece of pop ("Luanne"); but that's not what *Four* here is all about. It's all good gray unadorned stuff, unflashy and faceless, and it reassures everyone who maybe was getting a little worried that something might, er, um, change. It won't and FM radio can breathe easy at last; knowing, finally, just what the 80's will be like.

BOOK CHAPTER:

Notes on Cool: The Book Starts Here

Introduction to *The Catalog of Cool*, 1982

Now the roving gambler
He was very bored
Trying to create a next
world war
He found a promoter who
nearly fell off the floor
He said "I've never
engaged in this kind of
thing before"
　　—Bob Dylan, "Highway 61"

Right now, we feel a little like that promoter. Not that we're up to any-thing here as earth-shaking as the next world war, but we may drop some bombs, light a few fires. And Bob Dylan's a good place to start when cool's the topic. At his peak, writing and wailing "Highway 61" and "Like a Rolling Stone" at the world back in '65-'66, Dylan occupied a cool place like no one else. Rebellious, flip, overflowing with mystery, he stood there on the backs of those album jackets in stovepipes and fruit-boots, feeling behind those sunglasses like "some combination of sleepy john estes, jayne mansfield, humphrey bogart/mortimer snurd, murph the surf and so forth." Disengaged, out of time, resembling nothing that had come before, he stood alone, an incomparable icon of fresh style— cool.

But to get back to that promoter. We've never engaged in this kind of thing before, assembling all these personalities and pieces in one place and inviting everyone over. It's a pretty presumptuous gig. But some-body's got to do it.

"Hipsters, Flipsters and Fingerpoppin' Daddies, knock me your lobes!" roars the late great rapper Lord Buckley in his hip-talk tribute to Shakespeare's *Julius Caesar*. "I came here to lay Caesar out, not to hip you to him!" *The Catalog of Cool* comes to hip you to hundreds of items of enduring cool—books, magazines, movies, records, clothes, cars, diversions. Some may be familiar. Others have collected too much dust and not enough deserved attention and will come as surprises. There are lots of opportunities for discovery. You'll be formally introduced to the cool world of "correct" sunglasses; to the Cadillac Ranch, Cabazon's dinosaurs, and Louis Prima's "gleeby rhythms"; to customized Levis, paper dresses, Plastic Man; to Lenny Bruce's greatest riffs and Raymond Loewy's 1953 Studebaker Starliner coupe, "the most beautiful car ever made in America" (see Chapter 8, Wheels).

The Catalog has a practical side too. Each of the book's eight sections contains a 'Shop Around' guide offering where-to-buy leads, addresses, and advice. If you discover something here, we're assuming you'll want to learn more about it.

So, just what is cool anyway? Well, one look around will tell you what isn't cool: sponge-soft record charts, soapy translated-from-the-TV movies, non-books and non-magazines. It's no secret. American culture is up to its pectorals in mediocrity, swamped with the second-rate. Brooke Shields passes for beauty. Humor is snickering en masse at sly marijuana references passed back and forth between lame disc jockeys and "hip" comedians. Individual expression? Cal Klein and Jordache haul out a tire pump, inflate the image of a basic low-fashion garment (blue jeans) to bursting, then sell you the airburger as instant style. Here, have a bite.

In such an uncool world, true style—actions committed with some flair and cut with an edge, deeds that throw sparks or dare to display wit publicly—is hard to find.

Cool is not a fad or a fashion. Therefore, cool's enemies are not "preppy" or "punk" or next month's unearthed or invented sensibilities. Cool's beef is with misapplied style, false expression—attitudes and tastes that have nothing to do with the person who adopts them. Thousand-buck togs, cowboy ensembles, idle jet-setters who send nanny out to find them New Wave togs for the cocktail party, "Fatigue Chic." (You want khaki parachute pants? Enlist.)

To the outsider, the manifestations of cool may look arbitrary. That's because cool is selective in the way it reveals itself. It isn't elitist, but it knows its own. Cool never takes to the streets or billboards to proselytize; if you've got the goods, the mountain will eventually come to you.

True cool is eternal. Its independence from prevailing tastes is just one indication that cool follows its own mind for a reason. Like any deep faith, cool's flame burns, vanishes, reappears. Cool runs underground much of the time, but it never slows up. Like lightning, it links its past practitioners to its present with a flash and a fingersnap. Duchamp shakes hands with Dizzy Gillespie. Lenny Bruce cracks a line, Dylan cribs it in scribbling a song. A hundred years later, some seventeen-year-old girl poet will name a magazine after the song and publish a photo of Diz and Duchamp slapping five at Birdland. Cool reinvents its own wheel. It's a groove.

Cool has nothing to do with being "with it" or "in" by contemporary standards. If anything, like the holy fool, cool is often out of step. It's misunderstood (see our profile on George Hunter), persecuted (Bruce), or simply ignored in its time. True cool is nothing more (or less) than the fullest expression of what it is that's different or unique about a person. That's how the cool books get written, the cool movies made. Someone taps his uniqueness and liberally invests his creations with it. When those creations or expressions achieve maximum impact, that's cool.

Imagination counts.

"Uniqueness"? "Fullest expression"? We'd better stop now, before we devolve into pop psych and start soliciting memberships and taking up collections.

The point here should be fairly obvious: Learning everything that's between these covers won't *make you cool*, any more than it's made any of us cool. (Just look!) You are cool if you go away from here and invent your own version of cool.

That's what most of the characters celebrated in the *Catalog* did. That's why they're here, portrayed (hopefully) at the top of their distinctive forms. We'll hip you to Sam Peckinpah's warped Western series (see Chapter 7, Tube), to the Shanels' Japanese doowop music (Chapter 1, Sounds). Our Ink chapter clues you in to Doris Piserchia's sci-fi P.I. Mr. Justice and to that Terry Southern story about Boris and Priscilla and their pals pushing that gone globe of mercury around the floor.

We start, appropriately, at the beginning—with jazz. In New York. In the late Forties. Our man was there and wants to tell you about it in an essay entitled "The Birth of the Cool."

It falls to the grand Lord Richard Buckley to provide our invocation. As Mr. Rabadee said to the All Hip Mahatma, "Straighten me, 'cause I'm ready!"

FEATURE:

The Fine Art of TV Villainy

Featuring J.R., JD's, Psycho-Killers and Those Fun-lovin' Windbreaker Hoods

From *The Catalog of Cool*, 1982

Ask anybody. The best thing about so-called "drama" on television is not deeply touching stories (there aren't any), hotshot acting (none of that either), or *auteur*-type direction (where?). The best thing is Bad Guys. And now Bad Girls. Heavies. You know, low-ball cutthroats and cheats, swindlers and crazed maniacs. They're almost always preferable to good guys in terms of pure entertainment and, at least over the last thirty years on the best cop shows—where they're oversimplified and often overacted with a finesse approaching pure art—they get the coolest lines.

Think of it. J.R. on *Dallas* throwing on that smug, happy face when he tells the cartel boys those stock certificates he's sold them aren't worth a liter of gasohol. Or those menacing pinstripe punks on *Cannon* or *Mannix* who catch their extortion-victim daddy as he's leaving for work and tell him, "Real nice family you got there, mister. Sure be a shame if anything were to ... *happen* to them."

Heh heh heh. The sniggers echo way back to the ghoulish Crypt-keeper and all those horror comic hosts. Face it: He's not blond, but Snidely Whiplash has more fun than you'll ever have. Believe it.

Where did it all start? The Fifties, probably. Richard Boone's Paladin character on *Have Gun Will Travel* ("a knight without armor in a savage land") was a black-dressed avenging angel, a bounty hunter with a boss business card and a tendency to let his pearl-handle do his talking. This was back from '57 to '63. Even before that, TV's first cop and detective series ran with stock baddies—lots of goons with five o'clock shadow, pencil moustaches, and light ties on dark suits crimed it up on programs like *Boston Blackie*.

But it wasn't until '57 or '58 that the first significant trend in tele-villainy popped up. We're talking about the juvenile delinquent. He was a convention borrowed, as were most of the rest, from the movies (*Blackboard Jungle*, *The Cool and the Crazy*, *High School Confidential*), and from '57 through about '60, he was hurriedly written into every cop show script that required thoroughly repugnant antisocial behavior and a touch of relevance. "Hey, *maan*," the Vic Morrow clone sneers as he flicks open his switchblade, "you goin' someplace?" With its usual style, television softened even these hard guys in the name of family interest. If the widescreen version was puff-faced John Davis Chandler and pals swaggering down the sidewalk casually kicking over a baby carriage in *The Young Savages* (people scream and flee; the buggy cradled only a doll), TV was Edd "Kookie" Byrnes hot-wiring a T-bird and skating for the malt shop. It's not widely known, but Byrnes, Mr. Cool to millions in '59 and '60, began his *77 Sunset Strip* career as a JD. In the pilot ep-isode, he played a psychopathic teen killer who watched color cartoons in between mayhem sprees. Even as a heavy, Kookie was such a hit that the show's producers were forced to bring him back as a regular—as a reformed hood who parked cars rather than stole them.

From there, it was only a matter of ten years before the Fonz blew into town, proving that, just because a guy wore a ducktail, engineer boots, and ratty black leather, there was no reason he Couldn't counsel teens and patch up domestic discord like some free-lance Danny Thom-as. Heeyyyy ...

Real JD villains vanished from the air as the Sixties dawned. A final few were located idling outside rural greasepits along *Route 66* or ha-rassing surfers in *The Aquanauts* and *Malibu Run*. They were politely ushered out with a wave of the hand when the fall '59-spring/ '60 season arrived, bringing with it a little Desilu number, a period piece on orga-nized crime fronting the greatest wooden actor of all space and time, Robert Stack. Stack was Eliot Ness, Ness was the tough talking Federal Prohibition agent, and *The Untouchables* became the first Sixties cop show smash. In its favor, the program made more creative use of pet-rol-powered vehicles crashing through doors, walls and abandoned ware-houses in a single episode than *Dukes of Hazzard* has in umpteen sea-sons. And its heavies—great thundering bad-asses such as Bruce Gordon (as Frank Nitti), Neville Brand (as 'Scarface' Capone), and Nehemiah

Persoff (as the slimy Jake 'Greasy Thumb' Guzik)—were tops, real mad dogs among mad dogs.

But wait! They all wore suits! Suits?! Right. Double-breasted, vested, tailored two-hundred-buck jobs. Regular guys they were, oiled crumbs just up from the rackets, and—granted, Greasy Thumb and Bugs and Big Al were now well off, but suits?—they looked downright respectable. And, unlike the sadismo hoods of '57-'60, these guys weren't kids. Pretty soon, every cop series was full of natty mobsters, manicured, pedigreed punks, dapper middle-aged cats who looked as if they'd just as soon buy a new Eldorado and move wife and kids into that big split-level down the block as slit your throat. Call Welcome Wagon; here they come—right next door to you. Like, what's happening?

What happened was inevitable. In no time, the cop shows themselves mutated into lawyer shows, and the criminal element moved further uptown, into courtrooms on *The Defenders* and its imitators. Upscale thugs ruled. Increasingly, their wrong-doing became more genteel, less violent. It wouldn't be long before *Bracken's World* (1969) and subsequently *Executive Suite* (1976) replaced knife-wielding scumbags with white-collar crooks, setting up audiences for J.R. Ewing's dastardly but graciously performed deeds.

The late Sixties did make one invaluable contribution to tube villainy, when they momentarily reversed the gentleman gangster trend in a single stroke and created a monstrous generic meanie, a character type I call the California Windbreaker Hood. He was surely a cousin to the juvie, and his emergence was certainly a nod to the westward tilt of the world. He might be a psycho Viet vet trafficking joy pills, a small-time con running a harmless fat-cat fleece, or some pimp engineering May-December marriages and accidental deaths for quick policy pay-offs. But one thing's sure: He trashed the three-piece heavies with what has got to be the coolest, most casual style to ever stalk the scan lines. The California Windbreaker Hood!

No one knows the exact point where he first appeared, mind you, but there are clues. Like that '67 or '68 *Mannix* episode "A Step in Time." A young woman is abducted by two thugs on the Malibu sand. Mannix and Peggy drive out to a seedy coffee pad (the Freak Out) to check leads. Peg: "Joe, this is where all the weirdos up and down the beach come to groove." Then it happens. Joe and Peg locate a witness who cops: "I saw them. One of them had on a longish black leather jacket. And the other had on a . .. a .. . a windbreaker!"

You bet he did. The navy MacGregor model, 100% cotton, with the midnight-blue knit collar and the two-button neck strap, the narrowed knit cuffs and alloy Talon Claw zipper. Like Ike wore battling the Nazis, but civvie, lightweight, and cool blue. And the creep would invariably have on the rest of the ensemble—white chinos, immaculate crew neck t-shirt (white), five-eyelet Ked deck shoes in blue, and impenetrable Balarama shades. And He'd have short hair. Neat. Cut clean. Like a block of ice. Suburban. Looked like the kind of guy you'd meet Saturday morning buying lawn seed or polishing the Evinrude on his power boat.

But no. The ranch-wagon exterior concealed an evil so insidious, so unpredictably malevolent, he was the closest image match TV has yet devised to Tony Perkins' tidy little Norman Bates in *Psycho*. Eventually, these sunburnt California bully boys took over televillainy, cropping up on *Cannon*, *Barnaby Jones*, every other *Mannix*, and most Quinn Martin shows. In fact, the all-time Windbreaker Hood performance was given by the late Steve Inhat on Q-M's *The F.B.I.* Inhat, a pioneering character heavy who played a chilling game of wits with detective Richard Widmark in the movie *Madigan*, buttoned up his Mac for dozens Of CWH parts in the late Sixties.

But here he leads a pack of leering jacket-boys into the Mojave Desert to hold all twelve inhabitants of a touristy ghost town hostage in a decrepit old house. Efrem Zimbalist, Jr., and company get the scent, so Inhat's gang plays a waiting game. They unzip their windbreakers to half mast, keep their pistols trained on their sweating hostages. When a distraught young woman begs Inhat to let her take one hostage, an infirm old geezer, to the nearest hospital, Inhat growls "Nobody leaves!" The woman decides to go for it and breaks for the door with the dying geezer. Inhat catches them, the old man stumbles then falls to the floor, conked out. "You killed him!" screams the woman. "It's your fault! He's dead!" Tight shot on Inhat's face. He breaks into a grin, looks at the hysterical gal. "People die," he says.

From there, it's all downhill. The last Windbreakers broke out on *Starsky & Hutch* and occasionally on *Vegas*. Nowadays the action has moved elsewhere—to Sunbelt power corridors where J.R. Ewing wheels and deals, to Denver where Blake Carrington's books, not his hands, run red with heinous deeds. Over on *Flamingo Road*, the maniacal Michael Tyron dabbled in voodoo, home-wrecking, and senator-buying, while Howard Duff's Sheriff Titus Semple bugged whorehouse bedrooms, framed innocent victims, and waved his cigar in the air while referring to all males as "Bub." Mild stuff. If the Eighties have vanquished the great goons, they've at least provided equal opportunities for women.

The past two or three seasons have witnessed the overdue arrival of a strong breed of female cutthroats—scheming sex kittens like *Dynasty's* Fallon Carrington and *Knots Landing's* Abby Cunningham, and the doddering gothic matriarch Angela Channing of *Falcon Crest*. But, above all the rest: Morgan Fairchild as Constance Carlyle on *Flamingo Road*, whose moist lips speak lust *and* larceny, and Joan Collins' satanic Alexis Carrington *(Dynasty)*. Collins' treachery knows no bounds; she's carefully plotted the ruin of ex-husband Blake's marriage and his business career, successfully caused Blake's new wife to abort, and, in the spring '82 season closer, literally loved Blake's archrival to death. In a steamy bedroom scene just this side of hard X,

Collins bedded the obsequious Cecil Colby inside Blake's on-premises guest house. The lovemaking grew too intense for middle-aged Cecil, who expired in the sack after a heart seizure. "You can't die on me now!" shouted Collins. "You've got to help me get back at Blake!"

Good stuff. And, hopefully, there'll be more to come, if low Nielsens and Moral Majoritarians don't intervene. Like some infernal bad seed, evil grows on in television land. Viva villainy.

LINER NOTES:

The 4 Seasons 25th Anniversary

Rhino Records, 1987

"... He turned on his record player, dressed up in his sharpest clothes, and practiced dancing as if as long as Kookie Byrnes or Cousin Brucie or Mad Daddy or Babalu or Murray the K or Dion or Frankie Valli could be heard, as long as there was some kind of hip ditty-bop noise, as long as there was boss action, as long as there was something to remind him of the nowness and coolness of being seventeen and hip, he was safe."

That's Richard Price, describing the mindset of one of the young mooks who populate his novel *The Wanderers*. For the record, the mook is an olive-skinned member of a North Bronx gang, circa 1963. But one needn't share his background to appreciate the litany of hipster saints recited above. The 4 Seasons' "ditty-bop noise"—at its best a series of sharp, ethno-urban thunderclaps—is the musical equivalent of Kookie's cocky grin or Murray's mouth on mike. "Rag Doll" and "Sherry" and "Stay" are, like "The Wanderer" or "Be My Baby," Pop of an extremely tough order. On those records rests the rep of Frankie Valli and the 4 Seasons. That includes a fine, private place in American rock history (as *the* hot link between Fifties and Sixties modes), and their enduring status as a Tri-state treasure: the Seasons are nothing less than the East Coast's Beach Boys, a heart-swelling home team with the stats to prove it. As in 90 million records in twenty years.

Like the Beach Boys, the 4 Seasons gave the Beatles a run for their money on the charts (racking up over forty chart records,) by updating a Fifties genre—vocal group 'doowop'—for the Sixties. Unlike the Wilson brothers, though, Frank Valli, Bob Gaudio, Nick Massi and Tommy DeVito were primarily singers, not a guitar-led rock & roll band. Which made the 4 Seasons trend-buckers and totally out-of-step once the Beatles came along to define the sound of the Sixties as precisely that.

Out-of-step they remained through much of that fabulous decade; when those around them touted lab-bred Nirvana and giggling gurus, or posed for albums with their private sectors publicly displayed, these guys just kept making records. Some of the greatest Pop records, in fact, to ever hit the tunedecks.

THE NAME GAME

The story gets under way in 1953. That's when young Frank Valli (originally Castelluccio), out of Newark, cut his first record. It was a version of 'Toastmaster General' Georgie Jessel's "My Mother's Eyes." It was on Mercury Records, and by-lined Frank Valley & the Travelers. It flopped but Valli rebounded, hooking up with a Jersey lounge act, the Variety Trio. He sang lead (and played standup bass or shook maracas), while Hank Majewski sang bass, Tommy DeVito played lead guitar and Tommy's brother Nick sang backup. The Trio worked steady through 1956, at joints like Newark's Silhouette Club and Passaic's Broadway Lounge, wowin' 'em with standards, Hit Parade covers and such neighb faves as "Come Si Bella" and the risqué "Italian Cowboy Song." The same year, they signed with RCA, rechristened themselves the 4 Lovers and cut "Apple of My Eye," written by "All Shook Up" and "Great Balls of Fire" scribe Otis Blackwell.

"Apple" got some action on the East Coast and the Lovers even did the Sullivan show. But they couldn't follow up their hit, not on RCA—not on Decca (as Frank Valley) or Cindy (as Frankie Vallie & the Romans) or Gone (as the 4 Seasons, named after a venerable Jersey lounge). By 1961, Valli, Tom DeVito and newcomers Nick Massi (singer/arranger) and Bob Gaudio (ex-Royal Teen, author of "Short Shorts") were reduced to doing backup vocals on other artists' records: everything from Danny & The Juniors' "Rock & Roll Is Here to Stay" to "More Lovin,' Less Talkin'" by Johnny Halo.

PERRY BABY

The backup work was the result of a two-year contract the Seasons had signed with Philly producer Bob Crewe, then swinging with Swan (he wrote Fred Cannon's "Tallahassee Lassie" and Billy & Lillie's "La Dee Dah") and Cameo (the Rays' "Silhouettes"). Valli and Gaudio were particularly dragged by the anonymity of backup, especially since

Gaudio had just written a tune he wanted the Seasons to cut, a little thing called "Sherry."

According to Seasons expert (and author of *Still White and All Right*) Ed Engel, Bob Crewe almost blew the Seasons' debut. Since he was now working for Perry Records, Crewe agreed to record the Seasons if they changed the title of Gaudio's song to "Perry," thinking the gender bend would be a real attention-getter. Cooler heads prevailed: Crewe cut, Vee Jay picked up the master and the group, and "Sherry" kicked off the 4 Seasons' career in the fall of '62.

With hindsight, we might be tempted to describe all Number One records as inevitable, even Joe Dowell's "Wooden Heart" (1961) or Player's "'Baby Come Back" (1978). But there is something instantly classic about "Sherry." Valli's vocal, the lean, taut strut of the melody stretched over that modified "La Dee Dah" rhythm—there was never any question of the impact it would have on Teenage America's ears, even when the competition included such boss discs as "The Loco Motion," "Party Lights" and "Green Onions."

Bob Gaudio and Crewe put their pens together for "Big Girls Don't Cry" while Nick Massi arranged the vocals; his "silly boy" bass line and the accordion-pleated harmonies on the chorus may be the record's secret stars. Another chart-topper.

The group's third consecutive Number One, "Walk Like a Man," was their most tense, toughest side yet. It piles layers of clean, crisp echo on the percussion and marches around like a ditty-bop general. "Walk" also intros one of the Seasons' most enduring themes: pride maintenance in the face of romantic rejection (cf. "Ronnie," "Big Man in Town"). Just the kind of inspirational medicine 15-year-old males could use in 1963; today they run to the misogyny of heavy metal. "Lucky Ladybug," the flip of "Walk," was a re-reading of Billie & Lily's 1959 Crewe tune.

TWINSPINS AND LABELSWITCHES

Fats Domino's 'Ain't That A Shame!," here updated with vocal-trumpet riffing and a *big* drum sound, is the first in a line of roots covers that includes Little Joe and the Thrillers' "Peanuts," Maurice Williams' "Stay," the Shepherd Sisters' "Alone" and, much later, the Shirelles' "Will You Love Me Tomorrow."

"Candy Girl"/ "Marlena" must surely rank as one of the choicest twin spins ever waxed. "Candy," a Top Five item from the summer of '63, is sublime, a woodblock samba with a razor-strop rhythm and one of Valli's most yearning vocals. The flip is both hard and sweet, with Frank pining for the same corner flirt Avalon fell for in "Gingerbread." Piano, claps, a rugged snare and Valli's "rupe-dupe-dooby-do"s make the fade all-time. For the follow-up to "Marlena" / "Candy Girl," Crewe and arranger Charles Calello came up with "New Mexican Rose." The spry, slightly campy mood piece ("Si, la gringo/I'll give you my ring-o") land-ed inside the Top 40 in the fall of '63. "Connie-0," "Big Girls'" B-side and a West Coast hit in its own right, is a neglected sleeper: melancholy, stunningly sparse, a state of mind straight from Cloud Nine.

Early the next year, the group left Vee Jay for Mercury's Phillips sub-sidiary. "Dawn," with its "Telstar" rhythm and heavy production, was the first Philips issue. It also established another popular Seasons theme: the vulnerability hidden beneath the chest-pounding pride of "Walk Like a Man." Here, as in "Bye, Bye, Baby (Baby Goodbye)," Frankie sends the gal away, explaining that, well, he's just not worthy: "Think what the future would be with a poor boy like me."

"Stay," its bottom deck "Peanuts," and "Alone," all hits from 1964, were lame-duck releases from Vee Jay's vaults. Nonetheless, "Stay" is a minor masterpiece, a whiplash chalypso from the very nexus of Italo-Su-damerican relations. It should really last just a little bit longer, though.

The Philips hit streak launched by "Dawn" continued with "Ron-nie": a driving Charlie Calello arrangement featuring homicidal drums, and Valli scaling a vocal wall of sound by the record's end. The streak peaked in "Rag Doll," the Seasons' most transcendent single. From the drum intro (same one that starts "Be My Baby") through Valli's soaring wordless fade, "Doll" is Superpop at its best: invigorating, emotional, kinetic. Number One the summer of '64, its observation of social in-equities pre-dates Dylan's pop arrival by six months (and Springsteen's bombastic odes to the virtues of poverty by a decade). Too much. Its B-side, Gaudio and Crewe's "Silence Is Golden," was a hit for England's Tremeloes three years later.

The Seasons closed out 1964 with a pair of aces from their new writ-ing team of Sandy Linzer and Denny Randell. While Crewe and Gaudio still produce, there's something different—fuller and more dramatic—about the sound of "Save It for Me" and "Big Man in Town." The latter begins with a melancholy harmonica out of a Sergio Leone flick, then opens onto a vista of surging drums and wailing Valli. A widescreen rock opera in 2:47.

The parade march "Bye, Bye, Baby (Baby Goodbye)" and the more sedate "Toy Soldier" presage another Seasonal cornerstone: their strings-laden melodrama suggests the move to the middle of the road is not far off. Before the M.O.R. wave hit, there were still classics to catch. "Toy Soldier's" flip, "Betrayed," and July '65's "Girl Come Running" are good, but December's "Let's Hang On" is great; its jagged guitar winks at punk while the tune itself nods deeply to Motown.

THREE IN ONE

As with everyone else in those days, changes visited the 4 Seasons in 1966. Nick Massi was replaced by Joe Long, and Valli began moonlighting as a solo. The latter development—along with a stone-rolling spoof record—accounted for the group enjoying hits under three different names during '64. Frankie Valli received sole credit on "The Sun Ain't Gonna Shine (Anymore)," "(You're Gonna) Hurt Yourself," "You're Ready Now" and Cole Porter's "I've Got You Under My Skin." The Seasons continued to click, with "Little Boy (In Grown Up Clothes)," the 4 Tops-ish "Working My Way Back to You" and "Opus 17 (Don't Worry 'Bout Me)." Meanwhile, a marred outtake from the group's *Sing Big Hits by Bacharach, David and Dylan* album, "Don't Think Twice"—credited to The Wonder Who—drew laughs and chart bullets. (The Wonder Who's real joke opus, "On the Good Ship Lollipop," is not included here, but hungry fans can trek down that "Lonesome Road" on Side Six.)

As Frankie's solo career geared itself to an older Easy Listening crowd, the Seasons stretched out and toughened up, delivering some of their most adventurous sides. 1967's "Tell It to the Rain" and "Beggin'" are fast and fuzzboxed, the former featuring an unusual midsong breakdown of piano and blues guitar. "C'mon Marianne," Top Ten in the Summer of Love, is rough and edgy, and further proof that the group could take chances with the best of them. The Doors copped the "Marianne" riff for 1969's "Touch Me." While Valli rounded out '67 with "I Make a Fool of Myself," the Seasons went psychedelic, sort of. "Watch The Flowers Grow" is light and spacy, still pop but sprinkled with quirky effects to create the mood of a gentle mind excursion. It works, nicely.

Although there were surely voices pleading "Let's Hang On!," "Bye, Bye, Baby" was the dominant theme of the Seasons' career from 1968 to 1970. Frankie enjoyed more solo success with "To Give (The Reason I Live)" and "The Girl I'll Never Know (Angels Never Fly This Low)." The group scored with "Electric Stories" (a psycho-vaudevillian ditty of the type Micky Dolenz handled in the Monkees) and "Will You Love Me Tomorrow." The latter signaled something of a return to form, but sounded even then like a swan song; hearing it now, it seems still more bittersweet and poignant.

The last Seasons chart singles (until 1975), "And That Reminds Me" and "Patch Of Blue," came appropriately enough, from *Half And Half*, the 1970 album that devoted a side apiece to Frankie and the Seasons. By then, Massi and DeVito were both gone, and Gaudio was devoting increasing time to such outside projects as *Genuine Imitation Life Gazette* (an imaginative but unsuccessful Seasons concept LP) and *Watertown*, the shamefully underappreciated Frank Sinatra album he co-wrote and produced. *Genuine Imitation Life Gazette* is represented by two selections, both from Bob Gaudio's adventurous songwriting partnership with Jake Holmes. A chart hit that spring, "Idaho" is a curious deadpan paean to the land of "thrilling checker games/Spelling bees... cherry trees." "Saturday's Father" somewhat recalls McCartney's "She's Leaving Home," but this broken home tale is infinitely less sweet, much more real.

RETURN TO GLORY

It's probably not coincidental that, during the years 1970 to 1975— generally acknowledged as the blandest, least lively in recent Pop history—there were no new 4 Seasons records on the radio. In the tie-dyed era of Taylor and Denver, there was really very little place for the powerful urban Pop at which the Seasons excelled. But strange things happen— and savvy record men are often there to take advantage of them.

In this case, it was the public's preoccupation with ballads and disco that provided the launching pad for Frankie Valli's return, with the biggest records of his solo career. After some stalled attempts at Motown, Valli and Bob Crewe found Larry Uttal's enterprising Private Stock label, which in 1975 released Frankie languorous "My Eyes Adored You" (another Number One), and the disco-fied "Swearin' to God" and "Our Day Will Come."

Happily, Valli's new success inspired Gaudio to go for the double play. The same year, he recruited a new 4 Seasons around Frankie and sold them to Warner-Curb Records, which promptly enjoyed two of their biggest smashes. "Who Loves You" was a doubly satisfying radio treat: its strength and spirit blew most other hits of the day out the door, and it signified the overdue return of a cherished American favorite. To many ears, "December, 1963 (Oh, What a Night)," the Seasons' final Number One (March '76), bests "Who Loves You."

And it is a killer, Valli trading verses with Gerry Polci, synth swirling around pounding piano and bass. "Silver Star," the third single from the *Who Loves You* LP, may sound like an unlikely candidate for hits-ville. Nonetheless, the mini-western (replete with acoustic strum and "Apache" solo) galloped two-thirds of the way up the Hot 100 during the Bicentennial summer. Two years later, Frankie delivered one last Number One, the theme from the musical *Grease*, which effectively capped the recording career of the 4 Seasons and Frankie Valli.

Last, though, is a word we ought to be wary of using in connection with the 4 Seasons. Hardly a month passes without rumors of reunion or new projects, and the future may be less silent and more golden than any Seasons fan dare imagine. Regardless, the 4 Seasons have left us an embarrassment of riches, a wealth of stirring, supremely American music. Listen to "Rag Doll" and "Ronnie" and "Let's Hang On!" and "Marianne." Dig the hip ditty-bop legacy and know: It Will Stand.

LINER NOTES:

Madonna *The Immaculate Collection*

Sire Records, 1990

"The Coolest Queen of White Heat"… "An outrageous blend of Little Orphan Annie, Margaret Thatcher and Mae West"… "Narcissistic, brazen, comic… the Goddess of the Nineties…"

And that's just the tip of the iceberg of what's been said about Madonna since she arrived in 1983. The complete press file would probably yield enough recyclable pulp to keep what's left of the Amazon rainforest from the saw for several months. And yet, in all that ink and column inches, most of what's been written has addressed the way she looks, acts, earns, and conducts her personal life. A breathless *Time* cover story, for example, concluded with four pages devoted to Madonna's comments on 22 pithy topics the magazine had chosen—everything from Fame and Femininity to Parents, Virginity, Catholicism and Belly Buttons. Apparently, *Time's* editors didn't think anyone cared to read what Madonna had to say about her specialty, the preeminent thing it is that she makes: Music.

In the years since, the ensuing hoopla has further fogged the issue of Madonna's music. It's easy to forget that before her hit singles became Events, they were great records, the best of which hit pop's cosmic G-spot, got a groove, and literally shook the world. Collected in one place and listened to as a body of work, those records 1) document the musical career-in-progress of an artist with an uncommon capacity for growth and change, and 2) sound as good as and often immeasurably better than ever.

The party started officially in October 1982, when Sire Records released a 12-inch of "Everybody." (Those who choose to see Madonna as a self-image mongerer might be surprised to learn that her likeness doesn't even appear on the sleeve of this first record.) It wasn't until almost a year later that Madonna really "broke," with the joyous "Holiday." Cougar and Culture Club were hot, the Police and Abba were cooling, and the marriage of New Wave and disco, hastily arranged by England's New Romantics, was on the rocks.

Onto this scene burst the two records that, by and large, invented what came to be called Dance Music: Shannon's "Let the Music Play" and "Holiday." The former turned the beat around with tough poly-rhythms, and the latter simply rocked—gently but insistently—with melodic sweetness and a "girl" playfully sending out party invites ("Ev-erybody spread the word... we're gonna have a celebration"). A synth bur-bles like some super fresh tributary of the Fountain of Youth and the girl, sexy and sure of herself, beckons us to "take one day out of life" "'cause we need that holiday, oh yeah, oh yeah." It's irresistible pop, and easily one of the most persuasive Let's-get-lost songs ever sung.

"Holiday" and the string of Madonna dance classics that fol-lowed—1984's sinewy, astro-bodied "Lucky Star" and "Borderline" (at Number Ten, her last single not to go Top Five) and 1985's 12-inch an-them "Into the Groove"—virtually defined the 80s' emerging sound. It was black-rooted, dressed sharp in custom production, physically attrac-tive. "Star" and "Groove" and "Dress You Up" and the rest forced radio to devise a whole new format to accommodate them ("Hot" or "Power" Radio, depending on where you listened). As Power flowered, the arrival of each new Dance Music hitmaker raised audience expectations about the genre's prime mover and shaker: what would Madonna do next?

Her first Number One single, crowned the third week of Novem-ber '84, gave an unequivocal answer. "Like A Virgin" shocked some, in-trigued others, and succeeded so thoroughly as an across-the-board pop smash (six weeks at the top) that it rendered the whole competition issue moot. From now on, this "shiny and new," coolly understated single an-nounced, Madonna records would confound all expectations, including those set by previous Madonna records. Like "Material Girl." The infec-tious, neo-Blue Beat romp resembles no other Madonna music before or since. Here, she comes on at once coquettish and self-determined, hence tantalizingly unreadable. Which probably explains the intense heat the disc drew once it hit (i.e. considerably more than Randy Newman's un-mistakably facetious "Short People" encountered a few years earlier). What to make of "Material Girl's" bucks-based dialectic? It's anyone's guess, but we ought to note that by the third verse she's counting her wealth in "experience," and that the end toward which she's been justi-fying her means turns out to be pretty benign and thoroughly pop: Boy

Attraction ("and now they're after me"). Roots bonus: when she chirps "That's right!" and "No way" on the second and fourth verses, she sounds uncannily like Lou Christie fading on "Two Faces Have I" (1963).

"Material's" unlikely follow-up, the *Vision Quest* ballad "Crazy For You" that Madonna treats with exceptional tenderness and a tinge of Country, presages a quartet of innovative, radiantly sung singles from her underrated 1986 *True Blue* album. She had a hand in writing all four highly dissimilar tracks. "La Isla Bonita" is as light and wistful as "Open Your Heart" is taut and determined. Both pivot from the subtlest of hooks into killer choruses, the former swelling and ebbing like some tropic tide, the latter driving like hard rain: "Don't try to run," she warns the unresponsive guy of her dreams, "I can keep up with you..." While the majestic "Like a Prayer" dwarfs it for sheer scope, "Papa Don't Preach" certainly ranks as one of Madonna's most compelling dramatic performances. She flat-out *sells* the song—from the inside—in a way that would have been unthinkable a year earlier. A new maturity is evident too in "Live to Tell." Her voice, full with loss and longing, sweeps across the stark arrangement of distant synth chords and lone guitar figures, seeking, holding secrets. "...It will burn inside of me...."

Nearly two years pass between 1987's "Who's That Girl" and the three *Like a Prayer* hits. The album, which critics waste no time in proclaiming Madonna's most frankly personal, even "confessional," yields more surprises—foremost among them a head-on confrontation with Catholicism and a re-embracing of her R&B roots. The title track doesn't just appropriate religious images: the words, and Madonna's impassioned delivery, actually sound Spirit-driven, rising from a whisper to a wailing soundwall. It keeps on pushin.' Only Madonna and co-writer Patrick Leonard know whether the song's theme is the redemptive power of romantic love or the Holy Ghost gig, or both (check the video). Either way, "Like a Prayer" Takes You There.

Madonna has called "Express Yourself" a tribute to Sly & The Family Stone, and it's surely her deepest soul dig since "Lucky Star." "You don't need diamond rings/Or 18-carat gold," the one-time Material Girl sings, recommending truth and self-respect ("Don't go for second best, baby") as infinitely better investments. "Cherish," the third single from *Like a Prayer*, simply swings. Credit Madonna's sunlit vocal and valentine lyrics. The Shirelles and Chiffons never had benefit of a better couplet than "Romeo and Juliet/They never felt this way I bet." A true tonic, "Cherish" bounces along as if it had the power to lift the darkest heart. If there's ever a successor to *You Can Dance* (the seamlessly segued anthology of Madonna dance mixes from '87), "Cherish" belongs there, in perpetual play, a joyous little whirl without end, amen.

Originally, the stylish "Vogue," her most recent Number One, was to have closed this collection. Of course it's here; the epochal dance-pose track is still inspiring musical (and video) imitations even as we write. Fittingly, the final honors now go to two just-cut Madonna originals, the dark and hauntingly poetic "Rescue Me" and "Justify My Love." Their inclusion is further proof that Madonna's interest lies not in what *has* happened, but rather in what's happening. "Vogue" collaborator Shep Pettibone co-wrote "Rescue Me." Writer-singer Lenny Kravitz was Madonna's partner on "Justify My Love".

Putting a lid on a collection of Madonna's greatest hits is a risky business at best. Like no other singer (or writer or producer) in recent memory, she continues to demonstrate an uncompromising commitment (hell, maybe an obsession) to never stay put. The experience of honoring that commitment has made the Material Girl "rich." It has also enriched popular music as a whole—pushing it to new limits, pulling apart preconceptions about what it can say and do. Best of all, there's our experience of the music she's made, itself so rich in wit and emotion, and so abundant with the undisguised joy she has taken in making it. That's one secret she's never been able to keep.

LINER NOTES:

Dion
Bronx Blues—The Columbia Recordings (1962-1963)

Sony/Columbia Records, 1991

"Rock 'n' roll *started* as rebellious music. It had an attitude, and in that attitude was a lot of stuff: anger, frustration, joy, and that whole sense of really shakin' things up. When it first exploded, it happened in a whole lot of different places at once. In Lubbock, Texas, it was Buddy Holly. In the San Fernando Valley it was Richie Valens. And the brand of it that I made comes from where I come from. That's why they call it Bronx blues."

In the fall of 1962 Dion took his Bronx blues to midtown Manhattan. After four years with Laurie Records (where he'd cut the doowop classics "I Wonder Why" and "Where Or When" with the Belmonts, the searing "Runaround Sue," "The Wanderer" and a dozen other hits), he signed with Columbia Records. While the label had fielded the occasional pop-rock hit, these were often confined to crossover artists signed by the label's country division (Johnny Horton, Jimmy Dean, rockabilly cat Ronnie Self) or to one-and two-hit wonders from Columbia's sister label, Epic (Roy Hamilton, Link Wray, Tony Orlando). Dion DiMucci, Pascuale and Frances' kid from East 183rd Street, was the prestigious label's first rock 'n' roll star.

"I was excited about going to Columbia," Dion recalls. "They really wanted me, and I wanted to be there. But I did have concerns about whether they'd understand my music." His concerns proved well founded. With no prior rock 'n' roll experience, his first producer, Robert Mersey, tried to steer Dion toward the ballads and standards that defined what used to be called "legit" music. This direction change was standard procedure in the pre-Beatles rock era; after establishing themselves with a few hits, young artists were expected to 'graduate' from the teen (45 rpm singles) market to the adult (album) market. The fact that only one rocker (Bobby Darin) ever succeeded at this alchemy did not stop A&R men from attempting it with scores of others. Dion made a passing effort at accommodating Mersey, as had labelmate Aretha Franklin, who hit with a remake of Al Jolson's "Rock-a-Bye Your Baby with a Dixie Melody" the year before Dion arrived. Ultimately, Mersey (and subsequent A&R men) agreed to let Dion produce himself, a decision that allowed him to experiment, explore old roots and rock's newer branches, and to produce some of the most satisfying music of his career.

"You want to know what goes into Bronx blues?" Dion asks earnestly, as if we're comparing recipes for *baccala* or *cioppino*. "You mix in R&B, street-corner doowop, some Hank Williams 'Honky Tonk Blues,' you filter it all through an Italian neighborhood full of wiseguys and all *that*, and it comes out with an attitude, like 'Yo!'"

"I've always loved this stuff," he says of the four doowop cuts that lead off this collection. His jubilant covers of the Cleftones' "Can't We Be Sweethearts" and "Little Girl of Mine," "Oh Happy Day" (all from the *Donna The Prima Donna* album) and the classic "A Sunday Kind of Love" (from his final Columbia LP, *Wonder Where I'm Bound*) were cut in one two-day stretch in March, 1963. Dion calls these songs "close to my heart. I mean, they're what I was listening to when I was 13 years old." The real sleeper among them is "Oh Happy Day"; a Top Five hit for 17-year-old Don Howard in 1952 (it was later covered by the Five Satins), the song here becomes a vehicle for one of Dion's most soulful ballad performances.

The driving "Gonna Make It Alone" (from the *Ruby Baby* album) and "Flim Flam" (off *Donna The Prima Donna*) bow less to earlier influences, sounding instead like pure Dion signatures. "I put a lot of time into those cuts," he explains, describing the former as "an attempt to proclaim my independence, after I cut loose from the Belmonts." The proclamation's a gem, particularly the obvious smile in his voice the second time he sings "I'll make some money in a rush/ Yeah, be too much." He's started performing "Gonna Make It Alone" again in concert lately. "Flim Flam" prefigures Dion's sharpest duo-syllabic move, 1963's single-only cover of the Drifters' "Drip Drop." He's at the top of his form on "Drip Drop": in charge, at ease, he moves through the arrangement like the King of Cool on an official visit. Dig the playful elongation of "roof" on the third chorus, and the way he transforms the Drifters' throwaway third verse into a major policy statement: "Now listen here, friend, I tell ya I'm hip, hip, hip...."

Both "Drip Drop" and Dion's other Drifters cover, "Ruby Baby," were "things I walked in with, that I'd been doing since the Belmonts days." The latter was his first, and biggest, Columbia single, reaching Number Two on *Billboard's* Hot 100 less than a month after he'd recorded it at his first Columbia session (in December, 1962). His second hit was "This Little Girl," a song that started out with Dion and Carole King "messing around on guitar" up at the office she shared with Gerry Goffin.

"When I listen to it now" Dion says, "it sounds like I had a lot of resentment in me toward women. I guess I did. When you're young and frustrated trying to understand yourself and the opposite sex, this is how it comes out." Dion's third Columbia hit (Top 10, September 1963) was "Donna The Prima Donna," a fluid "Sue" remake written with frequent Laurie collaborator Ernie Maresca.

Among the other material included on the *Ruby* and *Donna* albums, Dion recalls working with Doc Pomus' co-writer, Mort Shuman, on the atmospheric "Troubled Mind" and putting Paul Anka's advice to work in the "Lonely Teenager"-ish "Will Love Ever Come My Way." "'Dion,' he used to say, 'you gotta write songs that make the girls feel sorry for you, that's the trick.' That's what we were trying to do here." It's "Sweet, Sweet Baby," though, from the *Donna* LP, that's the pivotal track among these cuts, since it's the one that presages Dion's deepening interest in roots blues. His actual epiphany took place in John Hammond's office. Columbia's legendary A&R man worked two doors over from Bob Mersey. "He'd heard me playing some things like 'Flim Flam' and 'Sweet, Sweet Baby,' and he said, "Dion, come in here for a minute..." Then he played me this Robert Johnson album he'd just put together. It had sold 12,000 copies just by word of mouth, and he really dug that. It was like he wanted to let me in on some great secret. When he played me the record, it just put me *out*, man. My first reaction was to be resentful: it was like 'Who's been keeping this stuff from me?'"

Hammond heard the strong blues feeling that had always been present in Dion's solo work, and he wondered where the pop/doowop singer had picked it up. Dion admits "It wasn't until then that I started thinking about this guy Willie. He was the janitor in our building when I was growing up. I was learning to play guitar, and I'd go down to his place and he'd show me how to play, teach me songs. When I heard Robert

Johnson [and dozens of other blues artists whose records Hammond lent him], it all sort of connected up. Willie was part of a musical community I hadn't even known existed." Dion smiles, remembering the John Lee Hooker song his first teacher used to play him. "It was 'Walking the Boogie,' where Hooker accompanies himself by just stomping his feet on the floor. I loved that so much, it sounded so primitive. That's where I got that stomping beat for 'Flim Flam' and 'Drip Drop.'"

By 1964, blues—both the rural acoustic variety and the amplified Chicago style—had become a near-obsession for Dion. Digging legends Lightning Hopkins and Muddy Waters at Greenwich Village clubs alternated with visits to Reverend Gary Davis' Bronx apartment for more lessons. (This new musical direction occasioned its share of culture clashes, like a disastrous gig at Long Island's Boulevard supper club. "I went in there with just myself on electric guitar and Buddy Lucas on harp," Dion laughs. "We're up there doing stone blues stuff, and all these people are walking in in tuxes, out for an elegant night on the town. They never booked me back after that!")

That spring, Dion began recording a number of blues covers and originals ("Most of them were done as demos. We'd usually go in, say 'OK, in the key of E' and just start playing"). The sessions featured mostly black jazz and R&B musicians, such as Buddy Lucas (who'd played sax on "The Wanderer" and other Laurie sides), saxophonist Jerome Richardson, and drummers Sticks Evans and Panama Francis. Guitarists Johnny Falbo (from Dion's road band) and Bucky Pizzarelli also contributed. While a few tracks such as "The Seventh Son" found their way onto the *Wonder Where I'm Bound* album, most have gone unissued until now.

As part of the first generation of white boys to 'play the blues' (most of whom gravitated to the music from the folk circuit), Dion was really alone among rock 'n' rollers in embracing rock's roots. (In 1964 the Stones were just starting to break; the Blues Project and the Paul Butterfield Blues Band were a year away). The fact that his efforts went unnoticed ("Spoonful" and an alternate version of "Two Ton Feather" were released as singles but didn't chart) does not diminish Dion's work. As represented here, his blues sound natural and confident, and are remarkably free of the husky 'blackface' posturing that afflicts so much white blues of the period.

"Sweet Papa Di" is probably the most affecting. Its lyrics, pretty standard blues boasting, barely seem up to the warmth and quiet strength of Dion's vocal. Buddy Lucas, who "had about a hundred songs he'd written stored underneath his bed," composed the song for Dion. Subtly arranged for two acoustic guitars and snare, Sonny Boy Williamson's "Don't Start Me Talkin'" comes across lean, relaxed, and unselfconsciously witty. Of the two Willie Dixon covers, "Spoonful," so often inflated and misshaped by rock bands, is kept sparse and space-filled here, Dion's reverbed vocal intruding only intermittently to add color.

The other Dixon tune, "The Seventh Son" (which Dion, like most singers, learned from Mose Allison's version), sounds deliberately dense and cloudy. Dion says the intent was "to get a Muddy Waters feel" to the track, though its pace and stinging guitar punctuation lend it a deliciously ominous tone more akin to Dylan's "Ballad of a Thin Man (Mr. Jones)." Dion recalls that "The Seventh Son"'s lyrics held the same appeal for him as "Hoochie Coochie Man" and "The Wanderer"—"that need, I don't know if it's Italian macho or something more healthy and universal, to stand alone and declare your independence, to say 'I'm a man, I can take care of myself.'"

The three remaining cuts, from the spring and fall of 1965, show Dion responding—with good humor and tough licks—to the gale-force winds of change then blowing through every quarter of the rock 'n' roll world. Dylan's the obvious influence on "Baby, I'm In the Mood for You." Dion couldn't remember how the song came his way, though its producer, Tom Wilson, also produced *Bringing It All Back Home* and "Like a Rolling Stone." "I may have actually heard Dylan recording or rehearsing it," Dion observes, noting that the two singers often crossed paths in Columbia's studios. Apart from appearing on an Odetta album some time back, "Mood" remained unheard until its inclusion on the Dylan anthology *Biograph*.

Tom Wilson also produced the R&B-styled "Two Ton Feather," whose message Dion summarizes as "Hey, don't hand me no bullshit." He credits guitarist Johnny Falbo with the Junior Wells-ish arrangement heard here. "Kickin' Child,' another collaboration with Buddy Lucas, "has a lot of attitude," Dion says. It's also got a free-swinging vocal ("Coast awhile...") and the unmistakable busy flavor of so much post-Brit mid-'60s rock: marching "She's About a Mover" rhythm, the flickering harp, and buzzing Fender lead.

Not long after recording "Two Ton Feather" and "Baby, I'm In the Mood for You," some three years after signing with Columbia, Dion left the label, largely to pursue the folk-blues phase of his career that, in 1968, landed him his next hit, "Abraham, Martin and John." Other triumphs followed (and continue), not the least of which was his 1989 induction into the Rock And Roll Hall Of Fame. "With rock 'n' roll," Dion says, "after you've been doing it a while, you've got five choices. You can die, you can burn out, you can go 100% showbiz, you can leave showbiz altogether... or you can realize that this music is something powerful, that it can communicate deep emotion and real thoughts, and you can go on to develop those parts of it. And you don't have to worry: the original rock 'n' roll attitude, that fire, the Bronx blues or whatever you want to call it, that will remain with you forever. Believe me." Indeed.

LINER NOTES:

Screamin' Jay Hawkins
Cow Fingers and Mosquito Pie

Sony/Epic Records, 1991

As with most successful artists, Screamin' Jay Hawkins career hung on lots of *ifs*... It might not have happened at all if his first manager hadn't sold the young blues singer's contract to another manager for $50... if an Epic A&R man hadn't heard something "weird and primitive" in Jay's ballad "I Put a Spell On You" and turned Jay's first OKeh recording session into a drunken soiree in order to set free the wildness in the song... if Alan Freed had stopped peeling hundreds off that roll of bills he was holding to persuade Jay to start his stage act by climbing out of a coffin...

It's 1991. Screamin' Jay Hawkins is 61 years old. He's working more than he has in ages, getting in more faces than ever, thanks to his performances in *Mystery Train* and *A Rage in Harlem*, on Arsenio and Carson, and in a series of Japanese Walkman commercials. At this point, a good 40 years into a career that just won't quit, all the *ifs* in the world have little to do with Screamin' Jay's success. It's unconditional and irrevocable. He's one of the last (and most active) of the great R&B shouters who came up in the early Fifties under such immortals as Roy Brown and Wynonie Harris, and he's a rock 'n' roll fixture. "I Put a Spell on You" has sold millions and sustained wildly varying interpretations by such acts as Sarah Vaughan, Alan Price, Them, and Creedence Clearwater Revival, and Screamin' Jay the showman has influenced everyone from A. Cooper and G. Clinton to all those metal-gloom-doom outfits talkin' voodoo and biting blood capsules. I mean, he *invented* flashpots, baby.

"I elected to be different," is how Jay puts it, "to be strange. If you want to call it crazy, do it. It makes sense to me, though, 'cause I can go to the bank on it." The powerful baritone made his first deposits in the wildness account early on. Born in Cleveland, an Amateur Golden Gloves champ who wanted to take on song and wail like his idols Paul Robeson and Enrico Caruso, Jay was barely 21 when he started performing with Tiny Grimes' Rockin' Highlanders. "I'd come out in a Scottish kilt, and I'd have these two small Carnation milk cans hanging off my chest, like tits. I sang 'Mama, He Treats Your Daughter Mean' and the cans would be jiggling all over the place. Ruth Brown came to see me. She said, 'This is the only bitch who can sing my song better than me.'" His subsequent solo career found Jay rocking Atlantic City clubs like Herman's nightly on 8 p.m. to 9 a.m. shifts, cutting up in color-coordinated outfits ("down to the socks and cuff links") of orange, pink and fluorescent blue. "I charged one club owner $1,500 a week and three suits," Jay laughs.

The commitment to high impact performing didn't stop at the stage either. "It was always my object to do whatever I had to, to capture the interest of people who were just casually listening to the radio; the housewife ironing, or whatever. I figured, if I could hold their attention for the first eight bars, I'd sold a record."

Jalacy J. Hawkins didn't sell a lot of records, though he cut a few, for such labels as Timely, Gotham, Mercury and Wing, and even Atlantic, between 1952 and 1955. Of his experience at the latter label, Jay recalls cutting (the still unissued) 'Screamin' the Blues' for Jerry Wexler. "He'd stopped me five times during the take. Finally he starts shouting, 'No, no, no, I want you to sing it just like Fats Domino, man!' I said, 'Now listen, Fats is off to a good start, he's doing okay. I'm singing here with Tiny Grimes, and I've got a chance to record the song I chose. If you want Fats Domino, then go out and get him.' He started up again and pow! I just punched him in the mouth."

Jay cut the original (ballad) version of "I Put a Spell on You," the first disc to bear the artist credit Screamin' Jay Hawkins, for Grand Records in 1949. The single started in Philly and Trenton, spread to Baltimore, then fizzled. While the dates are disputed (Jay claims it was 1952; label records say it was September 1956), the magic didn't start until Jay's first Epic (OKeh) session. Producer Arnold Maxin, an A&R staffer credited with having discovered Little Jimmy Scott, Big Maybelle and Little Joe & the Thrillers, insisted Jay's re-recording of "Spell" live up to its 'weird' title. His suggestion: turn the session into a picnic, supply Jay and the musicians with enough barbequed ribs and chicken, yams and sweet potato pie, wine, beer and whiskey, then turn on the tape.

"When we started recording, we started out with a slow version" is about all Jay can recall of the infamous recording date. "A week later I was sitting at home, and they bring me a 78 of the thing. I put it on, I played it again and again. I thought they'd lied to me: this couldn't possibly be me singing like that. So I tried to see if I could reproduce that style of singing. I contorted my mouth this way and that. I couldn't do it. Finally I poured myself some J&B Scotch, poured *that* down, and then I was able to do it like the record."

The performance—heavily liquified on disc, stone sober as Jay now wails it live—is a stunner. The delivery, particularly his snorting 'cannibalistic' coda, got "Spell" banned from radio stations across the country. (An edited version, minus the scarifying grunts and groans, replaced the original version. The original is included here.) The single never charted, but it sold throughout the late Fifties to eager teens anxious to embrace its spooky beauty and strangeness.

"I Put a Spell on You" remains Jay's prime piece of real estate, but as this collection—compiled from his OKeh singles, the Epic album *At Home with Screamin' Jay Hawkins* and various outtakes—makes clear, SJH covered a lot of territory during his brief tenure (1956-58) at the Epic label.

In many ways, hearing these tracks today is like listening to something from another planet several warp fields away. And not because they're so absurd or studiously strange (they're not), but because what they communicate—that unrestrained sense of fun that forms the core of the best first-era rock 'n' roll; the guts and joy and chops of someone who's lived, and not just learned about, blues and jump and R&B— seems so alien and in such short supply in today's music world.

There's much to dig. "Little Demon," the "Spell" single's flip, is an easy-gait rocker about another love-spurned critter who's "gonna run through the world till he understands his pain." The previously unreleased "You Ain't Foolin' Me," with a priceless false-start exchange between Jay and Arnold Maxin ("Howzat? Howzat?" "Take two." "Thank you!"), sports a big boss delivery that places Jay squarely in the ballsy jump tradition of Roy Brown and Joe Turner. Check Panama Francis' drum hits, the booting sax (Big Al Sears or Sam 'The Man' Taylor), Jay at the piano.

In his book, *More Funny People*, Steve Allen refers to certain comedians (Jonathan Winters, Sid Caesar, Robin Williams) who have what he calls a "Silly Center." Sure, Jay knew he could go to the bank on craziness, and he's always been canny about the business end, but plenty of the tracks here also prove that Jay's wired into Silly Central in a major fashion: "Hong Kong," "Yellow Coat," and his mad trashing of "I Love Paris" (why didn't they invite Jay to participate in that recent Cole Porter tribute?). "Hong Kong" belongs in the canon of Orient-fixated Fifties rock 'n' roll (the Five Keys' "Ling Ting Tong," the Five Discs' "My Chinese Girl," etc.), and Jay's wordless sputtering sounds like it may have inspired the Trashmen to do the same on *their* immortal slab of silly-rock, "Surfin' Bird." "Yellow Coat" may be the hippest of the trio, with mangled visual rhymes that'd do Dali proud, a self-referential inspirational verse to die for ("What walks on two feet and looks like a goat?/ That crazy Screamin' Jay in a bright yellow coat!") and a sneak preview of that "bright red leather suit" Jay used to steal scenes in *Mystery Train*.

"Coat" is also one of Jay's great grocery-list compositions, a noble tradition that includes "Alligator Wine," the *molto* macabre "There's Something Wrong with You" and (later) "Feast of the Mau Mau." "I would deliberately try to concoct lyrics that created weird images for the listener," he explains. "I'd go into drugstore soda fountains and steal menus, read advertising flyers from grocery stores, then sit down and see what I could come up with."

"I Love Paris" isn't the only standard or piece of 'good music' Jay took a whack at. "Frenzy" and "Temptation" get the axe (dig Jay refreshing his vocal chords at the top of the latter), as does "You Made Me Love You" ("I said, 'I like the song and I want to do it.' They said, 'How'd you like to approach it?' I said, 'Like a gay person.'"). "Orange Colored Sky" was another tune Jay picked for *At Home with*, "because I'd always dug its strange changes. O.B. Masingill, who was Roy Hamilton's arranger, arranged it." "Person to Person" shows anyone who hasn't already figured it out that there are chops behind all the clowning. One of the OKeh singles, it's a solid, tough blues that was also a hit for Eddie 'Cleanhead' Vinson.

"My mother liked the song," Jay says of "Take Me Back to My Boots and Saddle." "I first heard it by Gene Autry." It's unlikely that anyone with close ties to Autry's version would know what to make of Jay's rendition, including Jay's mom ("She wouldn't even listen to it!"). "Boots" may be the sleeper of the whole set, for it's so abundant in all the things that make Jay's music so enjoyable. Listen to it—a cornball choral arrangement (the Ray Charles Singers) fitted over smooth walking bass, crisp Mickey Baker guitar solo ("Ah, giddyup there!" yells Jay) with Jay's marvelously funny, powerful vocal ("Ropin' those steers on the ole Bar X/With my buddies Slim and Tex")... it's worth the price of admission just to hear him soar past the chorale on the bridge and growl those ridiculous "Woo-oohs!"

Like I said, there's much to dig. (Don't miss Jay's practice screaming—a sort of cross between a field holler and a zombie belch—in the hall outside the studio, just before "Darling, Please Forgive Me." Jay Hawkins and Epic parted company in '58, and he went on to new labels and new heights. There were lulls too, and a long stay in Hawaii, and a part in the Alan Freed biopic *American Hot Wax* (1978). But always there were memories of Screamin' Jay and "I Put a Spell on You." In 1983, director Jim Jarmusch used the song in *Stranger than Paradise*. *Mystery Train* followed, then the return to active touring, TV, commercials and, most recently, *A Rage in Harlem*. Happily, there's no end in sight. But when there is, many moons hence, Jay's got that wired too. "When I go, I don't want to be buried," he says. "I've been in too many damn coffins already!"

FEATURE:

Art for Sale:
A History of Music-Business Advertising

Billboard Magazine 100th anniversary issue, Nov. 1, 1994

*"Doing business without advertising is like winking at a girl in the dark.
You know what you are doing, but nobody else does."*
—Stewart Henderson Britt, New York Herald Tribune, Oct. 30,
1956

Much like nature, the artist abhors a vacuum. No musician, from the
most devoted choirmaster to the most despairing grunge rocker, creates
for the half-filled house or the untouched ear. The desire for a respon-
sive audience is the drive that takes an artist to a record company, and
advertising—be it the "free" promotion of radio exposure or the multiple
impressions of a print campaign—in turn delivers the artist's work to the
public.

From the beginning, advertisements have been among *Billboard*'s
most colorful features. The magazine's charts and news articles traffic
in the hard currency of verifiable fact and quantifiable data. Advertisements—appearing in the rented spaces between (and on) the covers—
also deal in these properties, but with an added dimension. Not just
the promoters of goods and services for sale, advertisements articulate
dreams; they try to infect those who read them with enthusiasm and
invite those readers to act in a spirit of mutual interest. Advertising also
reflects the ongoing parade of popular culture. It is no surprise that advertisements in *Billboard* have, for the past 100 years, signaled the arrival
of most of the world's major entertainment figures.

Over time, a certain consistency of technique has appeared in the
advertising pages of *Billboard*. A July 5, 1902, Barnum & Bailey ad pre-

figures the Lollapalooza festivals of the '90s, promising crowd-pleasing contortionists, grotesques, tumblers, leapers, and freaks, among other acts, while the artist-owned label is augured in an August 26, 1916, announcement of the new Mary Pickford Film Corporation ("World's Foremost Star of Motion Pictures Supreme Heads Her Own Company"). The modern "crossover" star who exploits notoriety in one media realm to storm another (for example, Howard Stern or G. Gordon Liddy) belongs to a long line that stretches back (at least) to famed prohibitionist Carrie Nation. "Wanted ... Wanted," proclaims a March 19, 1904, ad, "Every Manager Of Fairs, Parks, Etc. To Know That Clark Ball Is Now Booking Ahead For The Coming Summer Carrie Nation Of Saloon Smashing Notoriety."

Publishers and song pluggers touted their wares in *Billboard* throughout the teens and '20s (and a one-column August 13, 1927, spot pitched "World's Hottest Cornet Breaks & Choruses... Two Books By Louis Armstrong"), but it was not until the '30s that ads promoting recording artists began to appear regularly. By 1936, record labels had started buying space near the weekly 10 Best Records chart — mainly to promote their releases, not to retailers but to jukebox operators, whose public players were among the era's most potent means of exposure. "Fats Waller At The Top!" crows a small Victor/Blue Bird ad of August 1, 1936, that advises the operators to "Put These [Record Releases] In Your Machine And Watch The Nickels Roll In!"

A full-page Jan. 8, 1938, back-cover ad for Wurlitzer Automatic Phonographs shows both the primacy of jukebox promotion in the '30s and presages the "bundling techniques" employed to sell CD-ROMs in the '90s. The ad's copy and stylish deco design use Duke Ellington ("The Creator Of A New Vogue Of Jazz Music") to sell both hardware and software. "He Plays Wherever There Is A Wurlitzer," reads the headline, and an adjacent balloon touts the composer/bandleader's latest Brunswick discs, including "Caravan" and "The New East St. Louis Toodle-o."

Record advertising became more widespread with the ascent of such major "diskeries" as Columbia, Decca, and Victor in the '40s. Big-band leaders and star soloists took the spotlight (a five-page spread in 1942 proclaims Glenn Miller & His Orchestra "America's Number 1 Band ... Over 6,000,000 Records Sold In The Past Year"), but just as common were roster ads that promoted a given label's current releases — often over an A&R landscape of staggering diversity. Two June 6, 1948, roster ads plugged Capitol's "Hot Hits" (everything from Nat King Cole's pop chart-topping "Nature Boy" to Tex Ritter's western classic "Deck

Of Cards" and Nellie Lutcher's "sepia" hit "Fine Brown Frame") and RCA Victor's "Climbers" (which ranged from Dennis Day's Hibernian hit "Clancy Lowered The Boom" to Dizzy Gillespie's "Ool-Ya-Koo" and Spade Cooley's "Oklahoma Waltz").

The changing of the pop-cultural guard in the '50s was also played out on the magazine's ad pages. Significantly, the dozens of upstart R&B and rock 'n' roll labels often utilized *Billboard* chart data in their advertisements—as if to convince fellow tradespeople of their legitimacy and stability in a music field derided by mainstream society as fraudulent and ephemeral.

In one ad, Imperial Records awards Fats Domino's "Ain't It A Shame" the "Triple Crown," citing the single's No. 1 status on Billboard's Most Played By Jockeys, Most Played In Juke Boxes, and Best Sellers In Stores charts for the week of July 16, 1955.

The new music's rise from the smalltime to big business was dramatic. Within weeks of a Dallas Booker's homespun playbill for a tour featuring Carl Perkins, Sonny James, and the Texas Stampers came RCA Victor's announcement of a fully coordinated rollout of the first Elvis Presley campaign (*Billboard*, March 31, 1956), promising radio and print support, ad mats, and promotional materials ("for walls, windows, [and] listening booths!").

With the expansion of the economy in the '60s, the volume and ambitions of music advertising grew. Bold new stories required imaginative telling. Few today would doubt the wisdom of Capitol's Jan. 4, 1964, spread inviting the American industry to "Meet the Beatles!" or Columbia's provocative two-pager (July 10, 1965) inquiring, "A 6-Minute Single? Why Not! When You Have 6 Minutes Of Bob Dylan Singing His Great New Song 'Like A Rolling Stone.'" Less judicious, but no less expressive of their creators' ardent intentions, were extravagant '60s campaigns for a host of since-vanished aspirants ("Bobby Jameson Is Here" shouts a July 25, 1964, gatefold that depicts a young singer standing atop his limo in the center of a motorcade and clutching a guitar in one outstretched arm).

The colorful procession of introductions and arrivals continues through the '60s and '70s. With it, advertising in *Billboard* shows the record companies reacting to change, as artists, audiences, and an industry grew up fast together. Motown drops the "Little" tag from its Stevie Wonder ads; Reprise recovers from the misstep of introducing the Jimi Hendrix Experience as "67's Foremost Soul Exponent!," and the once-dominant 7-inch single recedes into the album's shadow (as such acts as the

Doors, the Grateful Dead, and Led Zeppelin debut with LP ads).

In the '70s, the maturing industry learned new ways of addressing itself-and of positioning products for a broader, but more fragmented, audience. An Aug. 30, 1975, Columbia spread capitalizes on an intense rocker's accumulation of critical success to promote his new album, "Born To Run" ("Finally. The World Is Ready For Bruce Springsteen"), while Island's announcement for Bob Marley's "Survival" (Nov. 3, 1979) acknowledges the reggae star's emerging status as a cultural leader who, through an impassioned "roots journey ... delivers a lesson in life."

Self-awareness permeates Stan Cornyn and Pete Johnson's clever, early '70s image ads for Warner Bros. (a current-release announcement is headlined "The Mo Ostin Experience"), as well as the self-congrat-ulatory, late '70s multiplatinum announcements that bathed countless trains, taxis, phone booths, and album icons in silver. (Warners appar-ently found the music tradesfolk of the day rather less hip than the music consumer. The label's wry, self-kidding ads in *Billboard* were but the business end outgrowth of a much more provocative series that had first run in *Rolling Stone* in the late '60s; these gave away Randy Newman's first album, bemoaned Joni Mitchell's slowness in delivering her soph-omore LP, and promoted New York's notorious underground trio with a "Win A Fug Dream Date" contest.)

The past fifteen years have reflected their share of precious-metal gleam and shining accomplishments. In view of their respective titles' re-cord-shattering tallies, the copy-light announcements for Michael Jack-son's Epic album "Thriller" (Jan. 11, 1982) and Madonna's Sire album "Like A Virgin" (Nov. 17, 1984) seem remarkably understated.

Ads from the '80s and early '90s informed *Billboard* readers of a growing number of musical and technological advances — among them the supplanting of the LP format by the CD (though the "album" des-ignation, dating from the '40s, persists); rap's move into the mainstream ("Hammer Is On A Roll," states an April 4, 1992, Capitol ad enumerat-ing the star's worldwide achievements); and the internationalization of pop (the steady growth in pages promoting Julio Iglesias, John Secada, even the Benedictine Monks of Santa Domingo De Silos).

Advertising has signaled both the arrival of country music's new tra-ditionalists (with the April 25, 1987, ad for Dwight Yoakam's "Guitars, Cadillacs, Etc., Etc.") and the ascendance of its new wave ("He Opened The Door," declares a Sept. 12, 1992, Warner Bros. spread crediting Randy Travis with spearheading the young-talent movement).

If recent music advertising in *Billboard* seems more focused and

strategically directed, its aims remain true to those of its earliest predecessors: to inspire confidence in an artist or project, enlist believers, and
tell a tale. "One Year, Three Albums," proclaims Death Row Records'
anniversary ad in the June 4, 1994, issue of *Billboard*. Set against a background of unadorned steel, the ad concludes, "10 Million Units Sold. It's
Only Just Begun ..."

On May 9, 1992, hot on the heels of the Hot Country Singles &
Tracks success of "Achy Breaky Heart," Mercury Nashville announced
Billy Ray Cyrus' debut album ("In Store May 19th"). Two weeks later,
a modified ad touted the single's rapid assault on the Hot 100 ("47 to 24
to 18") and the album's sales ("Approaching Gold"). The sense of an
impending phenomenon is unmistakable and, the advertiser must have
hoped, irresistible. By August 1, the label toasted the album's triple-plat-
inum stature, the single's historic deed ("The First Platinum Country
Single In Nearly a Decade"), and the artist's imminent video, which
"Will Ship Double Platinum!"

Not at all like winking in the dark.

FEATURE:

Beguiled By Bruno:
My Great-Lost-Album Trip

Scram magazine, 1998

It's lonely out here.

Apart from the people who recorded it, I've never met anyone who's ever really known about this unusual album, first released 30 years ago.

I initially encountered it in an ad in the premiere issue (Oct. 1967) of a long-forgotten youth-culture slick, being hawked alongside one of the coolest debut albums ever made, under the headline "Catch a Batch of THE IN SOUND!!!" On the left, the LP cover to Buddah BDS 5001, *Safe as Milk*, the sharp, fish-eyed shot of short-haired, smartly tailored Captain Beefheart & His Magic Band. On the right, BDS 5002: a muscled Mediterranean guy with tattooed forearms, grabbing a chicken-wire fence in a suburban backyard while socks from a clothesline dangle over his head. Above him, in hot pink script: *The Beauty of Bruno*.

Now here was a gift. If Beefheart's natty, almost formal cover presented an intriguing alternative to the design fashions of the day (groups of ill-clad long-hairs burning their Knowing Acid Look into the faces of the prospective buyer) and suggested there was something truly unorthodox about the music within—then what to make of the even more skewed sleeve of *The Beauty Of Bruno*?

Like most *Scram* readers, I've spent an unhealthy amount of time seeking out lost left-of-center records. I know the joy of Brute Force's *Confections of Love*, Tupper Saussy's Neon Philharmonic and *Commercials to Cringe By*. But *The Beauty of Bruno*, whatever it was, eluded me. I had to have it, to hear it, but it was always ahead of me, one too many thrift shops away.

I finally found it, in the early eighties. A small record store in Santa

Monica was closing and selling its stock; rifling through the B's, I picked up two Baja Marimba Band LPs, and then I saw it! Once I got home and played it, *Beauty* didn't exactly jolt me into the Wolfe-ian epiphany all those years of searching had led me to expect. It stymied me, dosed me with context virus (how was one to take this—as revved-up Vegas? toned-down R&B? a total goof?) and ultimately convinced me that it is one of the Sixties' most delicious misfires. It still mystifies me, as something that adds up to much more than the sum of its parts—even after I've thoroughly quizzed its creators about how and why they made it.

The man behind the beauty got into the game by accident. "I was hangin' around the Brill Building in New York, takin' action for this bookie from New Jersey," Tony Bruno recalls. "I was doing pretty well, so he set me up with an office, and we pretended it was a record label; I had my desk, a small turntable and eight or nine phones." In 1959, the building was the center of the rock 'n' roll biz, so it wasn't long before a young blues singer entered the door of "Nomar Records" (an anagram formed from the letters of the Jersey bookie's surname) with an acetate, wanting to sign with the label.

One thing led to another, and Tony Bruno went legit, producing Maxine Brown's simmering soul hit "All in My Mind." It sold 800,000 copies, spawned a follow-up smash and launched his pop career. He wrote and cut countless sides in the decade that followed, among them the Bacharach-esque R&B classic "Tell Him (Her) I'm Not Home" (recorded by Chuck Jackson and later Tina Turner), Gene Pitney's "Last Chance to Turn Around" and Soupy Sales' "The Mighty Clem" ("It was a 'Big Bad John' type thing," Tony says), as well as items by such gone near greats as Victor & The Spoils, the Shalimars, Rick Lancelot, and Vinnie Zen & The Rogues.

Fate and good fortune again got cozy one chilly night early in 1967. When soul singer Phil Flowers failed to show for a session Bruno had booked at Manhattan's Bell Sound studios, the producer stepped in and sang the song himself. Buddah/Kama Sutra exec Artie Ripp dug the track and suggested they round up some material for a Tony Bruno album.

One of the reasons I find *The Beauty of Bruno* so beguiling is that it's simultaneously such a product of its time and so obviously out of step with it. The years '66 to '68 in pop functioned as a sort of creative gyroscope, rotating with wild ideas: if Top 40 could accommodate the Beatles' art-rock, Nancy Sinatra's sado-maso and Sgt. Barry Sadler, then why not Tiny Tim's "Tulips," the Fruitgum Co.'s Freudian nursery-rock and a Trini Lopez album titled *The Whole Enchilada*? What label in its right mind would demur when Bruno & co. started work on what might best be described as a post-rock Vegas lounge record?

Here's what makes it so juicy. The album has the requisite standards ("Yesterday," "That Lucky Old Sun"), but it's too in-your-face loud, too R&B, too knowing and suggestive of a world beyond Middle Of The Road to really have played to all those moms and dads doing the town on their Caesar's/Harrah's/Hilton getaways. Pete Anders, who co-wrote three of the best pieces on *The Beauty of Bruno*, says there was a shared interest in writing classic "Billie Holiday-type songs," and Tony notes that certain tunes were earmarked as potential covers for Dean Martin and Jack Jones. But what was the comfy middle-aged audience to make of "My Yellow Bird," which starts as a lazy banjo blues and evolves into clamorous Dixieland over crashing brass and drums as Tony tackles the vocal in a style uncannily like that of Handsome Dick Manitoba—all the while making Jolsonesque asides to his aviary amigo ("Is that you, birdie? Sing to me, baby!")?

Or "The Grass Will Sing for You," a thick slab of Spectorian pop whose beefy, button-popping vocal equals, if not surpasses, similar efforts by such bombasticators as the Walker Bros. and P.J. Proby (one trade review tagged T.B. "a HE-male stylist who combines virility and pathos"). So confident is Tony that he just laughs—incongruously, gleefully—in the midst of the heavily emoted final chorus: "And in your heart you'll feel a glow/That's when you'll know—Ha-ha!—my love for you." "We had a lot of fun making that record," he explains.

The 16-ounce Porterhouse "Hard to Get Thing Called Love" and the anti-rural rant "Small Town Bringdown" are other highlights. As is the covert seduction tale "What's Yesterday." At the bridge, Tony's interjections ("Do it!") punctuate the full band's brass/ strings/ glockenspiel crescendos, which break abruptly—just long enough for him to utter a husky "Let's dance," after which the two-step tempo politely resumes. You can practically see him thrust his left arm out, clutch his right to his chest and glide across the dance floor, chin forward. The moment, like so much of *Beauty*, is at once camp, fresh, and utterly appropriate.

I'll refrain from going on at length about the record's other virtues, except to cite Artie Butler's imaginative arrangements, often built around the unlikely combination of banjo and trombone (would you expect less from a guy who arranged for the Shangri-Las?), and the genuinely high level of songcraft. One composition actually uses the word "apoplectic" and it scans perfectly naturally.

And that Lothario-under-the-laundry album cover? Ripp's idea, says

Tony, was that "The beauty of the performer is not what you see on the surface, but what's inside."

Like the sleeve, what's inside proved too hip for the room on either side of the generational divide. Despite an album-premiere party at the Beverly Hills Hotel with Count Basie's Band, TV appearances and a stint at the Frontier Hotel in Vegas, the middle-management types stayed away. So did the Middle Earthers, despite the extended joint-toke that kicks the LP off and segues into "My Yellow Bird."

When the album flopped, Ripp sold the master to Capitol Records, which re-released it in 1968 as *An Original by Bruno—The Most Compelling Song Stylist of the Decade*, with a non-ironic crooner cover and without the dope-drag intro. (This version of the record, ST 2857, is the one more commonly found in used-record bins today.)

Tony Bruno's pop sojourn continued through the next decade. Capitol issued *I'm Feeling It Now* in 1969. More firmly in the File Under: Male Vocal bag, it nonetheless sports kinks of its own; there among the "Little Green Apples" and "Didn't We's" is the corrosive "Rhoda Mendelbaum" ("You're the kind of girl who likes to toy with young boys' hearts, like packing love in a needle/ stick it in their arms"). That same year saw our man move into film scoring, most notably *Hell's Angels 69*, a Tom Stern-Jeremy Slate cycle saga in which he sings on screen in a puffy shirt and medallion. There were also some "30 or 40" X-rated movies to which he contributed soundtracks (under various pseudonyms) and *The Last Porn Flick*, an R-rated spoof of the genre (1974) that sometimes runs on cable as *The Mad Movie-Makers*. And there was the infamous "Stickball," an underground hit Tony wrote, performed and distributed in 1972. What starts as a spoken-word reminiscence on childhood games spontaneously combusts into a scurrilous sex rap that would make Luke Skywalker blanch. Sales exploded when "Stickball" was accidentally mislabeled (and shipped to stores) as the Partridge Family single "Breaking Up Is Hard to Do."

Tony left the record business in 1985, around the time I found my copy of his first album. Nowadays, living in Florida, running his own company, he "plays around with guitar and keyboard" and feels blessed for the fun he had making music, particularly *The Beauty Of Bruno*.

Me too. It's a unique cultural curio whose charm I don't expect will ever diminish.

Is that you, birdie?

LINER NOTES:

Frank Sinatra *Lucky Numbers*

Reprise Records, 1998

Let's cut to the chase: The theme of this album is good times. And no one has sung about them as persuasively as Frank Sinatra. This ten-tune stack finds him at his exuberant (and sometimes pensive) best, on a roll as he extols the many states of feeling great. Love's near the top of the list ("Pocketful of Miracles"), and so are serendipity ("Luck Be a Lady"), camaraderie ("The Boys' Night Out"), can-do attitude ("Come Blow Your Horn") and compassion ("Here's to the Losers").

The good times start, fittingly, In "New York, New York." The theme from Scorsese's 1977 movie of the same name, included on 1979's *Trilogy* album, provides the occasion for a salute to one of just two "cities that never sleep" (think southern Nevada; Danny Ocean swung there). The big-stakes burg has always been a metaphor for high times, and Sinatra's returning-champ reading convincingly conjures up a land of opportunity and abundance, options and action. It's where you want to be, Jack. Wherever you go, you'll have a better time if you take your friends. Sinatra's ice-cool escapades with Davis, Dino and Lawford, et. al. in Vegas in the 60's prove he practiced what he preaches on "The Boys' Night Out." Recorded in 1962, this guys (and dolls)-on-the-town anthem wasn't released until 1995's 20-CD set *The Complete Reprise Studio Recordings*. He glides with grace through Billy May's effects-laden arrangement (cowbells, police whistles, calliope riffs) to offer a nice and easy take on an almost too clever Cahn-Van Heusen number.

The same scribes contributed "Come Blow Your Horn" to the Sinatra canon. The tune goes boom from the start, Ol' Blue Eyes nudging reticent gusto-grabbers to flex their digits now. The band does just that, playing a brisk Riddle chart: Sinatra pours a strong, smooth vocal over it like scotch meeting ice in a tumbler. Splash. Inspirational Verse: "In the civilized jungle, females adore/ The lions who come on swingin'/ If you want to score...roar."

The next pair of tunes finds The Voice swinging from sing-along kid-stuff to the far reaches of worldliness, without the slightest cred loss on either end. Nineteen sixty-one's "Pocketful of Miracles" is an infectious ode to euphoria. You can get there from here, Chairman and pint-sized chorus seem to be saying—all you need is the love thing. A more adult concern—the fickle behavior of Dame Fortune—informs "Luck Be a Lady."

Sinatra's 1963 recording of the *Guys and Dolls* classic has him dutifully laying down Frank Loesser's etiquette lesson to the wayward miss ("A lady doesn't leave her escort...it isn't nice"), but it's most memorable for the fun he has with the pure sound of the song. It's worth the price of admission to hear him read the final verse with that internal rhyme on "guy's dice." Nice.

Despite the fact that they spring from disparate sectors of the 60's (the unsullied Camelot optimism of 1962 and the turbulent turning point year of 1966), "Pick Yourself Up" and "That's Life" share a common theme. Resilience is the riff: getting up, bouncing back, dusting oneself off for another go on the carousel. "Pick Yourself Up" comes from *Sinatra and Swingin' Brass,* and that kicky baroque-a-nova horn figure is Neal Hefti's. Sinatra strolls onto the shuffle-time scene and never stops. It's like he's dancing through all that brass and walking-bass.

He comes on knowing and bluesy on "That's Life," a Top-5 pop hit that shared chart space with the Beach Boys, Supremes and Monkees. It's really no surprise that Sinatra so unerringly finds the groove of what was originally a soul song (by O.C. Smith) and keeps on pushin' throughout. Dig the whole "I've been a puppet, a pauper, a pirate, a poet" bridge, and his conversational hipster delivery of "Many times I thought of cuttin' out/But my heart just wouldn't buy it." Cool and convincing, Clyde.

If "Luck Be a Lady" found our man imploring Ms. Chance to play by the rules and shine on him, 1962's "Pennies from Heaven" finds him laying back to enjoy whatever she bestows, knowing that It'll Work. Count Basie's guys' supple take on Hefti's relaxed arrangement suits Sinatra to a 'T.' Umbrellas up, glasses more than half full, everybody drives this one home. Following the solos, FS takes marvelous jazzy liberties with the melody, playfully stretching and shortening notes where he feels like it—and it feels great.

The set wraps with the thoughtful "Here's to the Losers" and "Winners." Everybody missteps, Sinatra acknowledges in the former, then goes on to offer a benediction ("Bless 'em all") and even a buck-up message to all the less fortunate Tom, Dick and Harrys ("Those torches you carry must be drowned in champagne"). From the same '63 album as the similarly inspirational "Come Blow Your Horn," *Softly as I Leave You.*

The sole full ballad here, "Winners" from 73's *Ol' Blue Eyes Is Back,* sports a lush Don Costa arrangement and a sentiment that bears repeating—that implicit in our enjoyment of good times should be the generosity of spirit to wish everyone else the same. Sinatra salutes the heroes and miracle-workers, but, in that assured late period voice that suggests he Means It, toasts "the winners we all can be." Back atcha,' baby.

In a recent review in the U.K. music magazine *Q*, writer Paul du-Noyer lauded Sinatra as "the global saloon singer" and "the voice of the 20th Century." The proof's as close as this ten-spot, marked by a master and guaranteed to pay off any and all listeners.

FEATURE:

Who Killed Rock 'n' Roll?

WFMU *newsletter* LCD November, 1999

Who's the perp? Somebody must've done this. The victim's been lying there on life-support for years. Once a big, strapping music, light on its feet, unstoppable in its ability to move and shake all kinds of listeners, it fades in and out of consciousness, listless and unfocused.

Even without invoking the golden days of two and three decades ago, popular music today—an enervating mix of a-melodic R&B, lachrymose little-girl songwriter schlock and brutish fratboy b.s.—and posing, ever more posing—pales against any measurement standard.

As the wise solon Andy Kim once inquired, "Baby, how'd we ever get this way?"

Well, some folks suspect corporate-driven record companies, others point to research-run radio. Those two've done their damage, sure, but I think the real culprit is myths. For almost 30 years, rock music's been a prisoner of some powerful, essentially bogus "natural laws" that have shaped artists' and audiences' perceptions and behavior. Unchecked and unchallenged, these myths have resulted in an ever-narrowing definition of what R&R is and how it works; they've gutted its vocabulary, limited its expressiveness and left us with the soul-numbing jive that now surrounds us.

Now, ladies and gentlemen, let's meet our myths.

MYTH #1: ROCK IS ART.

This nifty bondage outfit dates back to 1967. That's when the mainstream media declared legit the music it had dissed for more than a decade. *Sgt. Pepper* was, of course, High Art; no less a cultural court than *Newsweek*, in its review of the album (6/26/67), declared the Beatles the equal of Wordsworth, Eliot, Tennyson, Harold Pinter, Donald Barthelme, Charlie Chaplin and Edith Sitwell.

OK, rock did do some real growing up in the '60s: "Like a Rolling Stone"—one of the 20th Century's true cosmos-rattling works—was surely no "Teen Angel." But then "White Room" and "Marrakesh Express" were no "Like a Rolling Stone."

The Rock Is Art myth was largely institutionalized by the late '60s/early '70s advent of rock journalism: If rock was legit enough to be written about, it must be Saying Something. And unless it was Saying Something, it wasn't rock. Since the principal means of saying anything is words, the gradual ascent of lyrics over sound was assured (*Rolling Stone* found little to evaluate in the output of such lyrically irrelevant acts as Slade, T. Rex, the Dolls or Ramones—just as it would've been speechless on Big Joe Turner or the Trashmen or, for that matter, the Marcels). In time, audience and artists alike came to *assume* that pop music was supposed to carry content.

Which meant that, before long, you had only to present yourself as a poet—the jasmine-sniffing psychedelic clods, the prog-rockers, smug-ass solo Lennon or the gifted seer Jimbo M—to be taken as one. The Lizard King, in fact, created the Tortured Artist template for all who've followed. See his intense gaze and self-absorption, his irrefutable claim to be dropping science big-time, in Stipe and Sting, in Amos, Bono, Badu, and Vedder, and Ndegeocello and hundreds of others.

The irony is that now, after 30 years of Myth No. 1's dominance, the thousands of kids who yearly make pop music a career choice (you could've gotten committed for this in pre-Beatles days) probably think their songs (or "works") are going to change the world.

Either that or they're paying obeisance to...

MYTH #2: ROCK IS REBEL MUSIC.

"Everything is so tame and so driven by corporations. But it hasn't been possible for them to take over and use the images of serial killers. It's the only thing that's still truly underground and alternative."
—James, publisher of Pop Smear *magazine, quoted in the L.A.* Times, *8/4/99*

But of course. The fallout from Myth No. 2 is everywhere; you can't walk anywhere without stepping in it. Its origins, too, lie deep in the mainstream's earliest attempts to understand the music—i.e., Catholic and fundamentalist-clergy denunciations of r&r as a soundtrack for juvenile delinquency, Sinatra's pronouncements against Presley, racist tirades about the rise of "jungle music." And, as with the music's '60s adolescence, there's truth here: to old-line publishers, promoters and broadcasters, this new thing really was wild and threatening.

It wasn't until the '60s and '70s that the rock=rebellion myth was institutionalized and, it often seems, stamped into the genetic code of almost everyone who would ever listen to the music. Key players include Stones manager Andrew Oldham, who shrewdly marketed his act as the anti-Beatles, and, later, the rock-crit establishment. Pop-music histories of the '70s, '80s and '90s tell and retell the tale of rock's rebel routes—for example, reserving major props for Gene Vincent (pain-addled, pill-addicted, died poor) while skimming over Fats Domino (mild-mannered family man, made some of the most joyous r&r the world's ever heard). (In the liner notes to a recent Faces reissue, Dave Marsh feverishly recalls the band's concerts: "They took the stage the way a teenage gang takes over a corner." Careful with that truncheon, Roddy.)

By now, rock's parade of self-proclaimed rebels resembles a clogged freeway. Stuck in traffic: Jefferson Airplane and the MC5 (raised-fist leftist rants signifying nothing), the Metal nation (30 years of taking Halloween seriously), country-rock's "outlaw" movement (millionaire songwriters revolt against bridges and choruses), and first-gen punks (did anyone really expect Western society to slip into anarchy?). In the driver's seat today: gangsta rap (endless tales of unsavory behavior, inspired by fascinating "real life" experiences) and the "hard music" wing of Alternative Nation (white guys' tales of unsavory behavior, often inspired by an endless fascination with Chuck Manson). Memo to James of *Pop Smear*: Don't flatter yourself: Ford and GM will one day use images of Gacy and Dahmer to move tough trucks.

The net effect of these two myths has been a gradual strangulation of rock 'n' roll, ever tightening the popular definition of the music. An aesthetic freeze-out now rules: If the music you're making isn't Serious (self-fixated, "poetic" proclamations: Morissette is Jewel is Rollins) or Dangerous (NIN, Marilyn Manson, Korn, Rage), you're engaged in frivolous activity—in a word, "pop." (Fear of the p-word is epidemic: Dig the way so many alt-rock bands craft catchy-as-hell melodies, then sing them with deliberately 'off' vocals—to make sure you know they're not trying to be Anka or Astley.)

I'm not saying there's no room for introspection or anger. The drag is that the new rock orthodoxy excludes so many other elements that have made the music so enjoyable over the years: exuberance (over calculated provocation), wit (over misogyny), heart (over histrionics), aspirations to beauty ("We made sure Public Enemy was going to keep portraying ugly music"—canny marketer Chuck D, in the *L.A. Times*, 7/25/99). What audience niche/ radio format today would embrace "Be My Baby," *Pet Sounds*, "Peggy Sue," "Shout," "Blitzkrieg Bop" or "Wooly Bully"?

So, with the patient hanging on by a thread, is there a chance of recovery? Maybe. If artists can break the myth-mold and restore the musical vocabulary, they might find the inspiration to revive the old dame.

As a listener, I know that my favorite rock 'n' roll CDs lately are albums that were either produced before the rule of Myths 1 and 2, or, because of cultural lag-time, transcend them altogether. Norton's reissue of Detroit soulster Gino Washington's lost catalog is a pre-myth monster: melodic, celebratory, so raggedly noisy it's almost out of control. *Bossa Cubana*, by Cuba's '50s/early '60s vocal group Los Zafiros, is sublimely beautiful (if *Happy Days* stereotyping has stood in the way of your appreciating the soul and sonic sculpture of doowop, try this). "Gear Blues," by Japan's contemporary four-piece Thee Michelle Gun Elephant (one theory suggests the name's a misreading of "Machine Gun Etiquette"), relentlessly rocks out with Dictators/MC5 fury—and you needn't understand a syllable to catch the fire.

Are any of these records Saying Something about life today or man's fate? Probably not. Are they dangerous acts of rebellion? In a world so suspicious of spontaneity, unfaked emotion and fun, you bet they are.

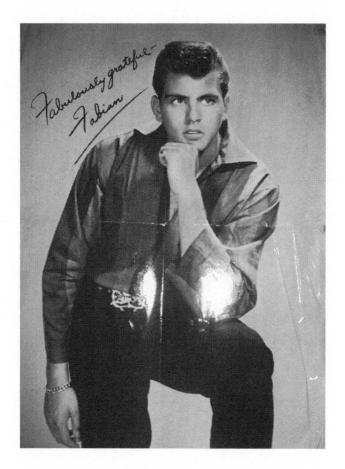

Just how fast is Justin Bieber allowed to grow up?

THE AUGHTS / AUGHT-TENS

How about that new millennium, eh? Who would have thought that 50-plus years into it, writing about music could be more fun than ever? It's a truism, but the Internet created vastly more venues for rock criticism. Now everyone can enthuse without restraint (or much remuneration) over their fave picks and peccadillos. Fanzines, both the online and hard-copy kind, and, especially, the now defunct writers' blog at Rock's Backpages, have been a godsend, allowing me to pop off on esoteric topics that never would have passed an editorial pitch in the grand old days (see "Do Knock the Rock" or "The Seventies' '50s Revival"). In 2012, I even did an e-book, Dark Stars & Anti-Matter: 40 Years of Loving, Leaving and Making Up with the Music of the Grateful Dead, *still available, the last I looked, on Amazon. Thankfully, there are still paying assignments; more significantly, there remain plenty of places to opine and tell strangers and friends about rock and roll.*

FEATURE:

The All-Time Top 10 'Next Dylans'

Monkee, Punkers, Bubblegum King: They Wished that for Just One Time They Could Stand Inside His Shoes

Scram magazine, Winter 2000

A funny thing about revolutions: Once they're won, it's hard to find anyone who opposed them. Paris, 1789: *"Mais oui!* My servants will tell you: For me, it was always *liberte, egalite, fraternite!"* Seattle, 1991: "I always dug flannel. That spandex belongs to my sister." Few cultural traditions are more time-honored than bandwagon-jumping, as P. Edwin Letcher's piece on faux Beatles (*Scram* #12) proved. Thirty-five summers ago, perhaps the most cataclysmic "arrival" in pop—Bob Dylan's, as reshaper of American song, world's unlikeliest rock 'n' roll star and irresistible force—set off a wondrous flood of fakery and imitation. Over the years, few musicians have remained untouched by his influence: Lennon, Prince, Jagger-Richards, Motown, Springsteen, V.U. Lou, Sheryl Crow imitating Stealer's Wheel imitating Dylan, etc. But the real fun was the gate-storming party-crash that occurred when they first opened up that new stretch of Highway 61. Once he roared past, it seemed like *everybody* wanted to be Bob Dylan, especially the 10 heroic aspirants revved up here on Simulation Row.

10. MICHAEL BLESSING (NESMITH)

As the early-'60s headquarters of TV-pop (Shelley Fabares, Paul Petersen, James Darren), it's perhaps not surprising that Colpix Records was the future Monkee's first label-stop. The surprise is his 1965 single, "What Seems to Be the Trouble, Officer," an outright sendup of Dylan's version of "Baby Let Me Follow You Down." It's all there: thick-strummed 12-string, rudimentary harmonica and M.N. talk-singing his way through a series of nonsequitirs in a voice somewhere between early Dyl and very late Walter Brennan. The song climaxes with the hippie equivalent of a standup's rim-shot: "First hard time I ever had was a policeman stopped me," drawls Nesmith. "He asked me if he could see some papers. I said, 'What you want, man, Bambu or Zigzag?'"

9. JOEY VINE (LEVINE)

On the single "The Out Of Towner," the lead singer of the Ohio Express/Kasenetz-Katz Singing Orchestral Circus wraps his eternally adenoidal cords around an early-Dylan-style 'protest' number. A jagged guitar riff plays tag with the vocal as J.V. inveighs against a hypocritical suburbanite who seeks sinful pleasures in the big city; "skyscrapers" and "tranquilizers" figure prominently in this gem of an outlaw blues from '65. (4 Seasons arranger Charlie Calello produced; hear that group's superb Dyl-crib, "Everybody Knows My Name," on their *Working My Way Back to You* album.)

8. TIE: THE TRASHMEN AND THE LOVE SOCIETY

Thank heaven the Surfin' Birdmen never bowed to sacred cows. Otherwise, they might not have given us "(Why Do You Give Me) The Same Lines," a '66 rocker that mocks their famous fellow Minnesotan to a 'D.' Talk about colliding visions of youth culture! The T-men cop the vocal kinks of the Poet of the '60s to tell what's basically a '50s teen tale: the singer's upset with a girl who won't hang with him at the malt shop. Only advanced voice-print technology could prove that the singer of the Love Society's "You Know How I Feel"' isn't his Bobness; an amazing resemblance, courtesy of this Wisconsin band's one-off RCA single from '68.

7. BUTCH HANCOCK

The gifted Austin songwriter and founder (with Jimmie Dale Gilmore and Joe Ely) of early alt-folkers the Flatlanders went delirious from the Dyl heat in '77, offering the fevered solo set *The Wind's Dominion*. The sprawling double-album resembles a hot-wired *Blood on the Tracks*: endless verses breathlessly sung, vacuum-packed with shadow figures (Cockroach Man, the Shrimpboat Captain, "the queen's daughter's lover," etc.). A solid hoot, even, it seems, for its creator.

6. MOUSE & THE TRAPS

From the same Nugget-y ranks as the Trashmen, Ronnie 'Mouse' Weiss and his East Texas Traps are easily the hardest-rockin' exponents of faux Dylanism. The near-hit "A Public Execution" and the scorching "Maid of Sugar, Maid of Spice" burn *Highway 61* rubber, while "Nobody Cares" brandishes *Blonde* roots.

5. SONNY BONO

Newsweek anointed Donovan "Dylan's work-shirted, cloth-capped English counterpart," but the early period's most profound pretender was the Son-king. Adapting the Tambourine Man's vocal mannerisms to his own restricted range, he begat a pop-protest style of great power and stupidity in 1965's "(I'm Not) The Revolution Kind." Its predecessor, "Laugh at Me," poignantly dramatized the plight of an oppressed minority (the bellbottomed, bobcat-vested ex-promotion man—Sonny—who'd been hooted out of an industry watering-hole by promo men in suits); it also set in motion the bizarre double-helix that found Ian Hunter borrowing Sonny's Dylan adaptation to forge Mott the Hoople's even more Dylanesque style five years later.

4. P.F. SLOAN AND BARRY McGUIRE

"Eve of Destruction" composer P.F. Sloan, 19, allows that his inspiration comes from being 'bugged most of the time,'" *Time* reported in 1965. Something made the composer of Jan & Dean's "Theme from the T.A.M.I. Show" and "One-Piece Topless Bathing Suit" swap his baggies for a Hans Brinker cap and life as a sim-Zim. Not so much a sound-alike as a write-alike, P.F. aped every Dylan song-style, from apocalyptic anthems ("Upon a Painted Ocean" = "When the Ship Comes In") and declarations of independence ("Let Me Be"= "It Ain't Me, Babe") to Burroughsian cut-and-paste ("Patterns, Seg. 4" = "Subterranean Homesick Blues"). His second LP, *12 More Times*, contains the great "Halloween Mary," whose witchy, wig-hatted protagonist is "riding on a sports-broom, actin' like nothin' is real." Sloan penned much of Barry McGuire's *Eve of Destruction* and *This Precious Time* LPs—most notably the Dylan dreamscape "Mr. Man on the Street—Act One" and the probing "Don't

You Ever Wonder Where It's At."

3. THE CHANGIN' TIMES

Despite a limited output (four Philips singles), former Brill Bldg. scribes Steve Duboff and Artie Kornfeld ("Deadman's Curve," tunes for the Turtles and Lesley Gore) snag the 'show' spot by virtue of the sheer crassness of their work. The duo's late-'65 "Pied Piper" (Crispian St. Peters' cover version went top five) is deliriously Dyl-derivative: an overcooked stew of deliberately flat vocals, clattering drums and reedy harp intrusions. True "babe magnets," Steve and Artie repeat Dylan's stock gal-phrase some 18 times over the course of "Piper" and its flip, "Thank You, Babe." Self-plagiaristic follow-ups like "Aladdin" and the fuzzed-out, prom-queen putdown "How Is the Air Up There" almost best the team's debut. "It didn't come from the Dylan song," the boys assured *Song Hits* magazine. "We chose 'Changin' Times' because it seemed to signify the present atmosphere of society." Whew!

2. DAVID BLUE

The heavyweights start here. One of Dylan's early Greenwich Village cronies, Blue was among the first to express his devotion on a full-length album. Looking on the cover of *David Blue* (Elektra, 1966) like Mickey Rourke playing some Dickensian scalawag in an off-Broadway *Oliver!*, on disc he slurs his way across a littered imagistic landscape, taffy-pulling syllables to the accompaniment of Dylan sidemen. "If Your Monkey Can't Get It" is "From a Buick 6" sideways, with sawing Velvets guitars, eagles in the hallway and Superman at the window. "Arcade Love Machine" tilts vertiginously, loaded as it is with dreaming streetlights, bleeding automats and "the hot-dog underground." On the fade, Blue gives one of those trademark Dylan cries of anguish: "Whoooahhh!!" Catch the late DB in the opening scenes of B.D's marathon movie *Renaldo & Clara*, nattering nervously as he plays (what else) a pinball machine.

1. DICK CAMPBELL

More bugged than Sloan, with better diction than Blue, this intense Chicagoan produced the sole masterpiece of the fake-Dylan field, *Dick Campbell Sings Where It's At* (Mercury, 1966). Modest talent and immodest ambitions provide the fuel for Dick to build a fire on Main Street

and shoot it full of holes; Dylan readymades (word choice, chord changes) form the DNA of the entire album, which, Dick's liner notes explain, is heavily informed by his volatile relationship with his girlfriend,
Sandi. Cases in point: the cringe-worthy "Blues Peddlers" ("I won't be
capitulating/ You're going to lose a few points in your ratings") and the
"Rolling Stone"-washed "Approximately Four Minutes of Feeling Sorry
for D.C." (world-class line cramming, plus appearances by Judas, blind
men and the farmer's daughter). The whole LP, from "Despair's Cafete-
ria" to "Girls Named Misery," glints like cubic zirconium. But the high
point—the veritable Apex of Appropriation to which all below Dick as-
pire in vain—is "The People Planners (proudly waving their propaganda
banners)." Mike Bloomfield, Paul Butterfield and support staff kick up
an electrical storm as DC spits fire at the enemies of us all:

> Hey there, don't you scream
> 'Cause I didn't eat up all my ice cream
> Or turn off the light when I came downstairs
> Forgot to burn the rubbish or comb my hair
> Just shut up!

Out of print? Yes. Hard to find? Natch. Likely to be reissued on CD?
Never. But *Sings Where It's At* is worth any effort it takes to find. Never
has thievery sounded so sweet.

FEATURE:

The Last Cop Show:
Requiem for *Walker, Texas Ranger*

Scram magazine, Summer 2001

Historically, a good cop show—and, until the '80s, there used to be plenty (*5-0*, *Dragnet*, Angie D's *Police Woman*)—has always delivered a lot. Namely, crypto-Reaganite moralizing, juicy villains and wailin' action—in other words, fun stuff. In these impoverished times, it seems as though, much like Lorenzo Lamas' solo swordswinger *The Immortal*, there can be only one—traditional cop show. And that show would be *Walker, Texas Ranger*, produced by and starring kick-box capo Chuck Norris, now winding up its eighth and final season on CBS.

This appreciation is offered on the assumption that the series will continue to run on the USA Network and in syndication, thus maintaining its ability to stun and delight well into Y3K. Almost every episode of *Walker* is a guaranteed goof that works off the same simple concept. Talent that's overly underwhelming (Norris as Ranger Cordell Walker) or unseasonably Honeybaked (Walker's adversaries) grapples with absurd premises, thrashing toward the inevitable climax (Walker's boot-tipped triumph over evil). Norris' wondrous woodenness is abetted by his live-action *Clutch Cargo* speaking style, and danger dogs him like Huckleberry Hound; he and partner Ranger Trivette can scarcely swing open a tavern door without being set upon by irate bikers. The cherry atop it all is that the show is constructed *entirely* of cliches and stereotypes.

Every line, gesture and character is proven, richly overcooked and easily digested by any viewer (Seasons 7 and 8 appear to have been written for—and perhaps by—children. Like *The Dukes of Hazzard*, Lawd, it's broad! And its literal lack of irony (scripts are apparently vacuumed to remove all traces) make *WTR* perhaps the last pure-camp vehicle ever to traverse the American pop-cultural stage.

Here's a guide, loosely arranged by subject matter, to what to watch for when you're ridin' with the *Ranger*…

Gangs & Mobs. Cop-show code dictates that these come in but two varieties: Mexican and Italian. A full half-dozen episodes treat the former; each pits low-riding, watch-capped cholos trying to recruit a hapless pre-teen ("*Ese*, come join us!") against the wishes of the youngster's poor but honest mom, who often works in a tortilla factory. Typical gang-episode resolution: the youth is saved from a life of violence by joining one of Walker's after-school boxing classes. Mob tales feature full-dress goombas in pricey suits and bling-bling, chauffeur-driven in sleek limos through the sagebrush. Neither their appearance nor their accents ever betray these hoods to the locals—until Walker uncovers them and kicks them back to Canarsie. (Ethnic/regional differences, however, are occasionally noted. When visiting N.Y.P.D. Sgt. Rossetti wraps a case with Walker, he announces he'll be "glad to get back to the Big Apple, where I can get a piece of steak that doesn't have sauce all over it!")

Terrorists & Teutons. At least two episodes address the timely issue of the IRA in Texas. In one, heavily brogue'd bro-and-sis freedom fighters drink, cry, recite poetry and toss *plastique* before diving out the window of a Houston high-rise. In one of the best of all *WTR* episodes, "Soul of Winter," storm-trooper fatso Stan Gorman burns churches, grimaces and orders his Sons of the Reich to find him "1000 new recruits by tomorrow!" (They get right on it, shanghai'ing unwary pedestrians and tossing them into their hate van.) At a key moment, one of Walker's Rangers gets the drop on a Son who's patrolling Gorman's arms depot—by yelling "Heil Hitler!" from behind a tree. When the goose-stepping guard drops his machinegun to salute, the Ranger decks him cold. Straight outta the Stooges.

Penal Reform & the Global Village. The finest of several prison episodes is "Fight or Die," in which Walker poses as a con in an Arkansas lockup—to uncover a corrupt warden who stages brutal cage matches between inmates and webcasts them around the world. Bad-ass guard Lt. Tracton, a sort of malevolent Brian Keith, chews scenery like some thespic Insinkerator. A mean multi-tasker, Tracton doesn't just MC the fights ("Here's some fresh meat, Hammer!," he bellows, throwing a new contender in the ring), he also directs the video from a studio as tricked out as Brokaw's or Rather's ("Camera 2, get in tight: go for the blood!"). The main card? Bare-chested, 61-year-old Walker vs. D Bloc's twentysomething Hammer (pro wrestler Randy Savage). No contest.

There's also recurring psycho Victor LaRue. No matter how many times he's put away by Walker's wife, D.A. Alex Cahill, he returns — like Scratchy to Itchy — to mug, maim and hold hostages. Wild-eyed and leering, LaRue (Wayne Pere) is so over-the-top he makes Jack Palance look like Pat Sajak. Mmmmmmmm good.

Space doesn't permit detailing such episodes as "Bachelor Party" (in the woods, Walker and his camping buddies are repeatedly attacked by a pissed-off grizzly, which Walker ultimately subdues with his boots and bare hands) or "Codename Dragonfly" (Walker's 'Nam nemesis, a peroxide ringer for Bill Clinton, strafes him with the ever-popular black helicopter!).

As the trad cop show's last stand, *Walker* delivers big-time. Dig it and be a part of history.

BOOK CHAPTER:

Gator in the Candy Lab:
A Brief History of Buddah Records

From *Bubblegum Music Is the Naked Truth*, edited by Kim Cooper & David Smay, 2001

The House That Gum Built started out as a second home. Buddah Records, official address of the 1910 Fruitgum Co., Ohio Express, the Lemon Pipers and a dozen lesser pop-tart combos, was initially a getaway
pad for business partners Phil Steinberg and Hy Mizrahi and producer
Artie Ripp (whose credits included Doris Troy's "Just One Look," Jay &
the Americans' "Come a Little Bit Closer" and the Shangri-Las' "Remember—Walkin' In The Sand"). Founded in 1965 as an offshoot of
the trio's Kama Sutra Productions, Kama Sutra Records had, one year
later, distinguished itself as America's hippest indie, notching hit after
hit by the Lovin' Spoonful and charting singles by the Sopwith Camel,
the Tradewinds and the Innocence. The label released a version of Bob
Dylan's "Can You Please Crawl Out Your Window" (by New York's Va-
cels) even before Dylan, and signed—then unsigned, at the point of a
shotgun—Frisco's psychedelic scene-starters, the Charlatans.

But by 1967 a rapidly souring distribution arrangement with MGM
Records had Ripp & co. looking for new digs. With backing from independent distributors, they founded Buddah Records, setting up shop at
1650 Broadway in NYC. "I concluded it was irreverent to spell 'Buddha'
like the religion," says Ripp of the Indo-Asian handle. "Besides, I could
never say 'ha' at the end of my name, but I could say 'ah'..." It was never
Buddah's mission to be the hothouse that grew the music America loved
to hate. Rather, the label was designed to attract talented writers and producers—Ripp already had Spector tunesmiths Pete Anders and Vinnie
Poncia (the Ronettes' "Do I Love You" and "The Best Part of Breakin'

Up") under contract, as well as Bo Gentry and Ritchie Cordell, who had produced Tommy James & the Shondells' "Mony Mony" and "I Think We're Alone Now"—and to accommodate unique artists with real prospects for long-term success.

West Coast A&R chief Bob Krasnow failed in his attempt to sign Frank Zappa's then-unaligned Bizarre Records imprint to Buddah, but he did snag Captain Beefheart & His Magic Band, whose early-1967 *Safe As Milk* (BDS LP 5001) officially introduced one of rock's most idiosyncratic and influential artists. Subsequent eccentricities such as organist Barry Goldberg's moody blues extrapolation *Reunion*, an early FM favorite, and Tony Bruno's tongue-in-cheek *The Beauty of Bruno* suggest Buddah might have taken off as a sort of left-of-center boutique version of Warner Bros. Then came Neil.

As counterpoint to the hip-clad Krasnow, Ripp hired a "young hot-shot" promotion man from Philadelphia's Cameo-Parkway Records. Neil Bogart was 24 when he became Buddah's VP/ general manager in 1967, and his founding philosophy, Ripp recalls, went something like this: "Having artists is a long-term game. Who knows how long it will take us in time and records to break these stars? So we need some real hit records." Bogart's aggressiveness is something Ripp knew well and admired, "having seen what he did with Question Mark & the Mysterians' '96 Tears' at Cameo. He could take that kind of super-basic record and just blow it out—bang-o!"

Among the records Bogart had blown out at Cameo was the Ohio Express' wiry "Louie Louie" rip, "Beg, Borrow and Steal," so, when he brought Buddah a new side by the producers of that garage nugget, Jerry Kasenetz and Jeff Katz, Ripp listened. "Neil plays me 'Simon Says' by the Fruitgum Co.," remembers Ripp. "I listen and I say, 'Boy, that sounds like a smash,' OK? Like it's a brand new trend. But I think we're gonna buy ourselves into a challenge: we're gonna all of a sudden have this badge on us if we chase this music. On the one hand, we'll be challenged as a label, putting out these records—which had no real artists—aimed at a very young head. On the other hand, we'd generate income and solidify the company right out of the gate." Ripp and his partners concluded that it was an acceptable risk.

"Simon Says" hit the Hot 100 in January 1968, eventually selling 2 million singles and rising to No. 4. By May, the Ohio Express' "Yummy Yummy" charted, on its way to the same peak: Buddha's foundation was down and the walls were going up fast, courtesy of Katz-Kasenetz's producing and Bogart's pushing. But, while the music's pre-teen target audiences clamored for gum, radio chewed slowly—and didn't always like the taste.

West Coast top-40 stations, particularly Bill Drake's powerful RKO chain (L.A.'s KHJ, San Francisco's KFRC), decided that, despite ringing request lines, Buddah's gooey goods did not fit the image they chose to project. 1968 saw the decade's most pitched battles between America's warring cultures; already hemorrhaging young-adult listeners to the new rock FM stations, the last thing AM top-40 wanted was to be seen as square—or to be left alone with a constituency of noisy 10-year-olds. Where radio refused to play Buddah's gum, Bogart's promo squad redoubled its efforts. "We just said, 'You guys have gotta be crazy,'" explains Ripp. "'Your ignoring this music is like they just dropped the atom bomb and your news department refuses to put the story on the air!'"

Radio eventually succumbed, thanks to the label's relentless promotional blitz—and a variety of marketing gimmicks designed to stoke customer demand for bubblegum music. Buddah backed dance contests (teams at eighty teenage Hullabaloo Nightclubs competed to devise the most original steps to "Simon Says"), in-house perks (a tie-in with American Air Lines rewarded sales staffers 50,000 bonus miles for their efforts on behalf of "Yummy Yummy") and retail promotions (a secret shopper—"Betty Buddah"—visited record stores, asking first for a non-Buddah record. If the salesclerk then tried to sell her a Buddah disk, Betty identified herself and handed the clerk $50).

Buddah celebrated its first anniversary in September 1968, as the nation's seventh-ranked label in single sales, a remarkable feat considering the then-crowded field. While it enjoyed success in the fields of general pop-rock (Lou Christie, Motherlode, the Brooklyn Bridge) and R&B (the Impressions, on Curtis Mayfield's Buddah-distributed Curtom Records; the Isley Brothers, through their T-Neck label), it was largely the sticky stuff that sealed the imprint's success. Within Buddah's bubblegum laboratory, it seemed as though teams of hook-canny creatives labored day and night, perfecting irresistible sugar-fixes. Katz-Kasenetz oversaw their own writing stable—Elliot Chiprut (the Fruitgum Co.'s "Simon Says," and "May I Take a Giant Step") and Levine & Resnick (the Express' "Yummy," "Chewy" and "Down at Lulu's," the Katz-Kasenetz Singing Orchestral Circus' "Quick Joey Small")—as well as "Artie's army," Ripp's original Kama Sutra composers (Bo Gentry, Ritchie Cordell and Bobby Bloom collaborated on the Fruitgum Co.'s "Indian Giver" and "Special Delivery").

The hectic work pace often occasioned the repurposing of both material and artists. Andrew Smith & the Hyannis Ports' satire on Robert F. Kennedy's Presidential bid, "Bobby Says," blatantly sampled "Simon Says." The Lemon Pipers, a bonafide band from Cincinnati whose repertoire included the extended psyche-funk workout "Fifty Year Void," were transformed into dutiful bubble-puppies by writer-producer Paul Leka, who fed them "Green Tambourine," "Rice Is Nice" and "Jelly Jungle." And, since Buddah's biggest records were being made by acts that didn't exist outside the studio anyway, who'd object if the lab cooked up a few more? The call for hits and the necessity of commanding shelf space almost demanded such chicanery. Brand identification was the goal. On what other label would one expect to find such fanciful concoctions as the Tidal Wave, Frosted Flakes, Salt Water Taffy, Lt. Garcia's Magic Music Box, J.C.W Rat Finks and The Rock And Roll Dubble Bubble Trading Card Company of Philadelphia 19141?

Bubblegum music prospered well into 1969 (the genre's signature work, "Sugar Sugar," charted that July), but the Buddah variety quickly lost its flavor. The label's last gum successes, the Ohio Express' "Mercy" and the Fruitgum Co.'s "Special Delivery," made the Hot 100 in May of '69—less than eight months after *Time* magazine had crowned Bogart king of pop's cotton-candy castle. By then, his crown had lost some of its luster, thanks to such fizzled Barnum-esque schemes as the Katz-Kasenetz Singing Orchestral Circus; the forty-member bubblegum supergroup played Carnegie Hall, but a subsequent tour and TV documentary drew scant response. There'd also been the shamelessly phony "Naked Truth" album campaign. The six nude bodies on the cover, Bogart told the press of the forthcoming LP, represented "the freedom of expression common to music today and the new attitude toward living." Upon its release, the front jacket of the anthology of bubblegum hits featured six cavorting toddlers; it failed to ignite controversy or sales.

Buddah's demise was surely hastened by its assembly-line approach (how were potential record-buyers to tell the difference between the Camel Drivers and the Carnaby Street Runners?). It was too-much-too-soon, but also not-enough-where-it-counts. Bogart's hit-city philosophy had generated a one-year streak of white-hot singles, but it had done little for album sales (of six *Billboard*-charting Fruitgum and Express LPs, the highest position posted was 129). "At the end of the day," explains Ripp, "if you were going to be a new Atlantic or Motown, you had to have the Arethas, the Ray Charles, the Bob Dylans—the stars who would keep you selling albums—and bubblegum music didn't have that." To say nothing of the reptilian payback monster Bogart's experiments had unleashed.

"When we again, finally [1969], sat down with Frank Zappa and [manager] Herbie Cohen to seriously discuss distributing Bizarre Records, which had now emerged as a very real thing," says Ripp, "the hit alligator bit me in the ass." Despite Buddah's initial braveness with Beefheart—and its early outreach to the hipster community (at Monterey Pop, a giant inflated Buddah served as both a signpost for festival-goers and an advertisement for the label)—Zappa passed. "How could I," Ripp remembers him asking, "allow Bizarre to be connected with Buddah, the home of bubblegum music?" The el supremo of avant-pop wound up taking his roster (the Mothers, Alice Cooper, Wildman Fischer, Jeff Simmons, the GTO's) to Warner/Reprise.

It was almost as if Buddah was fated to pay for its short-lived bubble of prosperity. The "badge" the label pinned on itself when it issued "Simon Says" seemed to ensure that the artist-attracting 'cool factor' Ripp sought would forever elude Buddah. The company did go on to sell albums (by Melanie, Gladys Knight & The Pips, and Curtis Mayfield, whose *Superfly* soundtrack came in through Curtom), but it sustained itself until its 1983 demise largely in the singles game ("Candles in the Rain," "Midnight Train to Georgia," the Andrea True Connection's "More More More").

By then, the architects of Buddah's early success had left the building. Artie Ripp exited in 1970, when the board of Viewlex Corporation, the educational-media company that bought the label in late 1969, refused to issue the (highly lucrative) Woodstock movie and soundtrack, to which he had acquired rights. The directors of the publicly-traded company had seen the TV-news coverage of sex, mud and rock & roll and decided an association with the festival was not in their best interests ("I told 'em," says Ripp, " 'You got involved with Kama Sutra and Buddah Records—did you think you were getting involved with the Vatican?'"). Ripp went on to discover and manage Billy Joel, and he remains active in entertainment today.

Neil Bogart quit Buddah in 1973 to found Casablanca Records. While the label's flagship act, Kiss, has proved to be among the most enduring in pop, the House That Disco Built was, like Buddah, hit-fixated and producer-driven; Giorgio Moroder and Jacques Morali, the minds behind Donna Summer and the Village People, respectively, called all the shots. (Bogart's Casablanca exploits and excesses get a full chapter in Frederick Dannen's 1991 music-biz exposé *Hit Men*. Bogart died of cancer in 1982, after founding the short-lived Boardwalk Entertainment.)

"The perception was that bubblegum music wasn't hip enough," reflects Ripp. "Yet the reality was that the gum songs and the dance groove of the records had a wonderful, fun aspect to them. It was something in the '60s that wasn't heavy or with a political agenda. It was, 'Smile, have a good time.' Everything is not so significant that you can't take a moment out to laugh. Everything doesn't have to be Einstein's theory or change the world."

Sometimes, though, it seems as if the world never will change, as if some bad reps—no matter how undeserved—are destined to stick to their wearers forever. As late as December 1999, more than a decade and a half after Buddah closed its doors for good, a *Washington Post* writer, reviewing a Beefheart reissue, wondered how the surrealist auteur ever could have consorted with "the label that specialized in bubblegum music—squeaky clean pop singles aimed directly at children and early adolescents. It was an odd place for the dada captain to begin..."

The same year, the BMG music conglomerate reactivated "Buddha" Records as an archival imprint, to mine its many acquired catalogs (including Buddah). For two years Buddha reissued albums by Melanie, Waylon Jennings, Duke Ellington, the Flamin' Groovies, Dr. Seuss and Henry Rollins. As we go to press comes the welcome news that they're compiling hits collections by the Ohio Express, Lemon Pipers and 1910 Fruitgum Company.

REVIEW:

Dorsey Burnette *Here & Now*

From the book *Lost in the Grooves*: Scram's
Guide to Capricious Music, 2004

By 1972, the middle-aged Memphian's Rockabilly Trio days were behind him. So were the hits he gave Ricky Nelson, his own pop stardom ("Tall Oak Tree," the affecting "Hey Little One") and his pill-fueled fall (his inability to say no suggests a Deep South Dennis Wilson). Burnette was saved—literally by religion and family, professionally by the early-seventies crossover tide that pushed country acts like Charlie Rich, Donna Fargo and Tanya Tucker up the pop charts in record numbers.

Back from the brink, Burnette sounds like a soul saved. *Here & Now*, his Capitol debut, is an L.A.-recorded, big-production countrypolitan album, the perfect habitat for that soulful booming baritone. Think P. J. Proby, minus the overt mannerisms, with a Tennessee accent. It's a joy to hear him take on "Daddy Don't You Walk So Fast," vocally supercharge the honky-tonk ballad "I Love You Because" and roll through the mid-tempo hit original "In the Spring (The Roses Always Turn Red)," itself a remarkable confessional to a late soulmate. But it's in the upbeat tunes that Dorsey excels—"Lonely to Be Alone," a dobro-powered, John Hartford-ish original, and, best of all, "I Just Couldn't Let Her Walk Away." Over a driving bass, banjo, chorale and pedal steel (the arrangement is almost bluegrass Spector), he just soars. By the last verse and chorus, riding the harmonies and rhythm, he and the whole massive track sound like they're about to lift off the terra altogether. It's a pure pop moment, really, in the midst of a country album: robust, real, life-filled, worth it.

The Dorsey Burnette album followed in 1973, and it's strong too ("Keep Out of My Dreams," "It Happens Every Time"). Burnette passed away in 1976.

REVIEW:

Muddy Waters' *Electric Mud* and Howlin' Wolf's *The Howlin' Wolf Album*

From *Lost in the Grooves*: Scram's *Capricious Guide to the Music You Missed*, 2004

First time I heard Shannon's great "Let the Music Play" (1984), the first thing the massively dense track reminded me of was this pair: two of the most widely denounced LPs of all time. Here's the backstory. In 1967, Chess Records junior honcho Marshall Chess thought he'd "update" the sound of the label's two blues giants. He hired arranger Charles Stepney, fresh from Rotary Connections psych-soul hits, and the two put Muddy in front of an eight-piece band featuring flute, amplified sax and mad ger-tar-slingers Pete Cosey and Phil Upchurch.

The result was a delicious noise-stew, thick with polyrhythms and fonked-up solos. Think David Axelrod's *Songs of Innocence* with more focus and meat and fat on its frame. Muddy—and later Wolf, whose set the same crew built—became mere bricks in the wall, like Darlene L. or Ronnie S. But what a wall!

Electric Mud's better, opening with a thunderous "I Just Want to Make Love to You" (it sounds like Cream and Sabbath jamming). On "Tom Cat," Gene Barge runs Coltrane riffs through a jungle of burry fuzz and wah-wah. Muddy catches the spirit on "Herbert Harper s Free Press News" (a salute to an underground paper), barking joyously as the guitarists hurl Hendrix and Cipollina licks against pulverizing piano, bass and drums. The rhythm seems to anticipate hip-hop by three decades.

The Howlin Wolf Album is something of a replay of *Electric Mud* with a few twists ("Smokestack Lightning" gets a flute and an echo chamber). The album, though, if you can find one, is worth its price for "Evil." Wolf's mean blues is reconfigured around a descending bass line and screaming guitar riffs that drop and scatter like a bag of marbles hitting the sidewalk. Talk about multitasking: the whole track wobbles, swings and rocks mightily.

Feature:

The Wanderer Walks with the Blues

Ambassador magazine, Fall 2005

It's a shame that these days a singer this good needs a qualifier. Until the arrival of Celine, there was only one Dion—Dion DiMucci, the voice behind the rock 'n' roll classics "I Wonder Why" (1958, with the Belmonts), "Runaround Sue" and "The Wanderer," "Ruby Baby" and "Donna the Prima Donna," and the era-defining "Abraham, Martin and John."

In many hearts and minds, there'll always be but one Dion. That said, the Bronx-born, Florida-residing singer and songwriter has always shown many sides, so that, in a sense, there've been many Dions. The latest shows up on *Bronx in Blue* (on The Orchard label), a new album of traditional blues that, for the most part, feature just the singer, his guitar and his uncommon affinity for one of America's most vital musical genres.

"I always said that my early rock 'n' roll was just black music filtered through an Italian neighborhood," Dion explains, "and it came out with an attitude." His association with the form began in the early 1950s, when "I'd tune into radio stations from the South, so I could hear people like Howlin' Wolf and Jimmy Reed." It took a while, though, before he felt confident enough to attempt playing the real 12-bar thing. "When I *first* listened to the blues, I never thought I could *do* that," he laughs. "I wouldn't think of copying Muddy Waters or those guys. But then, in the mid-'60s, the Stones came at it, and they sounded like Muddy Waters. I never wanted to copy the music, I just digested it all, and when I did it, it came out like me."

Indeed, after decades of white blues performers—many whose approach, it must be admitted, borders on blackface imitation—there's something unique and refreshingly natural about the music on *Bronx in*

Blue. "We went in and did the album in two days," says Dion. "I played the guitar and sang at the same time, then I went in and added some lead guitar to a few things, like on Robert Johnson's 'Walkin' Blues,' and on 'I Let My Baby Do That' [a playful double-entendre number, the album's one cut written by Dion], I picked it and sang, then went back and added the strumming guitar to it."

In addition to Johnson's "Walkin' Blues," the CD features, among others, the blues pioneer's "Crossroads" and "Terraplane Blues," Willie Dixon's "Built for Comfort," Lightnin' Hopkins' "You Better Watch Yourself" and Bo Diddley's much-recorded "Who Do You Love." "On that one," Dion laughs, "my voice—I couldn't get it up further, but I had to try, because I'm playing the guitar at the same time, and it's blaring into the microphone."

Among many highlights, Dion's rendition of Howlin' Wolf's "How Many More Years" may be the capper. What's always communicated in the best Dion performances is here—the ease of that voice gliding across the chords, melodic and free, the joy of his singing unmistakable to anyone within range.

His Italian-ness remains a source of pride for Dion, though it's something he had to develop.

"I used to see these people in my neighborhood, just hanging out on the street corner, Italians, and I thought, 'Wow, Italians are weird,' you know? Then when I went to Italy and I saw the poetry, the architecture and the spirituality, the humor and the love, and I said to myself, 'Hold on. I gotta take a second look at this.' So, from way back then, I saw my roots in a beautiful way."

Those roots go back to Abruzzi (on his father's side) and Calabria (on his mother's). His maternal grandfather, Dion recalls with great fondness, "was always teaching me the traditions, where we came from. I remember he said, 'Italians always want a son first. That's because we wanted someone to work in the fields. If we didn't have a son, we'd perish—we needed boys and men.' But then, he'd say, '*Then* we prayed for women—to grace the house.' He was a great man."

MOR's Adventures in the Lands of Pop and Rock

Scram magazine, 2005

Stan Cornyn's liner notes to *Buddy's in a Brand New Bag,* middle-of-the-road singer Buddy Greco's 1967 LP, tell it all: "Now the hip Mr. Greco focuses his talents on the pop music world. Where before the rhythms had been loose and lightly grooved, now they become driving, heavily orchestrated, massive. There are differences, most of which hit your ears immediately."

Well, sort of. Greco does cover Leiber & Stoller, Brill Bldg. lions Jack Keller and Howard Greenfield and Everly Bros. producer Dick Glasser, but *Buddy's in a Brand New Bag* should not be mistaken for *Perry Como Sings Esquerita.* It is, however, a good example of an overlooked Sixties trend that, by love's certain summer, had been going on for some time, with curious and often cool results: the alchemical process by which young pop bio-technicians tried to engineer a genetic match between old-line vocalists and the newly dominant teen-rock.

Like Mel Torme, who had no eyes to cut the song that gave him his only Top 40 hit (1962's "Comin' Home, Baby"), crooner Steve Lawrence was probably dragged kicking and shvitzing into the early Sixties sessions that produced the infectious pop-rock singles "Footsteps" (written by Barry Mann) and "Go Away Little Girl" (Goffin-King). Lawrence and wife Eydie Gorme scored with the uptempo "I Can't Stop Talking About You" and the ballad "I Want to Stay Here" (both Goffin-King), while she clicked solo with Mann and Weil's cha-cha-charming "Blame It on the Bossa Nova."

Most of the above were cut for Columbia Records, which seems to have mandated that its pre-rock acts get with the kids' new jive. A good thing, too, since the label was home to two of the graybeards-a-go-go genre's best records, both 1963 Terry Melcher productions of Jack Nitzsche arrangements. Frankie Laine's "Don't Make My Baby Blue" is a booming Mann-Weil masterpiece, a cavernous class-action suite of fuzz guitar, French horns and soaring chorus. Conceived by Nitzsche as a "white Ronettes" record, Doris Day's "Move Over Darling" delivers, with castanets, delicious Nitzsche string lines and Melcher's mom gamely belting. (Both are on the Nitzsche compilation *Hearing Is Believing*.)

Less dramatic but also sharp are Andy Williams' Doc Pomus-Mort Schuman sides (Columbia again, '63 and '64), the sparsely plucked "'Can't Get Used to Losing You" and the oddly syncopated "Wrong for Each Other," which seems to marry a slow-build Orbison ballad to a swinging Vince Guaraldi jazz waltz.

The genre brims, too, with one-offs, like Glenn Yarborough's "It's Gonna Be Fine" (1965). RCA's attempt to politely push the "Baby, The Rain Must Fall" tenor into folk-rock is a blast, a mid-tempo Spector-with-harpsichord entry, written by Mann-Weil and produced by David Gates.

All of the above are available on CD, as is Nat King Cole's "The Good Times," a guitar-y "Stand By Me" rip from his 1962 *Ramblin' Rose* album, and premature oldster Wayne Newton's great Gary Usher side, "Comin' on Too Strong."

You'll have to hunt, though, for a gem like "You Can't Lose Something You Never Had." Al Kooper's R&B-ish Bacharach entry, which here resembles a lighter-weight Walker Bros. track, turns up on young crooner Bruce Scott's *They're All Raving About Bruce Scott* (MGM, 1966). The LP's also the source for Mark "Pretty Flamingo" Barkan's Gene Pitney-meets-folk-rock piece, "So Much to Live For."

Two other Kooper items I've yet to find: Keely Smith's Reprise single "Goin' Through the Motions" (1963) and jazz singer Ernie Andrews' "Where Were You When I Needed You" (1965 Capitol 45). I have heard Buddy Greco do Leiber & Stoller's "Where's the Girl," and it's the least soulful version of this often covered ballad.

The whole MOR-goes-hip school closed its doors in late '67, when music modes changed so drastically that even the decade's preeminent pop tunesmiths were tossed out on their golden ears and a "progressive" new breed swept the shop clean. It was right around the time that Boyce & Hart produced Trini Lopez's *The Whole Enchilada* album (two years before, they'd contributed to Dean Martin's *Houston* album). I'm fine with hearing Mr. "Lemon Tree" work out to "I Wonder What She's Doing Tonight"—but covering "Sunshine of Your Love"? No, I don't think so.

FEATURE:

Suddenly Single:
When '60s Undergrounders
Made Peace with the Top 40

Scram magazine, 2006

A couple of *Scrams* ago (#21), we looked at the '60s phenomenon of middle-of-the-road acts trying to hip up their images by recording pop-rock material. A lesser examined but related event, it turns out, was taking place at roughly the same time, at the other end of the telescope.

It'd be hard to name a more tumultuous pop-music time frame than 1965-to-1967. Monthly, it seemed, new avenues of expression were being bulldozed across the landscape: Brit invaders, folk-rock, blues-rock, goodtime music, new Dylans, sunshine pop, acid-rock. Until late '67-'68, when the West Coast psychedelic movement, with its establishing of the LP as the coin of the realm and the advent of "underground" FM radio, toppled the age-old hegemony of hit singles, concessions to the old machine had to be made. A band needed a 45, as a sort of aesthetic business-card and introduction to the public. This requirement led to some fascinating records, on which the new boundary-stretching artists got a chance to show their creativity in a way that still fit the commercial strictures of the day.

The earliest example of this is probably the Yardbirds. An initial handful of straight blues covers failed as singles, and the decision to cut the cool but clearly un-Chess-like "For Your Love" (no slide guitar, plenty of harpsichord) precipitated a huge rift within the band. The group's first hit came from the pen of pop scribe Graham Gouldman (who provided Top-40 fodder to the Hollies and Hermits, later founded 10 cc and even made bubblegum records), which led directly to the departure of Muddier-than-thou guitarist Eric Clapton. GG next gave the 'birds the even poppier "Heart Full of Soul," while Manfred Mann drummer/vibist Mike Hugg contributed the socio-spiritual "(Mister) You're a Better Man Than I."

It would be a while before Clapton could shred freely and fill the Fillmores with 20-minute "Spoonfuls." While Cream's '66 debut album sported instrumental adventurousness and some truly unusual songwriting, it was preceded by the atypical "Wrapping Paper." Jack Bruce's sporty piano sortie sounds like a pleasant Sopwith Camel outtake or an entry by one of a dozen Lovin' Spoonful sound-alikes.

Other free-formers complied with the rules of the game too. The Grateful Dead's first album boasted a couple of extended cuts, but the bet hedge was Side 1 Track 1, the single "The Golden Road (to Unlimited Devotion)." The jubilant, two-minute cut features a tight, ringing Garcia solo, frequent choruses and old-time movie-serial organ on its intro and fade. The single's flip, "Cream Puff War," which I recall the band introducing as one of their first original compositions (from the Fillmore stage in 1966), is a breakneck rocker that mashes a Dyl-lite vocal with the spirit and sound of the Animals' "I'm Crying." (Sadly, the disc was a stiff, as was the band's second Warners seven-inch, a three-minute edit of their "Dark Star" opus.)

Seattle's Daily Flash were also improvisers (a bootleg CD offers their 13-minute version of Herbie Hancock's "Cantaloupe Island"), but their debut single pairs a feedback-packed blues adaptation ("Jack of Diamonds") with a familiar cover ("Queen Jane Approximately"). L.A.'s eclectic Kaleidoscope eschewed the often lengthy excursions of their live sets for a pair of 45's that aimed for radio-friendliness. "Please" b/w "If the Night" was a double deck of exceptional folk-rock (a later release coupled "Please" with "Elevator Man," which rather recalls the Stones' "Off the Hook"), and "Why Try" was a conventional pop tune, albeit with Middle Eastern accents. Its B-side nodded to the camp predilection of the day—"Little Orphan Nannie."

Blues bands, like their cousin psychedelicians, were obliged to pop up too. The (Barry) Goldberg- (Steve) Miller Blues Band cranked out the buzzing garage rocker "The Mother Song" in 1965 (Billy Sherrill, who recorded the Remains, produced) and appeared on *Hullabaloo* to promote it. Goldberg's subsequent Barry Goldberg Blues Band issued the noisy, attitudinal Dylan homage "Blowing My Mind." Even more interesting are the Blues Project singles. Early on, these relied on the dominant '65-'66 folk-rock trend. The A-sides of the first two issues were written by Donovan ("Catch the Wind") and Eric Andersen. The BP's rendition of the latter's crypto-Zimmy "Violets of Dawn" was one of several recorded in 1966 (others were done by the Robbs, Daily Flash and the Mitchell Trio).

Far more innovative was the Project's next pair, both composed by keyboarder Al Kooper. The former Royal Teen, Dylan accompanist and material source for various girl groups, Gary Lewis and Gene Pitney first delivered the smoldering "Where's There's Smoke There's Fire" (a collaboration with writing partners Irwin Levine and Bob Brass; the duo later penned Dawn's first hit, "Candida"). The Tokens (of "The Lion Sleeps Tonight") add vocal heft to the track, and it's a gem, but sadly a flopped 45. The same fate befell the rockin' "No Time Like the Right Time," cut in December '66. This one's got it all: an insistent melody, Kooper's Queens soul-patrol vocal and a mid-song instrumental breakdown (featuring AK on the spacey Ondioline keyboard), all of it perfectly in synch with the flavor of pre-*Pepper* psyche. The band's post-Kooper "Gentle Dreams" b/w "Lost in the Shuffle" couples a quirkily arranged A-side (its fussy arrangement almost suggests the BS&T of "Spinning Wheel") with an undistinguished Curtis Mayfield-derived blues.

The period, of course, subsequently saw real smashes originate from the new rock community; records like "White Rabbit," "Light My Fire" and "Piece of My Heart" would have been unthinkable visitors to the Hot 100 in 1965 or even '66. Eventually, the ascent of psychedelia and album-rock meant that hit singles were unnecessary, impossibly unhip and maybe even counterrevolutionary. Rather like the Byzantine contortions that govern the maintenance of indie-rock cred today, when you think about it.

One Kiss Can Lead to Another: *Girl Group Sounds*

Rhino Records 2005

Every little bit hurts. It does, you know. To see one of your favorite pop periods so ruthlessly maligned, as a matter of accepted, orthodox history, is painful. I'm referring, of course, to one of the most bad-rapped eras on record: early '60s rock 'n' roll.

You may be familiar with the charges: '50s rock was a wild and vital wellspring that gushed forth liberating attitudes and the first true youth culture, but then Elvis was drafted, Buddy Holly and Eddie Cochran died, Chuck Berry and Jerry Lee Lewis were missing in action, and an unrelieved drought ensued until the Beatles splashed ashore in '64.

It says so right here. Look. In *The Rolling Stone Illustrated History of Rock & Roll*, page 107: "[By the late '50 s) pop fell into the hands of those same old men of the music industry who had long sought to remove the unpredictability inherent in rock." And here, page 159: "In 1960, along with everything else going to hell in rock & roll ...," and 54 pages later: "[in1963) Rock & roll ... felt dull and stupid, a dead end."

Not to disparage the glory of the '50s or the still blazing sun storm that was the Beatles, but here's what I heard on the radio between 1960 and 1964: Dion, Del Shannon, The Drifters, Jackie Wilson, Brenda Lee, Etta James, Sam Cooke, Roy Orbison, the Beach Boys, Ike & Tina Turner, the Isley Brothers, Booker T. & the MG's, Maxine Brown, Marvin Gaye, the Everly Brothers, Mary Wells, Bobby Bland ...

... and, perhaps best of all, the Angels, the Butterflys, the Chiffons, the Cookies, the Crystals, Skeeter Davis, the Exciters, Lesley Gore, the Jelly Beans, Carole King, Little Eva, Darlene Love, the Marvelettes, the Ronettes, the Shangri-Las, the Shirelles, the Supremes, and many others.

Why this dissing of such a grand age? Because serious pop-music criticism developed in the later '60s—after The Beatles, Dylan, and others had seriously upgraded rock songwriting—and by the time the histories got written, people had been encouraged to have certain expectations about pop; namely to see it as a medium of expression for artists' (not mere performers') thoughts and ideas. These expectations, 40 years later more or less shared by everyone who produces and consumes pop music, would have been unthinkable in the pre-Beatles world.

In that world, this music was, like a moving symphony or a free-flying jazz jam, mainly about a feel: a sound. It had words, yes, but they were never intended to get in the way of the overall impact of a record.

Girl group music, I think, had an especially hard time gaining respect, since, with hindsight, its content seems so retrograde by modern standards ("It's my party, and I'll cry if I want to," "My boyfriend's back, and you're gonna be in trouble"). But that's missing the point, which is that, like the work of the other acts name-checked above, the best girl group records are simply some of the most joyous manifestations of being young/in love/out of love—hell, alive—ever committed to tape.

I don't know about you, but when I listen to Dorothy Berry's "You're So Fine" or the Girlfriends' "My One and Only, Jimmy Boy," I feel like I can walk through walls.

SOPHISTICATED BOOM

While its days in the sun were the mid-'60s, girl groups' origins rest squarely in '50s rock 'n' roll—particularly the distaff doowop of the Chantels (Arlene Smith's impossibly soulful lead on 1958's "Maybe" may well be the inspiration for the whole school) and the Shirelles, a New Jersey quartet best known for "Tonight's the Night" and "Will You Love Me Tomorrow," but who first clicked with "I Met Him on a Sunday," in 1958. Others served as early inspiration too: the lip-smacking Chordettes of "Lollipop" fame and the boys-and-girls-together Tune Weavers ("Happy, Happy Birthday Baby"), the Fleetwoods ("Come Softly to Me"), and the Teddy Bears ("To Know Him Is to Love Him").

By 1963-'64, the '50s fire-starters—the rangy rockabilly cats and street-corner harmony groups—were or being shaped into something sonically louder and more dramatic by a corps of hip, young professional songwriters, producers, and arrangers, many of them barely older than the adolescent audience who consumed their work on records.

The music that this youth crew was making wasn't anything like what had come before. The new rule of the day was *big*, booming singles, dense explorations of space like the Beach Boys' "Dance, Dance, Dance" or vast climactic zones like the Ronettes' "Walkin' in the Rain" or the 4 Seasons' "Rag Doll," ornate architectural undertakings like Jan & Dean's "Surf City" and overpowering furnace blasts like Martha & the Vandellas' "Heat Wave."

And there were a lot of people working long and hard to perfect these mini-masterpieces. Music publishers headquartered in Manhattan's legendary Brill Building (and similar Broadway warrens) kept songwriting teams busy spooling out potential A- and B-sides. Producers, label A&R representatives, and artists' managers sifted through writers' demos, choosing—with or without the performers' involvement—songs to record and release. Which is not to say that talent was incidental to the process or that female artists were necessarily permitted less participation than their male counterparts. Rather, it was the way the entire pop system worked then, unless an artist generated his or her own material (a distinct minority that included Dion, Del Shannon, the Beach Boys, and Roy Orbison) or had racked up a respectable batting average. By the time she cut "That's the Way Boys Are" (her fifth Top-15 single), Lesley Gore likely had enough clout to exercise veto power over the songs she was given to record.

Everyone in the Pool

The recording process itself was a community effort involving singers, arrangers, musicians, and engineers, yet in many ways pre-Beatles rock was a producer's game, much as it was during the '90s heyday of "boy bands." It was difficult to know if the vocalists behind the name on the spinning disc's label were organic, down-the-block groups (the Chiffons, Cookies, Angels, Reparata & the Delrons) or producer-recruited session singers convened for a one-time project (Cinderellas and Satisfactions, to name a pair).

The enormous popularity of the girl-group sound in 1963 (four Top 5 hits by Gore, the Ronettes' "Be My Baby," the Angels' "My Boyfriend's Back," the Chiffons' "He's So Fine" and "One Fine Day," the Raindrops' "The Kind Of Boy You Can't Forget," and more) ensured that every producer worth his headphones would soon try his hand at the genre. Between '63 and '64, a staggeringly varied roster of helmsmen waded into the wake of those initial hits. Among them: Motown's

Holland-Dozier-Holland team (the Supremes, the Velvelettes, Martha & the Vandellas), Chet Atkins (Skeeter Davis), Shadow Morton (the Shangri-Las, the Goodies), Brian Wilson (the Honeys), Ike Turner (the Ikettes), New York's Feldman-Goldstein-Gottehrer team (the Angels, the Pin-Ups), and Sonny Bono (Cher's "Dream Baby").

The 4 Seasons' producer Bob Crewe delivered tough, scorching sides by Diane Renay and Tracy Dey and big-voiced backup singer Shirley Matthews' "Big Town Boy." Spector arranger Jack Nitzsche oversaw Jackie DeShannon, the Satisfactions' cycle saga "Daddy, You Gotta Let Him In," and The Cake's haunting "Baby That's Me," while future Bread-winner David Gates hit two of the genre's heartiest non-hits straight out of the creative park (Dorothy Berry's "He's So Fine" and the Girlfriends' incendiary "My One And Only, Jimmy Boy"). In the U.K. producers Tony Hatch, Joe Meek and Ivor Raymonde worked similar wonders with Dusty Springfield, Petula Clark, and others.

Not the Revolution Kind

Nineteen sixty-five and '66 saw their share of girl group activity, but the school had surely graduated its most promising class the preceding season. Girl groups were just one of the previously sturdy vessels that began to founder as first folk-rock (1965), then psychedelic-rock (1966-'67) swamped the scene. Male vocal quartets and solo artists, soul men, instrumentalists, and garagers all experienced serious identity crises as introspection, outspoken social comment and cosmic puffery momentarily muscled affairs of the heart out of the way on the nation's tunedecks.

Some artists, like Cher and Marianne Faithfull , hitched comfortable, and fairly credible, rides on the folk-rock bus. Among the birds who gamely flew with flower-power were Lesley Gore (the tempo-changing, discordant "Brink of Disaster"), Goldie & the Gingerbreads (the sitar-strewn "Walking in Different Circles"), and the Chiffons (the genuinely trippy "Nobody Knows What's Goin' on [in My Mind But Me].") And by the later '60s and early '70s, some girl-group stalwarts morphed into romantic balladeers, most prominently Dusty Springfield and Diana Ross.

If respect has been slow in coming for the girl groups, scholarship hasn't. The principal proselytizer for the school was the late collector/editor/producer Alan Betrock, whose New York fanzine *The Rock Marketplace* was where much of the pioneering archaeology took place. Ken Barnes' column in Issue 7 (1974) alone heralded the discovery of such artifacts as the Cinderellas' "Please Don't Wake Me," the Cookies' "I Never Dreamed," and the Satisfactions' "Daddy, You Gotta Let Him In."

My own favorite historical-digging tales center on mid-'70s treks through the dusty, disorganized thrift shops and record-store backrooms of LA. with Ken. Once a wily San Gabriel Valley shop owner made us beg for admittance to his legendary storeroom (we were happy to), where thousands of 45s, stacked like Scrooge McDuck's coin stalagmites, awaited plucking. "Well, it's not worth me opening up [the room] unless you guys are prepared to spend some money there," he bluffed. Like craven junkies, we promised to throw down significantly, and he kept upping the dollar amount he'd need to unlock the vault. In the end, three of us guys must've spent $400 on singles, many of the yellow Red Bird and silver-blue Dimensions collected here, going for 25 cents apiece. Please don't wake me, indeed.

This compilation enables everyone to make similar discoveries to-day, without the travel expenses or greedy gatekeepers. These recordings, and many other sister hits, represent a true pop apex, both for their inher-ent beauty and their unquestionable influence on the records of so many artists who followed them. They deeply informed the songwriting of the Beatles (the group itself covered records by Ann-Margret, the Cookies, the Donays, Little Eva, and the Shirelles) and contributed much to the British Invasion, '80s New Wave, Euro -pop and dance pop, '90s R&B, and any number of records on last week's and next month's Hot 100. Like all of the best rock 'n' roll, this music radiates irresistible energy, heart, and soul, and its hooks dig and cling. In the end, when it comes to pop, I think I'd much rather be with the girls.

A Visit with Frankie Valli

Frankie Valli talks with *Ambassador magazine* about
the successful Broadway show, *Jersey Boys*, which is
based on the history of his band, the 4 Seasons

Ambassador magazine, 2006

Frankie Valli knows about comebacks and surprises. He'd labored in a succession of combos before finding "overnight" success with the Four Seasons, whose first record, "Sherry," in 1962 ignited one of the hottest hit streaks in pop music history. By the early '70s, the streak had cooled. But Valli reinvented himself, notching a No. 1 record in 1974's "My Eyes Adored You" and the following year's "Swearin' to God." Later that year, he and musical partner Bob Gaudio reconstituted the Seasons, scoring with "Who Loves You" and another chart-topper, "December 1963 (Oh What a Night)." Following a slight break in the action, Valli reemerged yet again, in 1978, with the hit theme to the movie *Grease*.

Valli's latest return to the spotlight is *Jersey Boys*, one of the smashes of the current Broadway season. Though he doesn't perform in it, Valli's story and songs are the heart of the musical, which traces the history of The Four Seasons, warts and all, from their '50 scuffling days to their 1990 induction into the Rock & Roll Hall of Fame. Recently, *Ambassador* music columnist Gene Sculatti caught up with Valli talked with him about his newest triumph.

Ambassador: Were you surprised by the success of *Jersey Boys*?
Valli: Well, It's something I always dreamed might happen, but for it to actually happen is really just a wonderful surprise.
A: How did the idea of a Four Seasons musical come about?

V: We had talked with NBC and CBS, and they wanted it to be a TV movie-of-the-week. But I just couldn't figure out how you could possibly cover 40 year of success in an hour or so. Eventually we said, "Maybe there's a possibility this could be a musical." We made some contacts, there was some interest, and ultimately it all happened and the show opened.

A: Did all of the Seasons [Valli, Gaudio, Tommy DeVito and Nick Massi] contribute to the play, in terms of providing background material for the playwrights?

V: Yes. Marshall Brickman and Rick Elice interviewed us. And they interviewed us separately.

A: Is what's up onstage fairly accurate?

V: I would say so, yeah. They do expand a bit, you know, but I would say most of it is accurate.

A: What's it like to see somebody portray your life?

V: The first time I saw it, it was a little strange. Not only to see somebody playing me, but, you know, I had no idea what each guy [in the Seasons] said in their interviews and what the writers used from those interviews. So that was a little weird. I got more comfortable after I'd seen it a few times.

A: Did you meet with John Lloyd Young, who plays you, and give him some tips?

V: You know, John did his homework, he really did. One of the things I found out later was that, when I was working in Vegas, he came out, without me knowing about it, and watched the show and took notes, which I was very impressed with.

A: What was it like for you guys to see some of the less flattering, more painful parts of your story depicted—like Tommy's gambling away your finances, and the Jersey mob?

V: Well, you know, everything in the play met with our approval. Those are the facts. Some of the facts in life are not flattering, and we all certainly have, each of us, skeletons in our closets. When we started, in the '60s, a lot of that was swept under the rug. Today it wouldn't matter. Today you have rappers who kill each other, and it hardly affects their career. And some things, when we came up, and for anybody who grew up in cities like Newark, were just naturals: If you were in the entertainment business, you worked in nightclubs, and nine out of 10 of them were owned by wiseguys.

A: It would have been hard not to brush up against them.

V: Absolutely. You worked in a place, a guy owned it. If you did good, he was terrific to you, he requested certain songs or he'd buy you a drink, and you were happy to have a job.

A: Has there been an uptick in attendance for your concerts since the premiere of *Jersey Boys*?

V: It's really seeping through now. You know, the play is not two months old yet, but it's doing very well, and probably by the middle of next year, there might be a road-company version.

A: How many dates do you do annually?

V: I'd say anywhere from 75 to 100 [laughs]. I don't want to do any more than that!

A: Can fans expect a new Frankie Valli record sometime soon?

V: Everything is possible. I've been playing around with a jazz project for almost two years now. I do it in my spare time. There's such a treasure of wonderful music that has been written: Cole Porter, the Gershwins, that's the kind of stuff I really want to do, unless there's some new writing that I really get excited about. I want to love what I do. If anybody's waiting for me to do "Sherry" or "Big Girls Don't Cry" again, I'm not going to do that kind. I love every second of everything I've recorded in the past, but I never really wanted to be a pop singer. Now I might have the chance to do some other things. Fortunately, I have a little studio of my own; I can go in and do whatever I want whenever I want, and if it's successful, fine, if it's not, I'm going to do it anyway. I owe it to myself at this particular point in time.

A: A standard question: Do you know where in Italy your family is from?

V: A small town outside Naples is the most I know about it. I probably have some third and fourth cousins there. My mother was born there, but my father was born here.

A: Have you ever visited the town?

V: You know, I've gone to Italy five or six times, and I start out in Rome, and when I go out I say I'm definitely going to visit each city there, but I've never been able to get past Rome! I get the feeling it would take years to really see Rome, so how do you go to Italy and just do two days in each place? There'd be nothing to bring back with you that you could remember. The way to do it is go somewhere and stay there for a month or two, and *then* you might want to go on to another place. There's so much there.

A: That's for sure. Thanks for talking with us.

V: Thank you.

BLOG POST:

Yesterday Once More:
Digging the Seventies' Fifties Revival

Rock's Back Pages Writers' Blog 2006

Any good student of pop-music history knows what happened in the Seventies: The broken bricks from the aesthetic street-fights of the Sixties were scooped up and mortared into a new edifice, "rock," which housed art- and prog-rock, heavy metal, sententious singer-songwriters and gray-faced corporate music. Then, in 1976, punk arrived and blew it all up real good, reinvigorating rock 'n roll.

Well, kind of. Actually, from the dawn of the decade another force had been quietly at work, chipping away at contemporary "rock," and its cumulative efforts may well have paved the way for punk's paramedic arrival. This was the revival of interest in Fifties rock and pop (which, arguably, can be said to have run from 1954 to 1964). When you examine the early Seventies, a lot was going, the effect of which was to legitimize pre-Beatles rock 'n' roll and thus challenge the notion that all the new hybrid rock forms constituted some inevitable forward motion or "growth"—which was precisely the thesis behind the Ramones-Pistols-Clash attack.

> "On Oct. 18, 1969, with backing provided by an office-partition manufacturer, Richard Nader presented the first edition of his Rock 'n' Roll Revival at New York's Felt Forum. Headlined by Bill Haley, Chuck Berry and the Shirelles, it was a sell-out, the first of nearly a hundred since… Nader's projection is that the Rock 'n' Roll Revival will keep kicking along until the next direction in music arrives in 1974."
> —Phonograph Record Magazine, November 1972

With hindsight we know that the first signs of a coming sea change *were* present in 1974 (proto-disco singles by the Hues Corporation and George McRae, the Ramones' CBGB debut), but these weren't apparent at the time. Back then the decade's next direction looked more like *Diamond Dogs* or *Tales from Topographic Oceans.*

By '74 the presence and impact of the Fifties revival was already six years old and growing. The phenomenon's parents may well have been Frank Zappa and Dr. Demento, whose twin 1968 projects almost appear conspiratorial. Where Zappa had been goofing on gooey teen ballads as early as 1966's *Freak Out!* (the Paragons' "Let's Start All Over Again," he told one interviewer, "has the unmitigated audacity to have the most moronic piano section I have ever heard"), with *Cruising with Ruben & the Jets* he delivered a smoochy satiric valentine to early rock 'n' roll, using his Mothers to perpetrate such send-ups as "Fountain of Love," "Stuff Up the Cracks" and "Jelly Roll Gum Drop." On *Doo-Wop*, its cover featuring a caricature of a hipster Fifties DJ, Barry Hansen (yet to become Demento) gathered a dozen vintage Specialty sides (Larry Williams' Beatles-covered "Bad Boy," Roy Montrell's "Mellow Saxophone," etc.) into the world's first serious oldies compilation. Scholarship and humor jelled: Both albums earned a good deal of play on the then-new rock-FM radio.

Sixty-eight also brought such harbingers as Fats Domino's acclaimed *Fats Is Back* LP and the Beatles' first consciously retro moves ("Back in the USSR," "Happiness Is a Warm Gun"). Little Richard, Eddie Cochran and Huey "Piano" Smith got covered on the Flamin' Groovies' *Supersnazz* debut, and a stretched-out version of Dale Hawkins' "Susie-Q" was the centerpiece of the first Creedence Clearwater Revival album.

Over the next four years, rekindled interest in early rock burst into a great ball of fire, one that was continuously stoked by archeological digging in *Creem* and *Phonograph Record Magazine* and, most importantly, in new history-conscious fanzines like *Who Put the Bomp.* United Artists Records took Barry Hansen's comp cue, issuing exquisite, double-LP *Legendary Masters* anthologies on Domino, Cochran, Jan & Dean and Ricky Nelson in 1971 (Lenny Kaye's epochal *Nuggets* arrived on Elektra the following year). Sha Na Na debuted (1969), Little Richard followed Fats with a pair of comeback albums, and Dave Edmunds charted with an unlikely cover of Smiley Lewis' "I Hear You Knocking" (1970), then cut half a dozen Spectorized remakes at his Rockfield studio. (Edmunds and Andy Kim each took a crack at the Ronettes' "Baby I Love You," with

Kim making it into the Top 10 in 1969.)

Fleetwood Mac, in its pre-pop blues-band incarnation, was a neo-'Fifties force of the first order. In '69 the group masqueraded as Earl Vince & the Valiants to wax the crypto-Ted anthem "Somebody's Gonna Get Their Head Kicked in Tonite"; a year later, guitarist Jeremy Spencer delivered an eponymous solo set that flipped a finger at prevailing rock tastes by affectionately covering disparaged vanilla-teen classics by Fabian ("String A-Long") and Johnny Restivo ("The Shape I'm In").

By '71 and '72, dedicated revivalist bands had moved in from the freak fringe to deliver their own albums: Detroit's Frut, Australia's Daddy Cool and Michigan/California's Commander Cody and His Lost Planet Airmen, whose '72 debut, *Lost in the Ozone*, threw off a hit single (a re-do of Johnny Bond's "Hot Rod Lincoln") and essayed a re-examination of rockabilly a full eight years before the Clash fishtailed their "Brand New Cadillac." If 1972 saw the less than stellar return of Chuck Berry in the chart-topping "My Ding-a-Ling," it also witnessed the rock 'n' roll resurrection of another royal in "Burning Love." The year produced Elton John's "Crocodile Rock," its central riff lifted from Pat Boone's "Speedy Gonzales" (1962), Johnny Rivers' smash cover of Huey Smith's "Rockin' Pneumonia—Boogie Woogie Flu" and the premiere of the *Grease* musical. Just as significantly, the mythos of early rock 'n' roll was addressed in such disparate hits as Don McLean's "American Pie" and B.J. Thomas' Beach Boys-inspired "Rock and Roll Lullaby." (Pre-Beatles elements were becoming visible in the work of more adventurous rockers too—the "primitive" riffs and modified Holly-isms of T. Rex, the stylistic nods on Bowie's *Ziggy Stardust*.)

But 1973 was when the movement really exploded. Ground zero in terms of impact was *American Graffiti*. The power-shifting paean to early-'60s adolescence was a movie blockbuster whose soundtrack eventually sold 3 million copies. The film transformed Wolfman Jack into an American icon (the Wolfman-hosted *Midnight Special* concert series always featured a roots-rock act) and launched the Fifties-fixed *Happy Days*. (In 1976, Steve Barri-produced duo Pratt & McLain scored with the show's faux-oldie theme song; Cyndi Greco did the same with the ersatz girl-group theme to sister show *Laverne and Shirley*, "Making Our Dreams Come True".)

AmGraff and its spawn took Fifties/early-Sixties nostalgia out of the "guilty pleasure" category for Boomers and introduced younger listeners to the joys of music before it got "heavy." The same year that produced *Dark Side of the Moon, Houses of the Holy* and Jethro Tull's *A Passion*

Play also threw one of the revival movement's more creative developments into high gear: new original music created in the oldies mode, what might be termed "nouveau-retro." The genre's foremost practitioner—to this day—would have to be Roy Wood. With the Move, Wood had covered everyone from Jerry Lee Lewis to Jackie Wilson and cut Fifties-styled rockers like "California Man," but in '73 he unleashed his inner JD, declaring unabashed love for the rowdy/pretty old stuff on such singles as "Angel Fingers" and the extravagant Spector homages "See My Baby Jive" and "I Wish It Could Be Christmas Every Day." Robert Plant revisited his Rosie & the Originals roots in Led Zep's "D'yer Mak'er."

In the wake of Sha Na Na's success, hundreds of neo-'Fifties groups strolled onto the scene—none, however, as imaginative as Colorado's Flash Cadillac & the Continental Kids, whose 1973 debut LP revealed them as promising adherents of nouveau-retro. The Cochran-esque "Betty Lou" was a typical FlashCad original: "Betty Lou, Betty Lou, won't you dance with me, so I can dance with you."

Seventy-three also returned Jerry Lee Lewis to the charts ("Drinkin' Wine Spo-Dee-O'-Dee" from *The London Sessions* scraped the Top 40), put Ringo atop the Hot 100 with a remake of Johnny Burnette's 1960 hit "You're Sixteen" (the following year he'd almost do it again with the Platters' "Only You") and saw the Osmonds corner the cuddly end of the market. Donny racked up hits covering Johnny Mathis ("Twelfth of Never"), Sonny James ("Young Love") and Jimmy Charles ("A Million to One"), while Marie grabbed gold redoing Anita Bryant's 1960 ballad "Paper Roses."

But the real measure of just how far the revival had advanced may have been the Carpenters' *Now & Then* album. The platinum LP, which hung around *Billboard*'s album listings almost a year, devoted a whole side to songs, all from 1962 to 1964, by the Beach Boys, Chiffons, Crystals, Bobby Vee and others. "Yesterday Once More," the album's hit single, didn't merely eulogize the bygone era as Don McLean or B.J. Thomas had; it celebrated the very revival movement itself:

> *Every sha-la-la-la*
> *Every wo-wo-wo still shines*
> *Every shing-a-ling-ling*
> *That they're starting to sing so fine*

The next two years saw early rock more deeply saturate the mainstream. Grand Funk notched a No. 1 record with Goffin-King's "Loco-Motion," John Lennon released *Rock 'N' Roll*, and Linda Ronstadt began a 1975-78 covers streak that posted more than seven Top-30 singles with tunes previously cut by Chuck Berry, Buddy Holly, the Everly Brothers, Betty Everett and others. Nouveau-retro prospered: First Class aped California pop on "Beach Baby," and Flash Cadillac turned in *Sons of the Beaches,* an entire album of surf-and-summer sounds (thus inventing the Barracudas). Billy Swan went early-'60s on "I Can Help," Carly Simon & James Taylor flew with Inez & Charlie Foxx's 1963 duet "Mockingbird," and Art Garfunkel further etherealized the Flamingos' "I Only Have Eyes for You." Kiss made its singles-chart debut with a reprise of Bobby Rydell's 1959 "Kissin' Time." Across the pond, Pete Wingfield did mock doowop on "Eighteen with a Bullet," and Mud saluted post-army Elvis with "The Secrets That You Keep." Roy Wood scaled new heights with the powerfully wimpy "This Is the Story of My Love" and *his* full nouveau-retro set, *Eddie & the Falcons.*

By 1975 and 1976, Fifties/early-Sixties revivalism had become, if not the dominant trend, a powerful presence in pop. John Denver, Fleetwood Mac and *Physical Graffiti* took top albums honors, but *Born to Run* (at No. 3) sold 4 million copies. Its sound was pure Spector, its subject the loss of innocence and its second single, "Tenth Avenue Freeze-Out," built in part upon the Orlons' "Wah-Watusi." The Four Seasons returned (after a seven-year hit drought), with the chart-topping "December 1963 (Oh What a Night)." So did the Beach Boys, whose cover of Chuck Berry's "Rock and Roll Music" anchored a new album, *15 Big Ones*, which sported covers of songs made famous by Freddy Cannon, the Five Satins, Dixie Cups and others. Long before the Seventies' Fifties revival—specifically 1964 on *All Summer Long*—the Beach Boys had honored their forefathers, in "Do You Remember (the guys that gave us rock and roll)," a song that stood solidly in line with such heroic defenses of the music as Danny & the Juniors' "Rock and Roll Is Here to Stay" and the Showmen's "It Will Stand" and may well have inspired the Ramones' "Do You Remember Rock and Roll Radio."

When they arrived in 1976, first-generation punk-rockers—as well as the pub-rockers who preceded them—were even more attuned to the essential charms of early rock 'n' roll, though the mid-'60s exerted an even stronger influence. Significantly, one of the Ramones and Pistols' main inspirations was the New York Dolls, whose 1973 and '74 albums showed considerable affection for Bo Diddley, the Cadets ("Stranded in the Jungle") and girl groups, as well as '65 Stones. And, of course, the Ramones covered Bobby Freeman and the Trashmen, and the Pistols worked over

Eddie Cochran and Chuck Berry in their formative period. And, once punk happened, it sparked all sorts of offshoots—not just electro-punk and the dance hybrids but numerous revivals of earlier forms, most notably rockabilly, ska, Brit R&B and, later, psychedelic and garage rock.

Although the revival had peaked, the remainder of the Seventies showed the movement's continuing strength as a repertoire source. With his 1977 interpretation of Jimmy Jones' 1959 "Handy Man," James Taylor began a side career in oldies covers, redoing Sam Cooke's "Wonderful World" (with Simon and Garfunkel), the Drifters' "Up on the Roof" and, with Carly Simon, the Everlys' "Devoted to You." Blondie did some gender transformation on a re-do of Randy & the Rainbows' "Denise" in 1977, the same year Shaun Cassidy took his re-do of "Da Doo Ron Ron" to No. 1, and Jackson Browne sang Maurice Williams' immortal "Stay" (1978). Around the corner in a new decade: the Stray Cats, the Pointer Sisters' girl-group redux "He's So Shy," Ronstadt's take on Little Anthony's "Hurt So Bad" and on and on...

LISTENING POINTERS:

Flash Cadillac's *Sons of the Beaches* is available on CD, though, sadly not their eponymous debut or the even better sophomore set, *No Face Like Chrome*. Roy Wood's solo, Wizzard and *Eddie and the Falcons* (which features the perfectly swinging "You Got Me Runnin'") are all on CD, but not Jeremy Spencer's first LP is not. Daddy Cool's *Eagle Rock* is a worthwhile Australian import. The Guess Who's *So Long Bannatyne* features Burton Cummings' nouveau-retro doowop classic "Life in the Bloodstream," and 2005's soundtrack to *Stubbs the Zombie* has some surprisingly cool covers by, among others, Death Cab for Cutie (the Penguins' "Earth Angel"), Ben Kweller (the Chordettes' "Lollipop") and the Walkmen (on the Drifters' "There Goes My Baby," singer Walter Martin sounds like Ian Hunter doing mock-Dylan on those early Mott records). Fleetwood Mac's Earl Vince & the Valiants record can be found on *The Immediate Singles Collection*. Intrepid wax-hunters will want to check out two delicious pop singles, Sha Na Na's "Maybe I'm Old Fashioned" (Kama Sutra, 1974, written by Alan Gordon of Bonner & fame), from the band's *The Hot Box* album, and "If I Could Only Be Your Love Again" (Mercury, 1973), written and produced by Frank Zappa for the Ruben and the Jets (an actual band, not the Mothers), which also led off the group's *For Real* LP.

FEATURE:

A Belated Valentine to Early-'60s KYA

Written for the Bay Area Radio Museum website, 2006

As most visitors to this site will freely acknowledge, the Bay Area has been home to some innovative, historically significant and just plain fun radio. In the early '60s, that meant broadcasters like Al Collins, spinning jazz and surreal raps from inside the imaginary Purple Grotto, and Don Sherwood, inventing an insane repertory of characters and bits every weekday morning—both of these shows on KSFO. It also meant Top-40 KYA, 1260 AM, "the Boss of the Bay."

KYA San Francisco, which became the region's second rock 'n' roll station in 1960 (following KOBY), always seemed to be in battle with Oakland's KEWB. Where I grew up (Napa Valley), most of my school-mates listened to the latter, if only because its signal penetrated further into the North Bay. But, really, there was no contest. While I've since come to deeply respect Chuck Blore's programming of Color Radio 91 and the talent of jocks like Gary Owens and Casey Kasem, KEWB was, no pun intended, square. It was high on silly, with cute ID's (a station mascot, Little Diane, squeaking "My mommy listens to KEWB!"), sound effects, jocks reading canned jokes and—worst of all—conveying little empathy with the sides they were spinning. It was almost as if the delicious seven-inchers that comprised their Fabulous 40 survey were interruptions, necessary digressions from their endless patter and shtick.

By contrast, KYA sold the music first. Under program director Les Crane, who arrived in 1961, it jettisoned the jingles, reduced the number of contests (DJ Norman Davis recalled when it had a dozen or so running at once) and expanded its playlist from the standard 40 to a Swingin' 60 Survey. This plus a nightly Battle of the New Sounds (listeners voted for one of five contenders—25 debut discs a week), a Radio KYAce of the Week and assorted Coming Attraction singles. The sta-

tion broke or re-started innumerable records (most notably the Byrds'
"Mr. Tambourine Man," but also the second go-rounds of the Isley Bros.'
"Shout" and the Shirelles' "Dedicated to the One I Love").

And, just as importantly, the best jocks, namely Bob Mitchell and
"Big Daddy" Tom Donahue, two refugees from WIBG Philly's 1959 pay-
ola scandals, sounded like they meant it when they intro'ed or outro'ed a
record. A vintage aircheck finds Mitchell creeping up to the post on those
solitary guitar notes that kick off the Miracles' "What's So Good About
Goodbye": "Brand new... the Ace of the Week...by the Miracles...Dig
it!" just as Smokey croons the first syllable, or following the slow fade of
the Shirelles' "Baby It's You": "Somethin' else, isn't it, that one by the
Shirelles? Fierce record, man...fierce." It was all you could do not to
stand up and salute, so commanding and convincing was Mitchell, even
doing spots for H-I-S A-1 Racer slacks or a special hamburger deal at San
Jose's Starlight Drive-in.

The sense of being leveled with and not being talked down to was
likewise present when these jocks *didn't* like something. Donahue on
a dance fad of the period: "Of the 100 or so records we get here at the
station every week, I'd say maybe 50% of them are Twist records... most
of them bad." And when there were jokes, they were subtle, sometimes
flying over the heads of their adolescent audience. There were obtuse
call-outs to local promotion men and jockeys at Bay Meadows racetrack,
asides about record-label salesmen getting hernias from carrying so many
free goods out of their warehouses. But even if you didn't know to whom
or what Mitchell and Donahue were referring, their straightforward, eminently hip manner seemed to imply inclusiveness, to say "You're in on
this too." When they announced a record hop at the American Legion
Hall in Redwood City or Spanish Hall in Hayward, it didn't matter that
the bill was stacked with non-hit local acts or that the "free 45" promised
to the first 100 people in the door was likely a stiff. You wanted to be
there.

There were other jocks too, though Donahue and Mitchell, who'd
of course leave KYA to found Autumn Records, discover Sly Stone and
have hits with Bobby Freeman and the Beau Brummels, were the best.
Young Norman Davis did the enormously popular dedication-and-re-
quest show (a phone-company audit logged 30,000 calls to the station
one night), affable ex-Atlantan Johnny Hayes handled midnight to six,
and Les Crane (as "Johnny Raven") and later KHJ/KFRC wunder-pro-
grammer Bill Drake did mornings. Tony Tremayne counted down the
fresh Swingin' 60 on weekends. (I recall anxiously rushing home from

school a couple of lunchtimes to try and catch Peter Tripp playing the
Drifters' "Sweets for My Sweet." When my folks and I left for the Seattle
World's Fair in August of '62, my great fear was never again hearing a
boss soul side Donahue had previewed only a week earlier, "Do You
Love Me" by the Contours.)

If the jocks were the gate-keepers and conduit to all these great
sounds, the Swingin' 60 survey, an 8-x-12 sheet (with "Official" embla-
zoned across the top) available weekly at record stores, was hard-copy
proof of the magic and movement taking place. Records on labels like
Atco, End, Legrand, Valiant and Caprice rose, fell, stalled, burned and
disappeared, only to be replaced by a new galaxy of discs as weeks passed.
The big stars of the day, of course, shone brightest—Sam Cooke, the
Drifters, Brenda Lee, Dick & Dee Dee—but so did only-in-Frisco hits
like "Candy Apple Red Impala" by Little "E" & the Mellotone Three
and Eddie Quinteros' Valens-ized "Come Dance with Me." And, again
largely due to the influence of Donahue and Mitchell but also because
KYA presumably commanded a healthy share of black listeners (KDIA
and later KSOL were the Top 40 R&B outlets), a lot of black music
got heavy rotation. Not just the Ike & Tina Turner and Jackie Wilson
hits, but Slim Harpo, Freddie King and Little Willie John and cuts like
McKinley Mitchell's proto-soul "The Town I Live In" (a Donahue favorite) and Charles McCullough's stark blues ballad "You Are My Girl" (a
Mitchell pick).

And not all of the fun was musical—or intentional. Many archivists
have heard the heavily fortified newscast by KYA reporter Lamar Sher-
lock, in which he struggles, unsuccessfully, to inform on the events of
the day (a turbulent integration march, an assassination in the Congo,
local happenings). What would you have expected from a newsman who
often rode his motor scooter, driving with one arm and a head full of
spirits, up the city's steep grades to KYA's Nob Hill studios? Less dramatic
but no less comic were newscasters Mark Adams and Terry Sullivan, who
intoned every bit they read off the wire service with way too much gravity
and sense of purpose.

From 1961 to about 1964, KYA seemed to have it all: much music,
a finger on the pulse of the tastes of the Bay Area's growing teen population, and a modern, non-kiddie way of doing Top 40. Times, of course,
changed, as did the music and the audience. Tom Donahue went on to
start "underground" rock-FM radio, first with KMPX and then KSAN.
Mitchell, slowly dying from Hodgkin's disease, moved his family to Los
Angeles and jocked as "Bobby Tripp" on Drake's booming RKO flagship,

KHJ. Their airchecks survive, as does a deep gratitude on the part of everyone privileged to have heard the Boss of the Bay when it swung like 60. Thank you, KYA.

LINER NOTES:

The Credibility Gap *A Great Gift Idea*

Reissue, 2008

Some folks' back pages read better than others.' Like the rest of us, performers who've gone on to greater glory have history: the false starts and flops, the dead ends encountered before their careers came to life. And often their history is just that—a collection of not so special experiences that merely form the preface to later, more luminous accomplishments that overshadow all that came before them.

That's not the case with the comedy of the early-'70s troupe the Credibility Gap. Its principal members, David L. Lander, Michael McKean and Harry Shearer (fourth member Richard Beebe died in 1998), went on to become American comedy and satire royalty. Lander and McKean made pop history as the dim-bulb JD's Lenny and Squiggy on the long-running sitcom *Laverne & Shirley*, while Shearer and McKean took the cluelessness and vanity of (some) musicians to new heights in *This Is Spinal Tap* and A *Mighty Wind*. Both continue to write and act, with Shearer entering his 20th year as the voice of Ned Flanders, Montgomery Burns, Smithers and other characters on *The Simpsons*.

But Lander, McKean and Shearer's work in the Credibility Gap is among their best, and A *Great Gift Idea*, originally issued by Reprise Records in 1973, is the Credibility Gap's best album.

The group formed in 1968, as part of the larger social upheaval just then beginning to exert its influence in the commercial sphere. Los Angeles radio station KRLA, challenged by a desire to maintain its traditional Top-40 audience while grabbing a slice of the countercultural pie simmering on the sill, convened the Gap (originally Beebe, news director Lew Irwin and others) to riff 15 minutes daily on items in the news. The group took its name from the period phrase denoting the often gargantuan gulf separating politicians' words from objective reality.

The Credibility Gap made a name for itself in Southern California with its current-events humor and (a bit later) its annual, largely fictive color commentary on the Rose Parade. By 1970, though, the troupe's KRLA time slot had been shortened and its personnel shrunk to Beebe, recently recruited actor-comedian Shearer (who, as a child, had appeared on *The Jack Benny Show*) and voice-mimic Lander. Lander brought in New York actor McKean, and the Gap really got going—mainly to Pasadena's first underground-FM station, KPCC-FM, which surely seemed a better fit than the culturally confused KRLA (eager to strap on sandals and march to a new tune, the AM outlet published a newspaper, *Gathers No Moss*, and ran ID's proclaiming "KRLA Gives Good Music").

Two Gap albums preceded this one (1968's *Political Pornography* on Blue Thumb and 1971's *Woodshtick* on Capitol), but it's *Gift Idea* that keeps on giving—and, really, that's what makes it such a rarity among comedy albums. In truth, most of them don't age well. For every *Button-Down Mind of Bob Newhart* there are a dozen *First Family*, Rich Little and David Frye (four albums of Nixon impersonations, 1969-73) sets that would elicit only shrugs from anyone who hadn't been there, heard that way back.

Being a product of its time (arguably a high-tide era for topical humor), *Gift Idea* might be expected to be stuffed with cultural barbs that have lost much of their sting—or puffed up with dope jokes, the Hamburger Helper of '70s comedy. But the album will have none of that. Apart from Lander's public service announcement on necrophilia, which seems included for mild shock value, everything else connects and, to these ears, sounds just as funny as it did 30 years ago. Well before '70s blaxploitation movies became common comedic currency (and, more recently, objects of reverence and serious study), the Credibility Gap nailed such films' ludicrous conceits and linguistic overkill in a trailer for *Kingpin*, which transforms the life of Martin Luther King into a kick-ass exploitation flick complete with craven honkies, sexy mamas and a post-soul score that flawlessly apes Curtis Mayfield's work in the genre ("He's a king, he's a pin...He's a kingpin"). Shearer's intro, as a black academic endorsing the bio-pic, is priceless, a combination of F.D.R. and Cornell West, and Beebe's narration dead-on ("If you want to get it together and see the film about the brother who predicted the weather, dress your mother in leather and see *Kingpin!*").

Other tracks skewer contemporary targets and deserving relics from previous ages (the '50s in general, an obvious field for boomer humorists). "16 Golden Bits" parodies off-channel spots for oldies-music compilations; here it's an anthology of stand-up comics, with the signature lines of Sahl, Berman, Nichols & May, even Britain's Goons, whizzing by in an audio eye-blink. "A Date with Danger" sends up square sex-education films of the '50s.

Among the album's extended bits, two stand out. Maybe it's just me, but both get me laughing out loud every time I hear them—and reaching for "Repeat." It's hard to say just what "Lance Learns to Box" is satirizing, but its utter silliness (achieved by the actors' consistently straight-faced characterizations) pushes incrementally toward the absolutely absurd. On the surface, the bit parodies the stereotypical domestic sitcom of the '50s. A perky mom sets dinner before son Lance (Lander) and anxious husband (Beebe: "Honey, I'm home!"), and the latter serves the plot: He's tired of Lance being a studious Stan and, to make a man of him, will teach his son the manly art of fisticuffs. When Lance demurs ("But I'm in training for the Math Bowl!"), blustery dad persists, eventually arranging to have the pre-teen go a few rounds with local hardware-store owner Bix Baker (McKean). Bix effortlessly topples Lance, prompting dad to excoriate his son, "C'mon! He's 20 years older and you've still got your reflexes!" Only after Lance is k.o.'ed in Round 2 does his father cut him some slack, noting that the boy's tight trunks may have been the culprit. Proud and clueless, Bix gets petulant ("Oh come on, the kid's just not ready for me!") before eagerly accepting the offer for a rematch.

The other tour de force is "Where's Johnny?," a 14-minute lampoon of Johnny Carson's *Tonight Show*. Much like the blaxploitation film, time has been especially kind to the late-night king, particularly since his death in 2005; his image retains much of the halo effect bestowed on popular figures who leave the party early. The savageness and pinpoint accuracy of this bit remind us that Carson wasn't always universally loved—that, to the Credibility Gap's young audience, his nightly talk-show often promoted an old, rapidly dating style of humor: booze jokes, cheap laughs extracted from sexist and homophobic attitudes. The Gap goes for the jugular here, presenting Carson, sycophantic Ed McMahon ("Yes, yes!") and a guest crew that includes a wholesome prostitute, an uncloseted Army lieutenant arguing against gay stereotyping, a deeply closeted author arguing against him, and Don Rickles ("That's good, John," he says when Carson gets off a line. "One for the Cornhusker!"). The bit succeeds not just on writing, but the actors' perfect timing and the ambience of the scene (post-joke rim shots, audience noise, guests restarting sentences when the crowd's laughter drowns them out).

The other extended segment, "An Evening with Sly Stone," relies on a more surreal conceit: Sly Stone hosting a *Playboy After Dark* episode as presented on PBS. "In Someone's Sneakers" allows Shearer to do a deadly impression of sentimental versifier "Rod McPoem"; here, as elsewhere, the Gap's capacity for letter-perfect parody is front and center (McPoem huskily intones about "a nosebleed that lingers on the hanky of dawn").

The Credibility Gap disbanded in 1976, with each of its members going their separate but equal ways—and recombining frequently on subsequent comedy projects. One last album, *The Bronze Age of Radio,* a collection of the group's KPCC broadcast bits, appeared in 1976.

Literal foot-note: The scene in *This Is Spinal Tap* in which a record-company promotion man who's failed to publicize an in-store appearance by the band invites them to apply their boots to his posterior was inspired by a real event. The original LP's inner sleeve lists a credit for Lou "Kick My Ass" Dennis, Warner/Reprise's national sales director at the time of the release of *A Great Gift Idea.*

REVIEW:

Various Artists *The T.A.M.I. Show*

Ugly Things magazine, 2009

First off, any regular reader of this publication whose home doesn't house a copy of this DVD—man, where are you at? Filmed before a Santa Monica Civic Auditorium audience of screaming teens, the late-'64 concert is the absolutely essential snapshot of '60s pop at its diverse, dizzying peak—a height as swiftly and irretrievably lost as it was inevitably scaled.

There are 47 live performances from 12 acts representing all that was vital and current within the youth-world then commonly referred to as "rock and roll": surf music (the Beach Boys, Jan & Dean), Motown (Miracles, Marvin Gaye, Supremes), Brill Building girl-group pop (Lesley Gore), Brit Invasion (Gerry & the Pacemakers, Billy J. Kramer and the Dakotas), roots rock (Chuck Berry), pre-soul (James Brown), proto-garage (the Barbarians).

With the exception of Kramer's listless set, they all come off well, showing what it was about their music that shook such action in the seats and on the charts. But let's be clear about this: There is but one cultural moment captured on this disc, a single five-song stretch that pulls the crowd's (and our) collective coat to the new business on its way into the world so insistently that everyone else—the soon-to-be-avant-angelic Beach Boys, the precision-drill rhythm king Brown, the conscious-soul metaphysician-in-waiting Gaye—might as well have been hoofing it across a vaudeville stage in high button shoes. It's, as Jan Berry introduces them in the concert's final segment, "those five fellows from England: the Rolling Stones!"

When I saw *The T.A.M.I. Show* in 1964, at a Northern California drive-in, the whole frenzied, high-voltage power grab from "Off the Hook" to "It's Alright" thoroughly blew me away. It still does, but with the added benefit of hindsight. The Beach Boys and Miracles sets had floored me, and Brown, it must be admitted, delivers a jaw-dropping performance. But that's principally what it is: superb showbiz. The Stones are the freakin' future, the sole glimpse of what it would soon *all* become: uncostumed, unchoreographed, disparate and clashing, provocative and unprecedented. Brown's cape and pirouettes didn't shoot up pop with Wolf-Waters-Diddley, didn't invent the Warlocks, Doors, Dolls, Stooges, Ramones, and send dozens of thousands of suburban kids into garages to hammer out the most potent r&r since the '50s. Sure, the Beatles played a part, but they rarely had that edge and they never brought the blues (and not for *instructive* purposes either: the Stones brought it, they themselves soon enough learned, for the express purpose of wrestling it to the ground, jacking the volume, bashing it into something that wasn't there before). This is the Modern World.

And, yes, what the Stones birthed has now gone bad: The whole globe seems awash in bad-boys (and girls) acting out and faux rebellions, misogyny and anti-romance. But that's not their fault, any more than Hendrix's experiments are to blame for decades of jag-off metal shredders. At their best, which they were within months of becoming when *The T.A.M.I. Show* was shot, the Rolling Stones were the most liberating, revolutionary act around. That's why they're to be cherished.

Other program highlights: the Miracles' singing/dancing/simian shtick during an extended "Mickey's Monkey"; Lesley Gore's opening "Maybe I Know"; the Beach Boys' manic "Dance, Dance, Dance"; everything Chuck Berry does but especially "Nadine," and the incontrovertible proof that what we now acknowledge as pop's classic period really happened, that the music of the artists seen here was all contemporaneous and embraced by a massive audience. Keep your eyes open. The chance won't come again.

Liner Notes:

Ben E. King
Supernatural and *Benny And Us*

Collector's Choice Music, 2009

By now it's a truism that F. Scott Fitzgerald got it wrong when he said, "There are no second acts in American lives." Sure, lots of artists and entertainers never really showed up for roll call after their initial flash of fame, but many others have come on like real cats. They may not have sprung back to life nine times, but several have come pretty close.

It's a tribute to Ben E. King's natural talent and the quality of his work that he holds some kind of reinvention record within popular music. Let's count the ways this singular singer, born Benjamin Earl Nelson in North Carolina, 1938, has made his mark on American culture and the world. First, there's his stint as the Drifters' lead vocalist (1958-1961), which served up such undimmed treasures as "There Goes My Baby," "Save the Last Dance for Me," "I Count the Tears" and "This Magic Moment." Concurrent with the latter part of that gig and continuing throughout the '60s, King soloed on the transcendent "Stand By Me" (which he co-wrote) and "Spanish Harlem," as well as "Amor," "Don't Play That Song" and "I (Who Have Nothing)."

In 1975, the baritone balladeer revealed a whole new side, placing the mega-funky "Supernatural Thing—Part I" in *Billboard*'s Top 5 (it topped the publication's R&B Singles chart). He followed with four more R&B hits, including two ("Get It Up" and "A Star in the Ghetto") with the Average White Band, then returned to the Top 10 in 1986 when "Stand By Me" was featured in the hit movie of the same name. Since then King has recorded with a disparate array of musicians, among them Mark Knopfler, jazz vibist Milt Jackson and Ray Charles-band mainstay David "Fathead" Newman.

King's "Supernatural Thing," and the *Supernatural* album from which it issued, may have been the most dramatic about-face of his career. And the whole project started off in the most unlikely fashion. Atlantic Records' founder saw King perform in a Florida club and invited him back to the label where he'd recorded all his previous hits.

"Ahmet had [arranger-producers] Tony Silvester and Bert DeCoteaux come up with this track, which he wanted me to record the standard 'Fever' over," recalls King. "I liked what they'd done and had started rehearsing, then Ahmet called and said, "We won't do 'Fever." I'm getting two writers [Gwen Guthrie and Patrick Grant] to write a new song to the track.' So 'Supernatural Thing' actually started out to be 'Fever.'

"It was a different kind of song for me," King admits. "I had never done a 'groove' thing like that before. Atlantic had Wilson Pickett and others doing that. But I liked the challenge of 'Supernatural' because it took me out of the E-flat, C and A keys that I had always worked in." The commercial success of his rise to the challenge almost took King by surprise. "I didn't know what to expect. We had a good groove, I liked the feel of it, and disco was just starting, so I thought, 'Wow, I'm in a place where this thing could happen.'"

The *Supernatural* album followed the single up the charts, as did "Do It in the Name of Love" (a top-five R&B single). "That one had a similar bounce to it," says King, likening it to "Supernatural." "I've heard it recorded since by other artists, and I thought, 'Well, I didn't make a bad demo!'" The tune was penned by the Grant-Guthrie team, who also contributed the disco-ish 'Your Lovin' Ain't Good Enough" (great lyric: "I hate to blow your mind/ But your lovin' ain't worth a dime"). Alabama soul singer Sam Dees (1974's "Worn Out Broken Heart") gave King two songs; his "Extra Extra" sounds like it could be a Thom Bell Philly Soul side, while "Drop My Heart Off" puts King in his familiar sweet-soul spot, complete with opening monologue. The latter tune was co-written with Stax singer-writer Frederick Knight (1972's "I've Been Lonely for So Long"). King collaborated with his son Ben E. King Jr. on the ballad "Imagination."

Supernatural sounds like it was a fun time all around. "The album didn't take long to do," King remembers, "only a couple weeks. One of the good things about that time—as opposed to now when you lay down a track, do a vocal, then come back to it—everything was more fast-paced. Also, it didn't take long to do because the people playing on it were good, so the results were good. We spent as much time laughing and eating sandwiches as anything else!"

Two years later, back on a roll with Atlantic after "Supernatural Thing," a second unlikely opportunity came King's way. "It was another brainstorm of Ahmet's," he says with a laugh. "Once again, he had a song he wanted to do. That was 'A Star in the Ghetto.' Originally he had in mind to do the music with some band in New York, but then he decided it needed something else—maybe a Philly or a Muscle Shoals feel. So he came up with the idea of AWB, who were vacationing in Florida at the time. He worked out a deal, flew me down to Miami, and we started work."

The work generated immediate results. "A Star in the Ghetto" sailed into the R&B Top 30, and sessions for a full Ben E. King-AWB collaboration, what became *Benny and Us*, began. "What was great about working with those guys," recalls King, "is that they just started throwing out ideas: 'Do you like this one?' 'How about this?', and, because they're right there playing the song in front of you, you get a feel for it right away. And they're such good musicians. All I had to do was sit in the middle of what they were doing and it was great."

What King and AWB did together was produce another best-selling long-player, well stocked with group originals and *simpatico* covers. "Get It Up for Love," which had appeared on singer-songwriter Ned Doheny's 1976 LP *Hard Candy*, became a solid soul hit, besting the chart performance of "A Star in the Ghetto." King absolutely shines on the ballad front—specifically on a Stax-ish remake of Mick Jones' "A Fool for You Anyway" (a non-single from Foreigner's 1977 debut album) and Donny Hathaway's "Someday We'll All Be Free." At AWB's urging, King also revisited his own 1966 single "What Is Soul," which had been an R&B but not a pop hit here. "Even now," says King, "I cannot go to Europe without doing that song. That record was a much bigger hit over there than it was here."

And then there's "Imagine," which offers some of the most moving moments on *Benny and Us*. "I think more people fell into the song after Lennon's passing," says King of the tune's subsequent ascent to contemporary-standard status; in 1977 it hadn't generated tons of cover versions. "I always admired Lennon as a songwriter," King, who initially met John in England well before Beatlemania broke, explains. "What impressed me more than anything was that he was a great writer who would also select songs by other writers to record."

"The Message" is one of King's favorites from *Benny and Us*. "That actually started out as a jam," he remembers. "The guys began playing, and I just started kind of chanting over it, and they said, 'Why don't we do this as a song? Keep doin' what you're doin'..." It was King who chose "Keepin' It to Myself," from the band's "white album" [1974's *Average White Band*], for a re-do.

The success of *Benny and Us* led to King's triumphant appearance at the Montreux Jazz Festival, and a subsequent European tour, on which he was backed by AWB. The singer and the band's affinity for each other remains an example of natural chemistry, and It's been the basis for a continuing friendship and mutual-admiration society.

Ben E. King followed *Supernatural* and *Benny and Us* with more accomplishments. He regularly tours Europe, Japan and domestically, in 1999 he released the big-band jazz set, *Shades of Blue*, working with Milt Jackson and "Fathead" Newman, and he's about to release a second jazz set ("a small-group record," he says, "more like what Tony Bennett has done recently"). King has also directed, for the last 12 years, the activities of the Ben E. King Stand By Me Foundation, which provides four-year financial support to musical students entering college. "We just signed an agreement with Berklee College of Music to bring the program there," he says with obvious pride.

Frisco, Where Art Thou?: Reassessing the Musical Legacy of the 60s' Psychedelic Capital

Rock's Back Pages Writers' Blog, 2010

Last Saturday afternoon, paging through an article on Robert Plant in the September issue of *Mojo*, I learned that, upon their initial meeting in a Dublin pub, the Zep master and his current bandmate, Buddy Miller, bonded over a shared interested in the West Coast music of... Moby Grape and Quicksilver Messenger Service.

How quaint that, and an unexpected pleasure.

On Sunday, I woke to the sound of a neighbor kid, aged 12 or 13, practicing a lick on electric guitar. It was familiar, not unpleasant, and soon revealed itself to be "Black Magic Woman," likely learned from the 1970 hit by Santana. In 1970, this kid's parents may or may not have just been born.

No one talks about San Francisco anymore. They do, but it tends to be dismissive, as if its joys long ago expired, their significance lost in a world now less naïve, more realistic, proudly tougher. The guitarist Wayne Kramer, in sleeve notes to a reissue of MC5 material: "West Coast hippie music had a gentleness: a goofy, 'la-la' kind of electrified folk music. [The bands] represented mass-marketed peace-and-flower-power crap. I think they all hated us because we kicked all their asses."

On the eve of the 45th anniversary of its birth, a look back at the '60s San Francisco scene might be in order. Did it leave any impressions? Does it deserve respect?

On Oct. 16th and 24th and Nov. 6, 1965, an ad hoc group of music freaks called the Family Dog threw three "dance concerts" at Longshoremen's Hall on Fishermen's Wharf. The name acts were the Lovin' Spoonful (from New York) and the Mothers (Los Angeles), but local action was the real draw: the Charlatans in dandified Victorian drag playing amplified jugband music, post-folk-rockers Jefferson Airplane, raga-drone primitives the Great Society, straight-outa-the-garage Quicksilver Messenger Service whiplashing Bo Diddley's back catalog.

Was this the very next wave in a pop world that in just over a year had been knocked silly by the Beatles, Stones and the 'British Invasion,' of America, Dylan-gone-electric, the Byrds' folk-rock, "protest" and "good-time music" and the truly unprecedented internationalization of pop?

It was.

Jazz critic and local booster Ralph J. Gleason wasn't far off when he proclaimed San Francisco "the Liverpool of the West." Both cities were cold, gray seaports, far from the cultural and commercial centers, where scenes sparked organically with little eye toward export. By 1967, the Bay Area was teeming, the Avalon Ballroom-Fillmore Auditorium circuit playing host to dozens of homegrown bands but also new arrivals who couldn't play as they pleased in Texas (Janis Joplin, the Sir Douglas Quintet, Mother Earth, and long-term visitors the 13th Floor Elevators), Chicago (the Steve Miller Blues Band) or New York (the Youngbloods).

Below the hip radar, San Francisco also birthed, in 1966 and '67, what was arguably the most hyperactive scene for what critics of the early-'70s would dub "punk rock." Packs of junior Jaggers and cod-Mersey combos steamed the teen canteens, among them such subsequently venerated acts as the Count Five, Chocolate Watchband, Syndicate of Sound and the Golliwogs, who, with a name change, would morph into Creedence Clearwater Revival. The same suburban club realm served as the training ground for Sly & the Family Stone.

What began at the Longshoremen's Hall soirees as a bunch of eager kids' backyard party soon caught the attention of adults—the record business. When the time came, the Frisco groups danced with commerce, but on their own terms. They were the first artists to contract to make full albums, not one-off singles or a limited number of "sides." Along with big-leaguers the Beatles, Stones and Beach Boys, they changed the exchange rate of pop from the single to the LP (it became the dominant configuration in the U.S. in 1967). They thus enjoyed an economic stimulus of their own. In late 1965 the Airplane signed with RCA Records for an unheard-of $25,000 advance. Barely a year later, Capitol handed the Steve Miller Band $60,000 plus a four-year multi-album option that, when exercised, awarded the quintet (which then included Boz Scaggs) a cool $75,000.

The San Francisco groups were also the first to demand, and most often get, creative control over the recording, packaging and promoting of their music. RCA assigned Jefferson Airplane a staff producer, but for their debut albums the Grateful Dead and Steve Miller picked their own (respectively, Rolling Stones engineer Dave Hassinger and future Who/Stones/Zep producer Glyn Johns).

Lightshows, colorful crowds and enhancing agents made psychedelic rock a live, had-to-be-there experience, but the high-stakes bets placed by the record labels left no doubt: These wagers were expected to pay off.

In retrospect, both the financial and creative expectations were met. Big Brother & the Holding Company's *Cheap Thrills* topped the U.S. chart for eight consecutive weeks, launching Janis Joplin as a major star. The Airplane placed five albums in the Top-20 from 1967 to 1969, including *Surrealistic Pillow* with its hits "White Rabbit" and "Somebody to Love." Santana kicked-started Latin-rock with *Santana* and *Abraxas* and the singles "Oye Como Va" and "Black Magic Woman." In 1969 and 1970 alone, Creedence batted five LPs into the Top 10, adding to the world's songbook such standards as "Proud Mary," "Green River," "Lodi," "Bad Moon Rising" and "Who'll Stop the Rain." Blue Cheer invented power-trio heavy metal ("Summertime Blues"), and acid-rock standards were set by the Dead's *Live/Dead*, Country Joe & the Fish's *Electric Music for the Mind and Body*, Quicksilver's *Happy Trails* and the Miller Band's *Children of the Future*. To some, *Moby Grape* (1967) stands as one of the strongest debuts by any American band of the era. Other Bay Area groups charted nationally as well, including the Sopwith Camel and It's A Beautiful Day.

At least three enduring, if now increasingly diminished, commercial institutions emerged from the city's '60s-music heyday—four if one counts the poster renaissance (and five if the poster artists' invention of underground comics is added in).

FM album-rock radio began in 1967 when ex-Top-40 DJ Tom Donahue bought time on an obscure ethnic-language outlet to program the music Top-40 AM wouldn't touch.

Fanzines like New York's *Crawdaddy* and San Francisco's *Mojo-Navigator Rock & Roll News* had launched roughly simultaneously a year earlier, but the birth of the modern rock press can be traced to the Nov. 11, 1967 inaugural issue of *Rolling Stone*.

The contemporary music-touring business likewise began in the city. Before San Francisco proved rock could fill ballrooms, pop concert venues were limited to multi-act Dick Clark-type caravans and local bars and teen clubs. The advent of the Avalon and the Fillmore, and the demand for West Coast, and later British, acts in other parts of the country created a virtual Pony Express route of what Frank Zappa ungenerously called "psychedelic dungeons popping up on every street"—in Los Angeles, New York, Boston, Philadelphia, Chicago, Detroit, Seattle, Denver and Vancouver, B.C. Convention centers, outdoor festivals and sports arenas came next.

(At the epicenter of activity, California concertgoers basked in the best bills. In one six-month stretch in 1967, the Fillmore boasted shows by Jimi Hendrix, Howlin' Wolf, the Byrds, the Doors, Chuck Berry, Buffalo Springfield, Martha & the Vandellas, Junior Wells, B.B. King, the Jim Kweskin Jug Band, the Blues Project, the Young Rascals, the Animals, Charles Lloyd, the Mothers, the Paul Butterfield Blues Band and The Who.)

And what of San Francisco's sins? It's tempting, and not entirely inaccurate, to list marathon guitar soloing and a lack of professionalism at the top of a short list. Yet the blueprint for instrumental stretching exercises had already been sketched out by the Yardbirds' blues rave-ups and the jazz-style guitar jams of Mike Bloomfield on the Paul Butterfield Band's *East-West* album. The lack of stage presence and the interminable instrument-tuning of early Dead and Big Brother sets qualify as the worst kind of amateurism, but it was an aspect of the musicians' Let's-just-get-up-and-play attitude, which itself seems to prefigure the unpretentiousness of punk a decade later.

The single most frequent charge against '60s Frisco music is that it advanced a sort of "goofy, la-la" sensibility, a brand built on naïve, if not altogether disingenuous, notions of universal peace and love. Images of the period (invariably a mini-skirted, high-on-something blonde lashing her long hair at an outdoor concert), and the pronouncements of any number of self-appointed hippie spokesmen of the later '60s, surely appear to support the charges.

But there's little of that in the music of San Francisco itself. Joplin essayed tortured-soul art over the almost psychotic guitar-playing of Jim Gurley in Big Brother. Grace Slick's acid tongue in caustic screeds like "White Rabbit" and "Somebody to Love" more than balance Marty Balin's romanticism in Jefferson Airplane. Quicksilver's soundscapes are positively gothic, and Country Joe & the Fish essayed edgy, hard-left politics well before the MC5 bravely bared their chest hair for the revolution. True, many of Robert Hunter's lyrics for the Grateful Dead leave him open to charges of cosmic puffery ("searchlights casting for faults in the clouds of delusion"), but he'd have no shortage of co-defendants at trial. Donovan comes to mind, as do Joni Mitchell, Jimi Hendrix, Traffic and a respected Liverpool foursome. "Get Together," the Youngbloods' San Francisco-identified anthem, preaches fraternal affection, an offense routinely committed by the world's major religions.

The la-la school of California rock seems to have been founded further south, in the blithe sunshine-pop of Los Angeles studio acts like the Mamas and the Papas, the Association, Harper's Bizarre, the Sunshine Company, Cowsills and others. In fact, the single most damaging and persistent strike against San Francisco's reputation is probably "San Francisco (Be Sure to Wear Flowers in Your Hair)." Scott McKenzie's global, summer-of-'67 hit lives in infamy, on oldies radio, and in every film and TV drama and documentary that purports to depict "the '60s." The song was written by head Papa John Phillips, recorded in Hollywood and sung by a Florida-born folksinger.

These days, it's not a tune you hear many teenaged guitarists practicing.

BLOG POST/OBIT:

The Dust Blows Forward, 'N The Dust Blows Back

Posted on the website RecordMecca.com, 2010

It's impossible for me to think what the world would be without Captain Beefheart's music in it. Amidst the bad news, the good is that his music is, and hopefully forever shall be, in the world.

This reminiscence is strictly personal. I had a little one-on-one interaction with Beefheart; mostly the relationship was between me and his powerful, funny, touching recordings and performances. I first encountered him in the spring of '66 at Frisco's Avalon Ballroom, when he and the Magic Band were the latest in a line of surprise visitors on the underground railway that weekly shuttled north L.A. bands like Love, the Rising Sons, Sons of Adam, etc. My late cousin and I, teenaged blues-heads (whose knowledge store then extended to the first Butterfield LP, *Muddy Waters at Newport* and Howlin' Wolf's 'rocking-chair' album), were floored by Don's act, which then consisted of spot-on versions of "Evil" and other catalog items, and his scary-good harp playing. We made it a point to catch him whenever his name appeared on a bill, and I bought the "Diddy Wah Diddy" single.

Some months later I hit the Avalon, and Beefheart and the Magic Band, like almost everything in those change-is-now days, had gotten magic-er and weirder and I-don't-know-what. But it was great: same bottom-heavy voice and slammin' band, but Beefheart was wearing Sun Ra-type shades and some kind of embroidered *Music Man* bandleader coat, knotting and retying the old blues chords into bizarre odes to confections like Abba Zabba and Kandy Korn (with the MB roaring behind him, he stalked the stage tossing the yellow and orange Halloween treats to the crowd). My God!

Then, sometime in '67 in a Berkeley record shop, I stumbled across the previously unannounced *Safe as Milk*. I'd never—no, I *have never* seen a cooler LP cover. Here, in the year of that famous summer and long, long, longer hair and suspect platitudes, as unpretentious dress slid into medieval costumery and cultivated slovenliness, CB & TMB were dressed in ties and tailored suits, casual but formidable, staring out from those redwood slats in Guy Webster's fish-eye photo as if to say, "What're *you* lookin' at?" The question would soon become "What're you *listening* to?" as friends, just as immersed as I was in the orthodoxies of the wild new world of Dead/Airplane/Dylan/Doors, wondered what were *these* bizarre howls and growls spinning on the Sears stereo about "Autumn's Child" and "Electricity"? Hey, what can I tell you? I was in love. With his voice, his inspired entanglements of verse and melody, the look, the aura of strangeness permeating the whole act, right down to the grinning-baby *Safe as Milk* bumper strip that fell out of that issue of *Rolling Stone*.

Like Jeff [Gold, RecordMecca site host], I count *Safe as Milk* as my favorite Beefheart set. But there is more. *Strictly Personal* upped the oddness ante but it also cooked ("Gimme Dat Harp Boy"). And *Trout Mask*!! This guy was giving notice: He was in the business of busting, following his muse to left turns no one else would even consider taking. So dazzled by *Trout Mask* was a roommate of mine that he kept a copy in his car—often instructing passengers to hold it up to the window as he gunned past slow-pokes, I guess to 'blow their minds' or something. *Clear Spot*: best meditation ever on female power ("Lo Yo Yo Stuff")...*Decals* and that whole hair-stacked look of *Spotlight Kid*... the fleeting pleasures of those Mercury LPs ("Sugar Bowl," "Upon the My-O-My"), and later *Doc at the Radar Station* and *Shiny Beast (Bat Chain Puller)*.

I was working at Warners by then, and my boss, Pete Johnson, took on the job of producing *Beast*. His reports from the studio suggested Don was now Pete's boss, and everybody's, but rough times yielded an underrated classic, where the Captain cuts a mean "Candle Mambo" outside the lesbian-run canteen of "Harry Irene" and leaves the world one of his funkiest gifts in "Tropical Hot Dog Night." Jesus!

It was around this time that I spent a bit of time with Beefheart. Frustrated that Warners wasn't pro-actively marketing some acts, co-editor Joe Robinson and I decided to use the label's house organ, *Waxpaper*, as a bully print-pulpit to pump up the volume on them: We'd utilize the publication's back cover to do our own ads. Which led to us taking our art director and a photographer up to Antelope Valley, meeting Don at a Denny's (he was already in a booth, sketching on a pad), then heading for cactus country, where we spent the day shooting away, enraptured by his rap and big heart. The ad ran in our Feb. 12, 1979 issue. "There's a Voice in the Wilderness. Captain Beefheart's," read the head, over a shot of Don standing in the fading desert light.

May that voice go on forever.

UNPUBLISHED BOOK CHAPTER:

Johnny Cash at Folsom Prison

Commissioned for book series on classic albums, 2011

They walk among us now, thick as thieves: the Rebels, their contempt
for orthodoxy proclaimed in a hail of tats and F-bombs, the proudly ten-
dered badges of cultural citizenship. Musicians, athletes, artists, authors,
politicians—all seem to feel the need to get over by convincing us of
their capacity for transgression. Don't tread on me, see?

In such times, it's hard to imagine how we might recognize a genuine iconoclast, someone who instinctually bucks custom simply because
it doesn't fit. *Johnny Cash at Folsom Prison* provided one early glimpse
of such a figure. Yes, Cash had been preceded by the anguished Bran-
do and the conflicted James Dean, by the sullen early Stones. And yes,
Columbia Records burnished the brand, polishing Cash's image as one
mean mother; "He's been in prison before," ran the label's ad copy for
the album. "Not always on a visit." And those chilling shouts that erupt
from the audience when Cash, in "Folsom Prison," sings, "I shot a man
in Reno just to watch him die"? Dubbed in during post-production, a
little lily-gilding taken out as insurance.

In truth, though, Johnny Cash *had* had it hard, and his response—
to regard life with wariness and sometimes dangerously walk his own
line—wasn't feigned. This was, after all, the man who'd written the un-
repentant "Folsom Prison Blues" in 1951, celebrated "The Rebel" in a
1961 country hit and "the whiskey-drinkin' Indian" antihero of "The Ballad of Ira Hayes" (1964), and sternly advised his woman to "Understand
Your Man" (1964). Many of *At Folsom Prison*'s tales of lost souls behind
bars—"I Got Stripes," "Cocaine Blues," "Give My Love to Rose," "25
Minutes to Go"—Cash had first recorded years before.

Cash's high-voltage performance and audience-friendly, author-
ity-hostile attitude (about prison guards: "They's mean bastards, ain't

they?") earned him legions of new fans when *Folsom* was issued in 1968. Not surprisingly, many were young Americans engaged in their own battles with the establishment, over its persecution of them for their opinions and habits and resistance to fighting a senseless war. This cohort was successfully captured by a Columbia marketing campaign that targeted the album to the then-new FM stations playing 'underground' rock.

But simply aligning Cash's *Folsom* bravado with the prevailing spirit of pop rebellion misses a larger point. What clearly distinguishes his music from Jagger's oversold satanic sympathies or the sloganeering of Jefferson Airplane ("We are forces of chaos and anarchy!") is something writer Mikal Gilmore caught in the 2004 *Rolling Stone* anthology *Cash*. "Nobody else in popular music," he wrote, "could match Cash for radical nerve *and* compassion."

All vinegar and no honey would not have allowed *At Folsom Prison* to make the kind of impact it made or sustain the legacy it enjoys more than 40 years later; it stayed on *Billboard*'s LP chart 122 weeks upon release, and the single, Cash's duet with June Carter on "Jackson," won a Grammy (Best Country Performance by a Duet, Trio or Group). In 2006 *Time* magazine rated *At Folsom Prison* among the 100 best albums of all time.

The record is saturated with a powerful mixture of the sacred and the profane. For every song of despair (Harlan Howard's "The Wall," Cash's own "Send a Picture of Mother") or orneriness (the title track, "Cocaine Blues," "25 Minutes to Go"), there's one of hope (the show-closing "Greystone Chapel," penned by Folsom inmate Glen Sherley) or undiminished love ("I Still Miss Someone"). There are songs of empathy and commiseration with which any breathing human can identify—Howard's "Busted," Merle Travis' miner's lament "Dark as a Dungeon"—and songs whose aim is nothing more than making listeners laugh: the "Jackson" duet with Carter, Jack Clement's twosome of "Dirty Old Egg-Sucking Dog" and "Flushed from the Bathroom of Your Heart."

The latter song discloses another clue to *Folsom*'s success: Cash's utterly modern sensibility, something that put him leagues ahead of most of his pop, rock or country contemporaries. Clearly, Clement intended "Flushed" as a send-up of the standard country weeper, but it's intimately related to other performances on the album in which Cash pulls humor from unintended sources: breaking up during the somber murder mystery "Long Black Veil," fluffing a line and wisecracking in the middle of the dead-serious "Dark as a Dungeon." These days, irony's a major mode of song, advertising, TV and film, even reportage, but goofing on country's sentimental streak—in effect dissing one of the cornerstones of a whole musical genre—wasn't that common in 1968, the broader novelties of Homer & Jethro and Roger Miller notwithstanding. On *Folsom*, Cash is confident enough to both kid traditional form and respect it (check his poignant treatment of "Greystone Chapel" or the straightforward reading he gives the maudlin "Green Green Grass of Home").

Cash's ability to acknowledge the merits of these competing sensibilities didn't just rejuvenate his career. It reinvigorated popular music. *At Folsom Prison* put Cash's contemporary—and thus cool—imprimatur on a genre that most members of the new album-buying generation had considered hopelessly square. Within months, the Byrds released *Sweetheart of the Rodeo*, the Band *Music from Big Pink*, and Bob Dylan readied *Nashville Skyline*. By the start of the '70s, country form and content were deeply informing the music of the Rolling Stones, Kinks, Neil Young and the Grateful Dead, providing part of the template for legions of singer-songwriters, and seeding country music's anti-Nashville "outlaw" movement. From 1969 to 1971, Cash hosted a weekly ABC Television series whose guests included Dylan, Ray Charles, Merle Haggard, Joni Mitchell and James Taylor.

Having "arrived" with *Folsom*, Cash was rarely absent from view until his death in 2003. He cut an even more commercially successful sequel, 1969's *At San Quentin*; toured and recorded successfully throughout the '70s and '80s (in the latter as part of the Highwaymen with Willie Nelson, Waylon Jennings and Kris Kristofferson), and won over a generation in the '90s with his stark and uncompromising series of American Recordings.

"I thought that people would take notice of men that have been forgotten in everybody's mind," he once said of his decision to record *At Folsom Prison*. "It would be good for them to hear the men's reaction." By all accounts, it was, is now and ever shall be good for us to hear *Johnny Cash at Folsom Prison*. The record's rebellious spirit perfectly suited its times, but its powerful redemptive message is what makes it an enduring document of another sort: an uncontestable testament to music's power to let a little sunshine into the most remote parts of the heart. Credit Cash.

BLOG POST:

Nostalgia and *The Nightfly*: Good Times Never Seemed So Good (or Real) as on Donald Fagen's First Solo Set

Rock's Back Pages Writers' Blog 2012

Item: A recent *Los Angeles Times* article reported that the city's Wende Museum, which houses more than 100,000 Cold War artifacts, had outgrown its present location.

Item: Last month marked the 30th anniversary of the release of Donald Fagen's first solo album, *The Nightfly*, whose songs its creator has said, house similar artifacts: "the fantasies that might have been entertained by a young man growing up in the remote suburbs of a Northeastern city during the late Fifties, i.e., one of my general height, weight and build."

Fagen has just issued his fourth solo set. It remains to be seen whether *Sunken Condos* will replicate the success of *The Nightfly*, which rose to No. 26 on *Billboard*'s LP chart, where it hung around half a year, spawned the hit single "I.G.Y. (What a Beautiful World)," and eventually went platinum.

Just why did *The Nightfly* strike such a nerve with audiences three decades ago? A *Village Voice* review of the time may have put it best: "Apparently, what Walter Becker brought to Steely Dan was an obscurantism that lost its relevance after the post-hippie era. On *The Nightfly*, words always mean everything they want to say." Not only did Fagen's aural autobio bristle with the literal. Its sober-eyed, sardonically Dan-ish takes on its material offered the first fresh rear-view look at the Fifties, which by 1982 had spent more than a decade imprisoned in the deep amber of '*Grease*'-coated poodle skirts and car backseats. *The Nightfly* admitted a more extensive notion of nostalgia. Listening to it now reveals just how rich, and honest, an album it is.

Like everyone else, Fagen was so much older then: a Fifties almost-teenager supremely confident in his worldviews, whether pessimistic or optimistic. In the hilarious, come-on-a-my-fallout shelter come-on "New Frontier," he informs his distaff target that if the Reds push the button, "the key word is survival." But he's just as sure, in the rose-tinted "I.G.Y.," that once the work of the future-focused scientists is done, "We'll be eternally free, yes, and young."

Young Donald's vision of hope-and-change colors "Green Flower Street" (despite intra-tribe suspicion, "joy is complete" for white guy and Asian gal) and even the Four Freshmen-ish "Maxine." Here, two young bohemian lovers visualize their escape from suburbia, planning to "move to Manhattan and fill the place with friends," and, just like Kerouac and Dean Moriarty, "drive to the coast and drive right back again."

The Nightfly swings too, deliciously, on the bop shuffle "Walk Between Raindrops" (Fagen's organ playing echoing Jimmy Smith, John Patton and all those Prestige grinders of the early Sixties) and the cover of "Ruby Baby"—itself no mean feat. So does the more subdued, comically sinister "Goodbye Look," in which a clueless Americano (envoy, spy or Batista-connected businessman) figures out—too late—what's really on the bill at the "small reception" they've arranged "just for me behind the big casino by the sea."

This is *The Nightfly*'s principal charm: that Fagen's affection for the period is sincere without being uncritical or sentimental, and actually a lot of fun if you've been there or ever wanted to be. The album cover (which ties into the title track), tells us much about who the aspiring young Fagen was. He wears his heart on his rolled-up white shirtsleeve, role-playing the hipster DJ from whom he heard the word, whose records still move and inspire our man far into adulthood.

REVIEW:

Everything's Jake on
A Lick and a Promise

On Rock's Backpages Writers' Blog 2012

The subtitle of a recently published book on Manhattan's Seventies punk scene is "Five Years in New York That Changed Music Forever." It's a sure bet no one would have thought of applying that descriptor to the New York music scene of the Sixties. Back then, all eyes and ears were on the West Coast. The Big Apple was a notoriously low-yield music field, a sort of patchy truck farm that couldn't compete with the more fertile San Francisco and Los Angeles scenes. Even today, it's widely agreed that New York's rock and roll legacy of that period rests solely on the Velvet Underground, a hitless if crucial combo whose full impact wasn't felt until a decade later.

There *was* other New York rock and roll in the Sixties, specifically the soul-fired Rascals and the effervescent Lovin' Spoonful, bands that came of age and changed music if not forever, then at least in those brief shining moments of '65-'66 before pop and rock were forever sundered. They were among the last acts of the music's adolescence, when the genre might still express joy and simple pleasures; soon such concerns would be put away in favor of introspection and world enlightenment.

Working alongside the Lovin' Spoonful in Greenwich Village clubs were the Magicians (who took their name from the Spoonful hit). In April of 1966 *Hit Parader* magazine touted the folk-rock quartet, newly signed to Columbia Records, as up-and-comers. Though the Magicians issued a handful of sparkling singles, the band never made it. But three quarters of its members did. John Townley went on to found Apostolic Studios, site of key recordings by the Mothers, Grateful Dead, Kenny Rogers and others. Gary Bonner and Alan Gordon became successful songwriters (the Turtles' "Happy Together" and "She'd Rather Be with Me," Three Dog Night's "Celebrate").

The fourth quarter, singer-guitarist Allan 'Jake' Jacobs, wasn't so lucky. His few albums—as Bunky & Jake (with singer Andrea 'Bunky' Skinner) and Jake & the Family Jewels—drew scant attention. But at the end of last year Jacobs broke a long hiatus and delivered *A Lick and a Promise*. It's credited to Jake and the Rest of the Jewels, but its sensibility is all Jacobs': winsome and heartfelt, flashing innocent wonder even as it acknowledges the pain of experience, and unerringly tuneful.

Among other things, *A Lick and a Promise* reveals Jacobs as a fan. He sends touching valentines to "Dusty" (Springfield), Ray Davies ("Kinky Afternoon") and Willie DeVille ("Willy and Toots," an easy-groove exercise that channels Betty Wright's "Clean Up Woman" and Van Morrison-style R&B). Which doesn't mean he's not an active participant in the proceedings. The ballad "For No One But the Moon" is Jacobs' personal recollection of vocalizing on New York street corners, and it'd be a strong contender for doowop's unofficial anthem if the genre didn't already have one in Kenny Vance's "Looking for an Echo."

"Annabelle" and album-opener "Rings" conjure the seamless convergence of folk and pop that characterized John Sebastian's best early work, and they're every bit as warm and convincing—no mean feat in these manifestly un-magical times. Jacobs addresses just that too, in "Just a Stone's Throw," a gentle yet hard-hitting series of sketches about people, like so many among us, who've been brought to the edge of calamity by the current downturn. Nor is he himself exempt: "So I feel all right on this bright summer mornin,' just me and this ole guitar workin' on a tune/ And I try real hard not to worry 'bout tomorrow/ Just live my life and do what I can do…just a stone's throw from the street." The song's sentiment resembles that of the Depression standard "Brother, Can You Spare a Dime," yet it's more hopeful. That quality seems to underlie most every note and nuanced lyric on *A Lick and a Promise*, rendering it very welcome record.

Rock and Roll Visuals:
Lights! Camera! Scowl!

Rock's Back Pages Writers' Blog 2012

Way back in 1966, the garage-y Brit quartet the Downliners Sect cut a searing single, a tune composed by a pre-Velvet Underground Lou Reed and John Cale titled "Why Don't You Smile Now." Gleefully anti-romantic in the best Jagger-Richards tradition, this record raised a question that's gone unanswered for some 40 years—at least when it comes to the way popular music is visually represented.

Unsmiling faces, framed by lowered brows and downturned, don't-mess-with-me mouths, have long been a dominant design element of pop album covers, whether the music within is made by scrappy indie outfits, howling grind corpsmen or easily aggravated hip-hoppers. Why so glum, chums? Sure, sleeves also feature objects, landscapes or illustrations, but when it comes to photographic captures, artists are often depicted as no-nonsense brooders whose gaze suggests they're conducting cold assessments of you the viewer.

Think about it, and please credit Stones manager Andrew Loog Oldham. Before his boys' debut LP, 1964's *England's Newest Hitmakers*, whose caught-in-the-cops'-spotlight cover shot seems to issue an "Are you lookin' at *me*?" challenge a decade before DeNiro's mirror turn in *Taxi Driver*, artists were portrayed as pleasers. Not just the cheery Fabs of the *Please Please Me* sleeve (though *With the Beatles/Meet the Beatles* opts for somberness, the effect is neutral, not hostile), but everyone in showbiz, from Sinatra (a wink and a finger-snap beckon you to *Come Fly with Me*) and Presley (a sexy grin for *Elvis Golden Records*) to the Beach Boys, Seasons, Supremes and the rest, aimed for an agreeable hook-up. The artists' eagerness to *Mach shau!* for potential consumers was never in doubt.

One could say that the Stones were selling disdain, and that we've loved them for it. They were. And we do. But there's more to that look and its enduring appeal. Historically, the reproachful posture was a defense—against the naysayers who scorned pop—and it's a statement that all of us, fans and critics alike, spent considerable effort making back then: This is serious stuff, not dismissible like the fluff that came before. Show some respect.

Forty years on, the defensiveness is hardly called for; we won, everything that preceded rock has been dethroned, all previous reigning cultural standards tossed. But the conceit that science is being dropped, that Something Big Is Being Said Here, still hangs heavy on covers, a sort of aesthetic ghost limb that obliges most of them to be strict no-smile zones.

Through the years, this approach has spawned numerous sub-schools. From today's perspective, perhaps the silliest was the late '60s/early '70s phenomenon that Howard Kaylan of the Turtles once described as "the Knowing Acid Look": all those medallioned, kaftan-ed junior yogis staring out from LP sleeves with a near-contemptuous regard for the poor shmuck considering his purchase. He should be grateful to pony up five bucks for all this long-play wisdom!

Next came the singer-songwriters, whose earnest faces suggested their shoulders were buckling under intense cogitation on politics, the environment, drug policies and that long-haired girl who messed up their minds.

The shadows deepened further still with heavy-metallers, who are usually depicted as simply more disgruntled versions of the Glimmer Twins. But that riff is now beyond redundant. It may explain why a preponderance of metal covers opt for gory illustrations over band photos. (At least it's a fertile field: a recent L.A. Weekly article on the genre listed 25 sub-styles, among them Skater Thrash, Tech-Death and Pornogrind.)

Ironically, while their music was refreshingly dumb and funny and the farthest from "heavy," visual representations of the Ramones—and of most punks who followed—hewed to the sullen template forged by the Stones. The message is clear: Anything labeled "rock and roll" had better look like this. Gloomy portraiture likewise thrived when metal met punk in Seattle grunge. Though the band itself never appeared on the front of Nirvana's three albums, Cobain and company were typically caught in downcast poses. Pearl Jam's Eddie Vedder, consistently solemn in the Nineties, now works out on ukulele, perhaps the only instrument that one cannot play without smiling.

It's with the rappers, though, that grimness reaches its apogee. Not just in the old-school glares of N.W.A or Ice Cube's isometric brow flexes, but with successive waves of glowering solipsists, bare-chested or in bespoke suits. Even now, as the charts swell with the forced glee of One Direction and the drowning irony of Katy Perry, hip-hoppers keep it real by keeping it serious. On the cover of his international No. 1 album *Take Care*, Drake stares inconsolably into the table, as drained as the empty goblet he halfheartedly clutches. Can nothing relieve his anguish?

It's a mean old world, this pop universe. But can't we all just lighten up?

BLOG POST:

Knock It Off: For Some, Second Best is More Than Good Enough

Rock's Back Pages Writers' Blog, 2012

Comic-Con, 2012. As I have for the last decade, I attended July's gargantuan tribe-gathering at San Diego's Convention Center. Not for me the trailer screenings, public cosplay or panels ("*American Dad*: Stars and producers preview next season's most hilarious moments"). I made straight for the hall's least glitzy quarter, where retail footage recedes annually at a rate rivaling the cryosphere's: the stalls where a handful of vendors sell old comic books.

No superheroes for me either, thanks. My beat is an exotic species of publication that enjoyed the briefest of shelf lives (1958-1958). I collect imitations of *Mad*, also-ran satire magazines with titles like *Loco*, *Crazy*, *Shook Up*, *Frenzy* and *Thimk*, most of which published out of small Manhattan design shops. Though clearly inferior to *Mad*, they wowed me at 12 and still do. Their anarchic covers, splash panels and crazy-font headlines ("I Was a Teenage Slob from Outer Space!," "Pagan Place: An Expose of the Sex Life of the New Englandian Savages") signified both a craven desire to cash in and an urgent need to catalog the uncountable cultural lightning bolts raining down on Americans in those wild mid-century years—Sputnik and rock & roll, fixed quiz shows, Castro and Bardot, drive-in banks and boat-size sedans.

More than that, the knock-off magazines' blatant mimicry—how different from Pope's *Imitations of Horace* or *Glass House* aping *Big Brother* aping MTV's *Real World*?—seemed somehow born of love. As a kid, it struck me that in brazenly nicking the styles of *Mad*'s artists and writers, even its masthead, indicia and mascot, the folks at *Frantic!* and *Nuts* were as jazzed as I was by the original and were thus crafting objects of intense affection. Isn't the wannabe's ardor the deepest? (In *Mad*'s case, imitation represented the sincerest self-flattery; to outflank an earlier wave of imitators, the magazine generated its own clone, *Panic*.)

In the mid-Sixties it was Dylan emulators. Like lots of guys my age, I would have given anything to be Dylan, so it was easy to recognize aspirational comrades in P.F. Sloan (he wrote "Eve of Destruction"), the Changin' Times, David Blue and a dozen others, their records overrun by ghosts of electricity and errant syllable-stuffing. They weren't him, babe, but longed to be. It was heaven when, in the Seventies, I found the best faux Dylan of them all: Dick Campbell, whose 1966 LP *Dick Campbell Sings Where It's At* jangled with gems like "The People Planners" and "Approximately Four Minutes of Feeling Sorry for D.C," the latter featuring appearances by Judas, the Pied Piper, blind men and farmers' daughters.

The Seventies is also when the guy initially derided as the most blatant Dylan pretender showed up, born to run down his predecessors in a fuel-injected, hemi-powered whatever. Springsteen inspired a parade of romantic street-sweepers, hearts stitched tautly to sleeves, brandishing their versions of his version of grandiose folk-rock. I had all their albums: Willie Nile's, Arlyn Gale's *Back to the Midwest Night*, Billy Falcon's *Burning Rose*, Desmond Child's *Runners in the Night*, D.B. Cooper's *Buy American*. Somewhat later came Elvis Costello's debut, *My Aim Is True*, trailing a long court of agitated popsters — Graham Parker, D.L. Byron, the Jags, and Scott Wilk + the Walls (their 1980 album resembles a slate of *Armed Forces* outtakes). And don't get me started on the Madonna-be's: Regina, Martika, Stacey Q, Debbie Gibson, E.G. Daily and the rest.

My passion for knockoffs has yet to flag (I've already registered for Comic-Con 2013 and updated my want list). The process and its practitioners still beguile me. Does this mean I think the imitator is greater than the original? Sometimes. After an apprenticeship spent strapping his style across someone else's engines, John Cougar Mellencamp on tracks like "Jack & Diane" and "Hurt So Good" bested his mentor, who seemed to have long since come up short at the melody pump. And there are surely other examples. But more to the point, what's ultimately appealing — and even touching — about the silly, now flaking pages of a *Cracked* parody or the quarter-century-old coyness of Regina's "Baby Love" is what they unintentionally reveal: the innately human impulse of, having seen what can be done, wanting to get up and do it ourselves. It's how we learn, pass along skills, make art, connect. It's really as simple, and as vital, as that.

BLOG POST:

Overcovering Pop: Are We There Yet?

What have we wrought, us guys and gals who write about pop music?

Rock's Back Pages Writers' Blog, 2012

It's an issue those of us in this game probably don't think about that often. But every once in a while something pops up that makes you wonder about the purpose of this whole enterprise of rock criticism, now celebrating its 46th birthday (*Crawdaddy* magazine debuted in 1966, *Rolling Stone* a year later).

What just popped up is a *New York Times* feature that broaches the vexing question "Just how fast is Justin Bieber allowed to grow up?" The piece spends 1600 words examining a crisis that's kept the windpipes of the world on lockdown far too long. Described as a pitiable "R&B aspirant trapped in a pop universe" who "has few options," Bieber is diagnosed with a malady that demands the hard focus of the major reviewer at a daily paper (circulation 1.6 million). Why is that?

I guess what got me was the photo, the one on the article's jump page: Bieber adorable and pompadoured, on one knee, gazing out from that teddy-bear/tiger space between innocence and manhood. The pose made it a kissing cousin to a glossy poster of Fabian that came with a 1960 greatest-hits LP. Across the poster, in the Fabe's own hand, was the inscription "Fabulously grateful."

In my day—at least in its earliest hours, now hurriedly receding from view—the notion of devoting *any* public space to the music of a pop star (I said "music," not sociological impact, which probably qualifies as news fit to print) would have been considered ludicrous. Until Tom Wolfe ID'ed Phil Spector to the masses (1965), the larger world barely knew or cared about pop's machinations. Sure, alerts like "Jack Nitzsche

Will Helm Sonny & Cher LP" or "Mickey Most's Playboys to Open for Gene Vincent in So. Africa" would have appeared in *Billboard* or *NME*. As for Sontag-ian exegeses on the texts of the Turtles or Showaddywaddy, forget it.

The advent of rock journalism was the first tub-thump on the tribal drum, relaying to 'our' community of interest news and information that barely rated a blip on mainstream radar. It necessarily legitimized music that had taken its knocks as unserious and insubstantial. But it's fair to ask, I think: Has something gone astray in the four decades since everyone (rightly) acknowledged Dylan and (insert your own pop worthy here)? Now, precious print and virtual real estate is routinely given up not just to recounting the naughty exploits of stars (that's been grandfathered into celebrity coverage since the Twenties) but to performing deep-tissue analysis on the music of every last act who charts.

My hunch is that it went wrong in the Sixties, around the time the first high-school teacher decided he had to hip up and, you know, "reach the kids." So he brought in Simon & Garfunkel's *Parsley, Sage, Rosemary and Thyme* for a little parsing and round-the-horn debate ("Diane, what is it you think they're trying to convey in 'The Dangling Conversation'?"). So now we have history-of-rock classes in high schools (not a bad thing, I guess), interdisciplinary majors in the study of pop-culture in college (well, OK) and prolonged chin-stroking and public cogitation on Justin Bieber's artistic dilemma.

I'll bet it won't surprise you to learn, as the *Times* has, that his new track "Boyfriend" is "spooky and minimal" and fittingly serves as "Mr. Bieber's formal coming-out party as an adult." Can a co-production with the top dozen rap stars and remixers, not to mention an epithet-strewn, video-captured set-to outside a trendy boite, be far behind? Next: an album of brutally frank, borderline-explicit songs addressing the set-to and excoriating those who hate on him for telling all, and Mr. Bieber's music will have fully matured.

Not to diss Bieber, but, beyond his many fans, who really cares if he "grows up" in his music? It may well matter mightily to them, but does such a concern fall under the need-to know interests of the general newspaper readership?

It's a problem Fabian never faced. No wonder he was so grateful.

REVIEW:

The Beach Boys:
Verizon Wireless Amphitheater,
Orange County

Writers' blog, *Rock's Backpages*, June 2012

"There's something ridiculous about a 70-year-old man going out there and singing 'Fun, Fun, Fun.'" So said my wife last week when I told her that a ticket to see the Beach Boys perform at an Orange County (California) amphitheater had dropped into my lap.

Is there?

My chance to find out came as I watched a visibly slower Mike Love, a slightly more-engaged-than-usual Brian Wilson, an energized Al Jardine, plus David Marks, Bruce Johnston and cohorts plow through two hours of hits, misses, rarities, and songs from a new, 50th anniversary album. By the time Love kicked off "Fun, Fun, Fun" (in the encore), the group, augmented by Dean Torrence of Jan & fame (he lives in Huntington Beach, a short hop away from the venue), Marsha's comment—indeed, all questions regarding the Hawthorne crew and their place in the pop firmament—had been rendered utterly useless.

Here's why. If one of the worst crimes anyone can commit these days is to have an "agenda," then Brian Wilson is a serial offender, booked as early as 1962 and '63 on multiple counts of trying to inflict massive, sustained amounts of beauty, exhilaration and positivism on the world ("In My Room," "Surfin' USA," "Catch a Wave," etc.).

The Beatles, Stones and Dylan may have begun, respectively, with aspirations to be the world's best rock 'n' roll band, to be the John the Baptists of the blues, or to dominate as a musical and cultural icon. Wilson's mission was far more basic and intuitive, and that's likely what's kept the best of his music—and, as the 50 or so songs in Sunday's show proved, there's so much of it—front and center so long for so many people. The Beach Boys' catalog tracks a half-century's worth of pop itself: from early, insidiously complex paeans to sea and strip (with immodesty in check: contrasted with today's chest-thumping stars, their most arrogant boast was "Well, I've got the fastest set of wheels in town") and folk flirtations like "Cotton Fields" and "Sloop John B," to *Pet Sounds* art-rock, good-vibed psychedelia and post-*Pepper* back-to-basics ("Do It Again").

From the audience you could indeed "feel the love," irony- and snark-free. Huge rushes of it burst forth from the loges, the down-front and terrace seats when the stage screens projected video of the late Dennis and Carl Wilson, their vocals on "Forever" and "God Only Knows" synched to the backup singing and music played onstage. And it wasn't just the 50- and 60-somethings who sang along to "Fun, Fun, Fun" because the tune is one of their (my) coming-of-age touchstones. There was the trio of teenage Latinas two seats over, up and frantically surf dancing through "Help Me Rhonda" and "Do You Wanna Dance," and the young Asian woman and her daughter one row down, singing every word of "Wouldn't It Be Nice." In the parking lot before the concert, as the ticket line snaked its way to the entry gates, an interracial acappella quartet harmonized on "And Your Dream Comes True" (last track on 1965's *Summer Days—And Summer Nights!* LP).

The show itself was enjoyable enough, but by its end what became clear was that, as good as the performers are/were, ultimately the enduring appeal of the Beach Boys resides as much in the songs as in the singers. Their abundant melodies, unifying harmonies and emotional range—from pure exhilaration at life's offerings to soul-wracking melancholy and grateful redemption—are what do it, and they all proceed from Wilson's singular agenda. He was made for these times, and those to come.

BLOG POST:

The Perception of Doors

SoFein.com, May 2013

Why not weigh on in the Doors, since everyone's doing it these first days after Ray Manzarek's passing? I have a slightly unorthodox take on them, much like the one I have on the Grateful Dead (earliest, quasi-garage-y stuff is best).

First time I saw the Doors (January, '67, Fillmore Auditorium), I almost thought they were a joke. I'm a Frisco guy, but I never bought into the town's notorious provincialism, so that doesn't explain my perception. Besides, I'd already enjoyed great shows by L.A. acts like Love, Captain Beefheart, Buffalo Springfield, Sons of Adam, etc.

No, what soured me on the Doors (and I hadn't heard their just-released album yet) was that, while the music was spooky good (though not as gothically dark as Quicksilver Messenger Service), their presentation flew starkly in the face of everything that defined the newly emerging 'rock.' Which is to say, the anti-pop'ness of it all. What was fresh about all these groups, no matter where they hailed from, was a certain unpretentiousness: go onstage in your street clothes, eschew crowd-pleasing patter, leave the showbiz at the door. Just play.

But the Doors...partway into a strong set, the lead singer, already working the mic with crypto-*Privilege* rock-star technique, fakes a fall, pretends to be hurt. Mister Mojo rises, acts disoriented, belts and croons some tunes. In the audience, I'm thinking, 'What is this—Euripides? Some choreographed set-piece/stage play?' Later there'd be the dramatic "The End." The music was great, the audience seemed to like it (I recall lots of us quizzing each other on our impressions after the show), but what to make of all this artifice?

Silly me: I had the same reaction two months later when I heard about the Who and Hendrix performances at Monterey. This seemed like Ed Sullivan Show stuff: flashy theatrics, maybe at the expense of music (though, to be frank, it never prevented either of those two acts from creating some of the best of the era). In time, of course, both the more improvised and studied 'rock' approaches came to coexist perfectly, until you get to today's pop, most of which wears its fakery proudly, seeming to claim rebellious rock-spirit by virtue of its craven unnaturalness.

There was plenty to dislike about Doors music (Jimbo's Lizard King variations and coy, do-you-wanna-see-my-pud? concert teases), but way more to like, if they did swipe "Touch Me" from the 4 Seasons' "C'mon Marianne." Krieger alone was one of the Sixties' great guitar stylists, and the band (and Jim) at their best cooked, and, owing to Manzarek and Krieger's gifts and dispositions, always made sure melody had a stage-front spot in their music. Break on through.

BLOG POST:

Louis Nye, Silly Guy

WFMU Ichiban, 2013

He would have turned a hundred this year. Gordon Hathaway. Sonny Drysdale. Raise a glass (better still, as Gordon advised on his *Heigh-Ho Madison* Avenue album, hoist some "Martinis and Miltown"). Or offer a heartfelt "Boola boola" as raccoon-coated Sonny did on more than one episode of *The Beverly Hillbillies*.

Steve Allen, it's been persuasively argued, was the first hip spy in the house of TV, abetting the earliest visitations by Elvis, Jerry Lee Lewis, Jack Kerouac, Frank Zappa, the Collins Kids and countless other outsiders to millions of American living room; he "had the true spirit of a comic anarchist fluttering like a red flag in his soul," wrote James Wolcott.

Louis Nye (1913-2005) was among the more subversive offerings of Allen's late-Fifties/early-Sixties show. Appearing weekly in skits and 'Man on the Street' bits, Nye's Gordon Hathaway wasn't merely funny, batting his eyes, cocking coy smiles, dropping Mad-Ave and Greenwich Village jargon into his exchanges with Allen. He was a cultural signifier of a half dozen things that, much like race and ethnicity, official America found too taboo to talk about. He was a louche aesthete and style cat, an uninhibited wit who couldn't tell you who won last week's big game, who was maybe gay, who hung with bohemians and cracked about getting high. Walking into frame in his thin tie, button-down Gant and Tyrolean hat, Gordon (whose shtick was usually written by Allen staffers Stan Burns and Herb Sargent) confounded prevailing notions of how guyhood was supposed to play. If Lord Buckley was the Fifties' avatar of the Sixties, Gordon Hathaway was, in his own way, the coal-mine canary that brought news of much that society would eventually accept and respect.

Nye's brief (1962) run as Clampett banker Mr. Drysdale's playboy son Sonny was juicy if wildly anachronistic; *The Beverly Hillbillies'* writers wrote the eternal college student as a prancing refuge from the Thirties. It was as Gordon Hathaway that Nye killed, with heavy doses of sly and silly—not just on Allen's show, but on singles like "Teenage Beatnik" ("I like to cha-cha in my Bermuda shorts") and LPs like *Heigh-ho Madison Avenue* and *Here's Nye in Your Eye*, where the proto-Mad Men tropes fly fast and furious ("Let's toss it down the well and check it for splash"). If you can find the latter set, dig "Hipster in a Bank" and be set free.

BLOG POST:

Do Knock the Rock: The Eternal Hipness of the Square-Biz Mind

WFMU Ichiban site, 2013

You know what I miss from the past? Sure, Moxie and men's spats, The Old Philosopher, pre-surgery Kris Kardashian, etc. But what I really miss the most is comedians who made fun of rock 'n' roll and pop music.

I was reminded of this by a clip I just came across on YouTube, from a Lloyd Thaxton TV show ca. 1965, in which Steve Allen and Milton Berle satirize the then-current fad of protest singers. In long-hair wigs and the fakest of beards, "Monty Mad" and "Billy Bitter" send up folk-rock with silly songs ("Grown-ups are old, youngsters are kid-ish/ If it wasn't for George Washington we'd all be British!") and typically Allen-style cheap jokes (Thaxton: "You play piano, but you have a guitar around your neck. Why is that? Allen: "Man, that's because the piano's too heavy!").

The beauty part is that their deliberate stoopidity in making fun of a form they despise is only a couple of feet removed from the stoopidity of the real deal, like Sonny Bono's "Laugh at Me" and "The Revolution Kind." I mean, they're practically brothers in bearskin. And it's a hoot, even if they were coming from what we might think of as a square place.

Back then, as the new kid on the block, rock had to endure the slurs of the ageing, but still dominant, Greatest Generation (the most cited examples being Dean Martin's unsubtle dissing of the Stones on *Hollywood Palace*). But why shouldn't pop be able to take a few sucker punches, especially when the punchers don't really get it that the Showmen were absolutely right when they proclaimed, in 1961, "It Will Stand"?

And that's the sad part. 'We' won. Our music (everything since the pre-rock Fifties) stood, and still stands, as the undisputed champ genre that itself is now above criticism. Where once Steve Allen had Elvis sing "Hound Dog" to a sad-eyed basset on national TV and Stan Freberg's "Sh-Boom" deliciously spoofed doowop's goofy syllable-stretching (check YouTube for both), now the *New Yorker* ponders, "The Meaning of Michael Jackson" and asks, "What to Make of Rhianna?" Yeah, what?

Sure, TMZ and catty blogs and awards-show emcees dish the stars, but implicit in the very attention they pay them is the notion that pop culture, above all, matters and means something. And that's an assumption the old-school rock-knockers, bless 'em, never made. It's what allowed them to use it as just more joke fuel—like mother-in-law jokes, *Gunsmoke* and drive-in banks—and, in some cases, like Sid Caesar, Carl Reiner and Howie Morris' Three Haircuts satires (YouTube), grab some of the very juice and crazed energy of their target itself. The Haircuts and hams like Freddie Cannon are almost brothers in Butch Wax.

One of the hippest comics ever is Pete Barbutti. Fans of first-rate rock-knocking should track down a copy of his VeeJay LP *Here's Pete Barbutti*. Like Allen and Berle's protest skit, it's from 1965, just about the last time anyone effectively skewered pop (outside of Mark Shipper's 1978 book *Paperback Writer*). In front of a club audience, Pete takes on "Disc Jockeys," explaining that "One of the reasons for the poor state of music in this day and age is that, no matter where you live, there's at least one radio station that plays nothing but rock 'n' roll music, song after song…" Thereafter follows his impersonation of motor-mouth Top-40 jocks and the music they play: each song sounds like the next, Pete's screeching vocals attacking caveman-dumb lyrics as he counts down the hits by "Mary & the Knee-Knockers," "Theresa & the Tree-Thumpers" and the rest. It's priceless.

LINER NOTES:

Mason Williams Phonograph Record

Real Gone Music, 2013

Two words crop up a lot when you're talking to Mason Williams about his work: "explore" and "experiment." Of one of his producers, he notes that, "He wanted to create hits, and I wanted to explore songwriting." A persistent drive to experiment with various art-forms led him to "decide to have a creative life and not a career, because a creative life is doing what you want to do, and a career is doing what *it* wants you to do."

What's remarkable about Williams is that he's managed to success-fully indulge the former impulse while enjoying the fruits of the latter for almost five decades now. Even a casual glance at his resume shows that, by following his instincts, the Texas-born, Oregon- and Oklahoma-raised musician-artist-writer has done rather a lot: earned two Grammys (and three more Grammy nominations) and an Emmy (plus two nomina-tions); had his work exhibited at New York's Museum of Modern Art, the Pasadena Art Museum and L.A.'s Norton Simon Museum; published 16 literary/art books; and issued 24 albums.

The world, of course, knows Mason Williams best for his singular hit. Released in February of 1968, "Classical Gas" rose to No. 2 on *Bill-board*'s chart, logged multiple millions of broadcast performances, and became the most recorded non-classical instrumental composition of all time (more than 100 cover versions and counting). It also serves as the centerpiece for one of the most diverse and beguiling debut albums of the Sixties. Folks who heard "Classical Gas" on Top 40 radio and bought *The Mason Williams Phonograph Record* expecting to hear a dozen "Classical Gas" sound-alikes were surely flummoxed once they set the stylus down on Side One. But that's getting ahead of the story.

By the time "Classical Gas" woke the world, Williams was already a very busy young man. Having moved, with his childhood pal the artist

Ed Ruscha, to Los Angeles in 1964, he'd been writing for TV since the fall of 1966, penning skits and songs for *The Smothers Brothers Comedy Hour* (where he cooked up the Pat Paulsen for President campaign) and shows starring Roger Miller, Petula Clark and Andy Williams. He'd also had his songs recorded by such acts as the Kingston Trio and Glenn Yarbrough, and published the *Bus* book (his life-size photograph of a Greyhound bus, which made its way into New York's MoMA).

"It was through Tommy Smothers that I got a chance to make my album," Williams recalls. "The Smothers Brothers show exposed a lot of new artists [among them the Doors, The Who, Jefferson Airplane and Buffalo Springfield], and many of them were on Warner Bros. Records. Someone there, maybe [president] Joe Smith, came to Tommy and said, 'You've done so much for our acts. What can we do for you?' And Tommy answered, 'Well, I think Mason would like to make a record...'"

Warners assigned Mike Post (subsequently the pen behind the themes for *The Rockford Files, Hill Street Blues* and *The Greatest American Hero*) to produce, allotted a budget of $30,000 ("A lot at the time," Williams notes), booked super-arranger Al Capps, and waited for The Golden Boy syndrome to kick in. "The Golden Boy is what Hollywood is always looking for," Williams explains. "They like to think you just showed up and wrote all this music in a month or so. But really what happens is you come to the table with years of songwriting and they get to pick the best from all of that. That was the case with *Phonograph Record*."

Still, what they picked, with Williams' help, was an impressive earful. It commenced with an overture, performed by a 37-piece orchestra, of the album's several musical themes, which then segued to a dozen serious and silly songs, half-minute poems and complex instrumental compositions. "I was experimenting," Williams acknowledges. The galloping, coolly arranged "All the Time" was "a bid to do something I usually wasn't interested in: a straight pop tune. Then I'd think, 'OK, I've done that. Time to move on to something else.'"

Something like, say, the 30-second epigrams "Dylan Thomas" and "Life Song," or maybe "Sunflower," the gorgeous, five-minute instrumental engendered by Williams' embrace of the chance-composition concept. "The idea is to roll the dice to come up with the intervals to form a piece," he explains. "Here I took the word 'cantilever' and gave each letter of the word a different pitch that I then used to make a melody from. I had to put it in a time signature and put chords to it, but the point was: the process gave me a melody I never would have thought of."

The inspiration for the song? In the summer of '67, Williams had hired a pilot to skywrite the stems and leaves of a flower in the sky below the sun, making the sun the blossom of a "Sun Flower." "It was two miles wide and three miles high," he says. "It lasted about 40 seconds."

While some of *Phonograph Record*'s tunes were catalog pieces (the romance-heavy "Wanderlove" was written in 1963, "Long Time Blues" — which he "always wanted to have Ray Charles sing" — a year later), much of the material was the result of Williams' day-to-day work on *The Smothers Brothers Comedy Hour*. The ba-ba-bah'ing "Baroque-A-Nova" and the somewhat Association-al "She's Gone Away," he explains, "came from the fact that we had a lot of vocal acts on the show, singing harmony and parts. Simon & Garfunkel were on, and the Anita Kerr Singers were regulars; all of that was an influence." "Here Am I" was more of a lyrical experiment, in which the verses focus on the futility of life ("As the universe spins to a desolate end/ in the doldrums of destiny's sea…") as the chorus revels in present-tense love ("And here am I, holding your hand"). "The last chorus," confides Williams, "was going to be 'Here am I, holding your zipper,' but …It would have been funnier, though."

"The Prince's Panties" (part of a five-part "Dada Trilogy") manages that feat. The brief saga of a monarch's vengeful pups is read by Williams in an ultra-fey voice; producer Post secretly stuck this take on the album in place of a more straightforward reading Williams had done. "I was going to go on *The Tonight Show*," he recalls, "and I said, 'I'd like to sing *this* song' and I performed it for the producers. Once I did, they decided not to have me on the show."

An entirely different fate befell an instrumental he'd composed a year earlier, something he considered mere "fuel" for a guitar pull. Hence the song's original title: "Classical Gasoline" (a music copyist inadvertently abbreviated it as "Gas"). With some arranging tweaks, the tune made the cut for the album and became its first single. "The interesting thing about the track," Williams says, "was that the musicians had rehearsed all the sections of it, and the first time they played them all together, that's the take we kept. It had the most excitement.

"A disc jockey in Houston started playing it every hour," he continues. "Then it got played in Boston and Denver. I'd be at work, writing the Smothers show, and I'd get a call from Warner Bros: 'Your record sold 40,000 copies yesterday.' Great! Then I'd go back to writing comedy for whoever was a guest on the show that week." By mid-August 1968, "Classical Gas" was bested only by the Doors' "Hello, I Love You" on a *Billboard* Top 10 that included "Jumpin' Jack Flash," "Sunshine of Your

Love" and "Stoned Soul Picnic."

"I did nothing to support the record," says Williams, "no interviews, no touring, because I was writing TV. You'd get in at 9 in the morning and not leave till midnight or later. I did, though, perform the song three times on the show." His absence from the usual rounds of record promotion didn't make a dent on the ascent of "Classical Gas." It won him two Grammys (1968's Best Instrumental Theme and Best Instrumental Performance) and Mike Post one (Best Instrumental Arrangement), became radio's most-played instrumental recording, and has been featured in numerous films and TV series—among them America's two favorite family shows, *The Simpsons* and *The Sopranos*.

The Mason Williams Phonograph Record spent almost six months on *Billboard's* LP chart, peaking at No. 14. In November 1968, Williams released his second Warners album (of five), *Ear Show* (also being reissued on CD by Real Gone Music), and embarked on a full-time career as a performing musician. But, Williams being Williams, there was still room for more television writing (*Saturday Night Live* in the Eighties, more Smothers Brothers specials), books (*Them Poems*) and a crate-load of collaborative and solo projects. He continues to conceive, compose and record in Oregon, where he now resides. For the full picture: www.masonwilliams-online.com.

REVIEW:

Devo
The Complete Truth About De-Evolution

Ugly Things magazine, Summer 2014

Like Dr. Pepper ("The World's Most Misunderstood Soft Drink"), the wackiest wing of Akron's new-wave army often battled inaccurate perceptions about who it was and what it was up to.

As Gerald Casale and Mark Mothersbaugh's commentary makes clear on this big fat compendium of videos, shorts and performance footage, the band itself made significant contributions to the ball of confusion surrounding its mission. It was never the two conceptualists' intent to be a band per se. Rather, Devo was an artful project that would make films pushing the members' contention that humankind had flummoxed a good thing: that man's ginormous ego, so consumed by its own drive toward power and pleasure, is spoiling the party for everyone—us, nature, the planet. Like Daylight Savings Time, we keep falling back, continuously devolving toward some ultimate base state.

Fair enough. But Devo was/is a band, which raises an all-important query: Did it rock? In a manner of speaking, yes (especially live). I have to admit to being only a part-time Devo-phile during the group's heyday, mostly on the basis of its 'rockist' leanings ("Mongoloid," "Jocko Homo," "Satisfaction"). Now, though, watching these 20 clips, I 'get it' in a fresh way, the fun Dada absurdity of the music (the sicko sendup of Reaganite cowboy machismo in "Whip It," inspired by the cover of a '50s dude-ranch magazine) and the messages (the irradiated band mishandling barrels of nuclear waste in "Worried Man").

Casual and hardcore fans alike get lots of goods here: all the clips, including "Secret Agent Man," "Girl U Want," "Come Back Jonee," "Beautiful World" and "Freedom of Choice," with Casale and Mothersbaugh's comments on each track—and on the group's slow rise to and quick fall from popularity; MTV, which Devo's clever clips could lay some claim to inventing, arrogantly dismissed their final video, "Post-Post Modern Man," as 'not what's happening now.' There's also Bruce Conner's 1978 film for "Mongoloid," an interview with director Chuck Statler, and various live performances ("Uncontrollable Urge," "Gates of Steel," etc.).

Not to get heavy, but the group's de-evolution theory has turned out to have pretty strong legs since it was first propounded in the mid-'70s. These guys were talking about the now-dominant cultural style of corporate fascism a decade before Janet Jackson's quasi-Nazi *Control* dance routines. Three decades later, phalanxes of robotic arm-thrusters pervade every pop clip and arena performance. They may hate to say it, but Devo told us so.

FEATURE:

Frank Sinatra's *Watertown*

For Trunkworthy site, Sept. 2014

Frank Sinatra knew from dark and downcast. Just check albums like *In the Wee Small Hours of the Morning* or tunes like "The One That Got Away" and "One for My Baby (And One More for the Road)"—wherein he taps the barkeep for a couple extra shots of liquid courage before, disconsolate over a flown dame, getting in his car and driving down your street.

But *Watertown*, the 1970 commercial-flop album conceived and produced by Jersey Boy Bob Gaudio, is in a whole other league. It's a sober affair, an eleven-song cycle about the dissolution of a marriage, sung from the perspective of the left-behind husband and dad (two sons: see the wrenching yet remarkably un-maudlin "Michael and Peter"). Sinatra is shattered, confused, regretful, resigned in performances that belong with his best—and here's why it works: he does it by refusing to overplay the pain. Yeah, he's hurt, but there's no Nick Cave self-laceration, no Scott Walker wallowing, no equating his straits with the collapse of the cosmos. *Watertown* connects because the all-time song-reader never abandons the perfectly human scale of Jake Holmes' lyrics and Gaudio's melodies. Listen: If this record doesn't grab you, maybe you're Robert Stack-ing it: untouchable.

The title track sets it all up: wife decamps for the city, packing dreams, leaving Frank and the boys stuck in smallville. "Goodbye" (She Quietly Says)" sketches the couple's anti-climactic final scene. Facing each other across a coffee-shop table, he half-gallantly proposes one last try but she's already gone. "There is no great big ending, no sunset in the sky/ No string ensemble, she doesn't even cry."

It's the small stuff that hits the heart, like the details of post-breakup life that accrue in "Michael and Peter." Sinatra seems to shudder at the quickened, frightening sense of time passing ("The roses that we planted last fall climbed the wall") and moves through a range of emotions as he ponders chucking much of what's left of his life: "All those years I've worked for Santa Fe, never missed a single day/ Just one more without a raise in pay—and I'm leaving."

Things, of course, don't end well. We learn this as the verses of "The Train" unwind, full of what turns out to be Frank's false hope of a rapprochement. And yet… If hard knocks left the hero of "My Way" wiser, perhaps he was also a little too prideful. *Watertown*'s guy learns just as much from painful experience—but emerges humbled and way more grateful. In what's arguably the album's high point, "I Would Be in Love (Anyway)," he's got the guts to come out and say it: If he knew at the start it would end this way, he'd still have done what he did: loved her, made a family, believed in a future.

The arrangements, by 4 Seasons vet Charlie Callelo, Joe Scott and Gaudio, are as simpatico as any Sinatra's ever had, sparse or orchestrally spacious as the songs call for. "I Would Be in Love (Anyway)" features a 12-string folk-rock underpinning, and piano and French horns and a stirring, Righteous Bros. build to the chorus. The strings on "Michael and Peter" slay me; so do the track's bass-string "Wichita Lineman" guitar lines and, in spots, the *Pet Sounds* ambience. None of the sensitive settings would mean a thing if they weren't surrounding these vocals by this singer on such moving compositions. Devastating loss may never have sounded so irresistible.

Maybe it's ironic that when he recorded *Watertown*, Sinatra was trying to prove he could again be hip and relevant. Concept albums were the rage in those post-*Pepper* days, so he cut one. It stiffed. But he created something that did the job far better than the Nehru jackets, love beads and Caesar-cut rugs: that rarity, a set of performances that, more and more, sounds timeless.

Liner Notes:

Ron Nagle *Bad Rice*

Omnivore Recordings, 2015

It's entirely possible that they hired the wrong guy to write these liner notes.

How can you trust someone to be the least bit rational about a record that's been the object of his unwavering affection for 40 years?

Actually, there are plenty of folks just as untrustworthy as me. In the late '90s, when *Billboard* magazine asked its readers which vinyl LPs they most wanted reissued on CD, *Bad Rice* topped the list. It showed up again in 2005 in the obscure-albums book *Lost in the Grooves*, which declared the album "a true original of Americana pop" and praised Ron Nagle's "brilliant writer's eye for the details of strange people's lives and times." A lot of us never stopped believing. We've clung to our battered copies of Warner Bros. WS 1902 all these years. But many potential fans were denied the pleasures of *Bad Rice* altogether. Until now.

This belated first-ever official reissue of *Bad Rice* (with bonus tracks yet) is thus an 'event.' And, because it's been a while, some historical perspective is called for, which means getting out the back-hoe and going all archaeological.

Ron Nagle, San Francisco native, came up in the real, non-Fonzie '50s, when a teen with the right radar could get knocked-out loaded by Tarheel Slim & Little Ann on the radio, scalloped pearlescent coupes down the block, buying the Drifters' "Money Honey" on Fillmore Street and firecrackers in Chinatown, doing the whole shades-on Boho roll at the Blackhawk jazz club, then, come Monday morning back in class again styling up in pegged Levis and polished oxblood wingtips. And he could, and did, move on, graduating from S.F. State, firing and glazing ceramics at the S.F. Art Institute, mixing it up at that crazy '65 Civic Auditorium Stones show, then, naturally, going out and forming a band—the maybe-too-clever-for-its-own-good, juice-headed Mystery Trend—that kick-started the scene beside the Charlatans and Airplane, then conked out, bequeathing the world a single seven-inch nugget of sound and fury tagged "Johnny Was a Good Boy."

By 1969, Nagle admits, "I was mostly getting drunk." But he was also deep into his longstanding twin avocations, his hands in clay, his head and heart full of the rock 'n' roll he'd always written and sung. "I had the opportunity to do my first one-man show at this gallery in town," Ron recalls. "The guy said, 'You can do anything you want to advertise it.' So I came up with this Chuckie character [the gap-toothed goon whose photo fills the back cover of the *Bad Rice* LP]. I said, 'I want a guy who's hideous and unappealing-looking, and I want to put his picture on the side of busses all over town, with a phone number on it.' So the gallery owner said, 'OK.' We printed up and distributed leaflets, and had signs on the sides of busses and streetcars all over town. The whole idea was to get people to call the number, which had a message telling them not to go to the show. I wanted a song to go along with the answering-machine message, so we recorded '61 Clay' [the address of the Dilexi Gallery was 6131 Clay St.], which was about this guy Chuckie, who kills his mother because he's been grounded and can't go out. Consequently, the show was packed."

The track, praised by *Rolling Stone* reviewer Ed Ward for possessing "the sense of sheer energy that's been missing in rock since the Stones last walked out of a studio," was the germ for *Bad Rice*. A tape of "61 Clay" made it to San Francisco's KSAN-FM, where DJ Tony Pigg passed it on to station manager and underground-radio regent 'Big Daddy' Tom Donahue. "Tom dug it and wound up funding the act," Nagle recalls, "which we called the Fast Bucks. But he only wanted to sign me, not the band, which caused some bitterness."

Donahue and his partner Bob Mitchell ran Frisco's pop music scene in the early and mid-'60s, discovering Sly Stone, logging the first sessions by the Grateful Dead and Grace Slick's Great Society, and charting Top-40 hits on their Autumn Records label with the Beau Brummels and Bobby Freeman. In 1966, the label and its acts were sold to Warner Bros., which quickly coined cash with Autumn alumni the Mojo Men ("Sit Down, I Think I Love You") and Harper's Bizarre ("59th St. Bridge Song [Feelin' Groovy]"). Three years later, Big Daddy had a production deal with Warners, and he got Nagle signed to the Burbank imprint, then the hottest in the business.

Things didn't proceed smoothly. "For one thing," Nagle says, "there was the whole issue of me going on the road to promote the album. I just knew I wouldn't make it two weeks if I had to tour, man. The main idea for me has always been to *make records*. That's something that nobody in [psychedelic-era] San Francisco gave a shit about." Another issue was Donahue's incurable case of too-many-irons-in-the-fire; among them the hippie-rock troupe Stoneground (built around Beau Brummels vocalist Sal Valentino), which he'd packaged, promoted and also just signed to Warners. "Tom *was* very connected," explains Nagle, and when the singer-songwriter said he needed a more hands-on producer, Donahue asked, "Who do you want?" "I said, 'Well, ideally, Jack Nitzsche,'" Ron recalls, "and Tom says, 'I might be able to do that.' It's a move he later regretted, but he made it happen."

"Donahue was Jack's connection in Northern California," says Denny Bruce, longtime Nitzsche associate and Nagle's subsequent manager. "Jack was looking to produce someone who wasn't the usual Bay Area jam band. For Jack, when he met Ron it was like the guy in prison just looking for that appeal attorney to overturn his case because he's innocent. He was so happy to meet a Ray Davies, Randy Newman type artist who cared about *songs* and *records*." One listen to Ron's demos of "Dolores" and "Frank's Store" and the legendary arranger-producer said, "OK, I'll do it."

The mutual admiration thrived. "Jack called me 'the best undiscovered songwriter around.' I'm still working under that title," cracks Nagle. But the criminal lack of acknowledgment for Nagle's talents surely wasn't the result of a lack of effort. Sessions for *Bad Rice* commenced in 1970, the majority of them at Wally Heider's San Francisco studio, with additional time spent at L.A.'s Sunset Sound; Nagle plays keyboards, John Blakeley most guitar, though Ry Cooder roils up a storm on the re-recorded "61 Clay" and "Capricorn Queen." Production was shared by Donahue and Nitzsche. The results were stunning: indelible melodies, hard-charging rock 'n' roll and heartbreaking ballads, a level of insight and lyric sophistication that, at its best, invests the songs with the depth and plot points of the most compelling short story. (*Rolling Stone*'s Ward found Nagle's tunes "as good as or better than the material that serves as the basis of such acts as James Taylor, Randy Newman or Elton John," adding that "his lyrics have Taylor's and Taupin's beat hands down.")

Much of the allure of the *Bad Rice* songs lies in their ambiguity, in the tantalizing sense of 'What's going on here?' that pulls the listener into the lives of Nagle's fascinating characters and their puzzling, jointly painful and humorous, circumstances. Like the ruined souls of the over-the-top cautionary "Marijuana Hell" ("Matilda loved to paint, she'd done the patron saints on a mural 'crossed her bedroom wall/ She sold a bust of Christ for a premium price but now she don't paint at all"). Nagle: "On Yahoo or one of these sites where people write in about discovering the record, one guy said, 'I've listened to this song over and over and I'm convinced that it's not satire.' Well," laughs Nagle, "that's the beauty of what we do here. I mean..."

An even better example of what Nagle does is the confounding "Party in L.A." If it sounds metaphorical, using a radical-politics face-off to describe a child-custody battle, it isn't. "My first wife had identity issues at the time," he says, "and she decided things were gonna get straight by her joining the Progressive Labor Party and leaving me, since I was just some bourgeois artist. She informed me, 'I'm moving to L.A. The party needs me, and I'm taking our son,' I was heartbroken. It turned out she only moved to San Jose, so I was able to take the train to San Jose and visit my kid. It was rough."

"Frank's Store" likewise has real-world origins. As much a fixture of San Francisco as summer fog, the Golden Gate Bridge and gaudy Victorians are the corner groceries that, until not long ago, dotted most residential neighborhoods—pocket shops whose contents Nagle nails with pointillist detail: "warmest beer in cans, day-old meat and toys made in Japan." "There was one down the hill from where we are," he explains, "and there was this guy, Eddie, I guess you'd call him 'mentally challenged,' who worked there. Got to wear Frank's apron, you know, 'Yeah, Frank lets me run the place.' I just had this idea: Well, what would make it tragic? Well, the store could burn down, so this guy has lost his whole identity because he got to wear the smock with Frank's name on it. It lent him dignity." The narrative, the chorus with the neighborhood kids trying to comfort the crying Eddie, Nitzsche's strings, the crack in Nagle's voice: to these ears, "Frank's Store" is one of the most moving songs in pop, miles from maudlin yet heartstrings-close.

Along with "61 Clay," the album's barn-burning rockers are "Sister Cora" and "Capricorn Queen." Nagle's "not sure where 'Sister Cora' came from," though the saga of a holy-rolling faith-healer sprang from "lines that I just heard, like having arthritis so bad that 'It hurts me just combing my hair.' It's that hair thing again," he says, of what's become a recurring Nagle theme. "I didn't even have any to comb!" He's not at all unclear about the origins of "Capricorn Queen": "It's about my wife, we've been together 40 years. I grew up in the '50s, where if you didn't drink you were really out of it. I used to drink. But around the time I wrote this, I just quit. My wife helped me. I would depend on her as a Capricorn to keep the Pisces man clean. I'm not an astrology guy, but one of the things they say about Pisces is they're creative and indecisive, not knowing which way to go, and there's a predilection to addiction. So we're a sensitive bunch."

By some stretch, "Somethin's Gotta Give Now" and "House of Mandia" could be considered genre pieces. The former, a doomed-relationship tune with a modified country flavor, features steel guitar played by the West Virginia Creeper of Commander Cody & His Lost Planet Airmen, while the latter goes tropical in a most un-Buffett manner, alternating its breeze-sway with a despair-haunted rock riff. "I wanted to have a song with two entirely separate feels to it," Nagle says of "Mandia." "There are images there from my childhood, like 'Joe Carioca' from the '40s Disney cartoon," as well as the influence of popular novelist James Michener, whose '50s novels exoticized Hawaii and the South Pacific. The song works equally well as the fantasy of a frustrated salary-man or as Nagle's personal recollection of, as *Lost in the Grooves* reviewer Brian Doherty put it, "the details of strange people's lives and times"—in this case Ron's parents. "They came up with all sorts of horror stories," Nagle explains. "One they used to tell me was that people like Glenn Miller and Amelia Earhart didn't really die, but that they went to a heavily guarded special home, because they were so disfigured that the public couldn't handle them. They lived the rest of their lives in this island-paradise kind of Shangri-La. And they *believed* it!"

Some of the same inspiration fuels "Family Style," one of the real sleeper cuts on *Bad Rice*. It's got the rowdy feel of a *Basement Tapes* Dylan outtake, thanks to Ron's barrelhouse piano and that wondrously ragged chorus (the "Won't you love me forever" part of it, for some reason, recalls Brian Wilson's rough-but-earnest "Back Home"). "Certain things in it are true," Nagle admits. "I did step on a parakeet and crushed him to death, and I had to throw the shoes away because I felt so guilty." When Uncle Frank dies of unknown causes, "Frankie's pretty wife prayed to heaven to give him life/ Purgatory was the best that he'd do"—"I grew up wanting to be Catholic," says Ron ruefully. "That's What Friends Are For" is another easily overlooked gem; it may lack the narrative sweep of "Frank's Store," but it brims with honest, painful sentiment and characteristic Nagle melancholy, all elements that have earned his writing the comparisons to Elton John and Taylor and Newman, and helped his ballads find their into the repertoires of Streisand, Michelle Phillips and others.

It's significant that Jack Nitzsche agreed to produce Nagle on the strength of the demos for "Frank's Store" and "Dolores," as these tracks represent the apex of the pair's collaboration. It's tempting to call the latter a tragic ballad, but the partially described, altogether unresolved 'affair' is not the crux of the song; the boy narrator's yearning and his frustration with trying to comprehend his situation are. Nitzsche's bittersweet strings perfectly underscore the character's unfulfilled desire. When he was 10 or 11, Nagle's family used to visit Lake Tahoe. "I'd go down to the beach from the Eldorado campground," he remembers, "and all of a sudden there's this girl there, maybe 19 or 20, and I just had a crush on her. I'd go down there every day hoping she'd show up. It was like, 'What is this I'm feeling?,' you know? She didn't really lead me on, and I didn't know anything about sex, but I was nuts about her. It's a kid's fantasy about the girl who's kind of egging him on, which isn't the case but he wishes it was. I took some liberties with what really happened. The girl's name wasn't Dolores. I took that from my favorite aunt, or maybe from Dolores Street in San Francisco."

And what about the album's unusual title? Nagle plucked that from experience too. "There was this guy, Gerald Gooch, at the California College of Arts and Crafts," Ron explains. "We were having a picnic and talking about the '50s, how we had been obsessed with black and Mexican style. You'd buy Lincoln Marine-green Cordova shoe polish and shine the toes of your wingtips, really buff them. It was like a showdown, man: Who's got the shiniest shoe? We're talking about this, and Gooch says, 'Yeah, I used to take the side of the shoe and bevel the edge till it was razor-sharp, so if anybody fucked with me I could do this—he made a karate swing with his foot—and slice 'em right at the Achilles tendon.' I said, 'That's pretty heavy.' He said, 'Bad rice, man, bad rice.' I'd never heard that before, but I thought, 'Wow, this is such a heavy term!' When I decided that was the album title, I built that [shadow-box] sculpture around the idea."

From a record-marketing viewpoint, an album cover that eschewed the conventional photo of the artist for a back-lit mound of basmati presented something of a challenge. The flipside of the cover, a Polaroid of the demented Chuckie of "61 Clay," probably didn't help. But Warner Bros. went ahead with LP WS 1902, even producing a *Bad Rice* radio spot and including "Family Style" on one of its loss-leader sampler albums (*Non-Dairy Creamer*, which also teased LPs by Little Feat, Zephyr, Tony Joe White and Peter Green). And it sent out review copies, which drew raves. In *Rolling Stone* Ed Ward praised Nagle for "synthesizing all that is great about rock and roll" and pronounced *Bad Rice* "blessed with melodies that stick in the listener's ears, brilliant playing and Nitzsche's incredible arrangements... Not since 'Gimme Shelter' have I heard a cut with as much surging power as 'Clay 61.'"

Despite fervid critical response, *Bad Rice* flopped. One theory lays its commercial failure to the evolving state of FM radio, at the time the key channel for exposing new albums. Reflecting market tastes, the format was abandoning its free-form origins and playing to extremes, its playlists leaded with hard-rock at one end and swabbed with singer-songwriters at the other. There was little room for an album that uncompromisingly, in Nagle's words, "tried to synthesize all that's great about rock and roll."

"It stiffed in about a week," says Nagle. "I was buying it in cut-out bins for a dollar. I went down to Warners, met with Mo [Ostin] and Joe [Smith] and said, 'What happened?' They just said, 'Look at these sales numbers.' Now, if you just go out on the road and help promote it, we can get something going.'" When that didn't happen, they agreed to let Nagle return to the studio to try and come up with something new. Though Warners promptly dropped him, Nagle's impressive response to that post-album offer is audible on the bonus cuts "Berberlang" and "Francine."

"Berberlang" originated, Nagle says, in "something Jack told me about. The berberlang was this mythic Filipino vampire he'd read about in a book called *Strange Facts*." The track, whose production represents a dramatic leap over *Bad Rice*, is among Nagle's finest, Ron's Bo Diddley-ish piano snaking through a funky, more energized version of early Dr. John and Little Feat style. It cooks, and Nagle delivers what may well be his strongest vocal ever, relating the sad/hilarious tale of a flamboyant waiter with "an infrared suntan and a blue bouffant" who stows away on a freighter to Manila. The ship's captain gets the best line: "I pleaded with him desperately to see my point of view/ He said that havin' me aboard just might excite the crew."

"I'm not sure how I came up with 'Francine,'" admits Nagle. "Two people tying each other up. I didn't have any idea of sadomasochism; why would anybody want to do that? So, once I became vicariously informed on it... There was a guy, one of my students, a closeted gay guy who I think was probably into it. He came by one day when we were rehearsing and gave me a whip, very proud of it. What the fuck am I gonna do with that, be Lash LaRue?"

The *Bad Rice* experience might have led a lesser man to throw up his hands and quit. Not Nagle. While fans of the failed album made like a cargo cult, patiently awaiting another beauty-drop from the heavens, he got to work. Through the later '70s and '80s, right up to the present, he's continued, most often with writing-producing saddle-mate Scott Mathews, to ride the sonic range. The Durocs album (Capitol, 1978) is only the best known of these later efforts, but there were also Nagle and Mathews' stint as the Profits (Radar Records' second single release), songs recorded by Streisand (on her *Superman* LP), Dave Edmunds, Michelle Phillips and the Tubes ("Don't Touch Me There"), the team's producing work (John Hiatt's *Riding with the King*), Nagle's ungodly sound-effects (with Nitzsche) for *The Exorcist* soundtrack and more. The remainder of the cuts on Disc Two, mostly song demos, come from the period immediately preceding and following *Bad Rice*, and illustrate how busy Nagle's muse kept him—and how wildly talented a musician he is, was and ever shall be... From the top...

- "From the Collection of Dorothy Tate": Another melodic pop construction that transcends form to become something more mysterious and beguiling: "It's about a girl I knew after I was getting over my divorce. She and her boyfriend were on the outs and she was just 'collecting' guys. I felt I was being used, at least that was my paranoid reasoning behind it."
- "61 Clay": Punk starts here: the original, rabid-fuzztone version of the song used to promote Nagle's Dilexi Gallery show.
- Excerpt from an early take featuring an alternate lead riff, here done with rabid fuzztone.
- "People Have Told Me": A ballad-in-progress. "Jim Barnett wrote it with Brad Sexton. There's a heavy Band influence there. To be honest, I have no idea what it's about."
- "Out in the Hall": Torrid rocker, a contender from the same stable as "Sister Cora" and "Capricorn Queen." "That one's about 80% Frank Robertson [co-writer of "Somethin's Gotta Give"]. We did a couple versions of this, but this one has more of a live feel."
- "Showdown": Midtempo meditation by a guy so fearful of commitment he can't even communicate with his love object from a distance—"My hands started shakin,' my pencil kept breakin'/ When I sat down to write her."
- "Say My Name": Great changes on a ballad with a warm, pre-rock standards feel and a touching truth at its core. In an about-face from "Showdown," the subject here *demands* commitment. "It's from an esoteric personal incident. When I was first going with my wife, I'd always call her 'Hon' or 'sweetie,' but I'd never say her name [Cindy]. To my credit, though, I never said 'Lady'! For a long time she had short

hair, and these guys at the gas station started calling her 'Bob.' I said, 'You know, I like that. That'll be your new nickname,' so I called her Bob for years. She decided she hated it, so now I call her Cindy."

- "Half as Much": Man, this guy has more sleepers than a Super Chief Pullman car! The track would have fit perfectly on the Durocs album, and its comic-tragic exposition of vulnerability puts the lachrymose public confessionals of most contemporary singer-writers to shame. Ron knows his gal's got another man: "I'll bet he's thinner than me, I'll bet he's got all his hair/ "I'll bet he says you look nice when you're too tired to care."

- "Who You Gonna Tell": A subdued ballad-with-strings about negotiating the space between hope and despair.

- "So Long Johnny": The pacific uke-and-steel strum belie the painful true story of an early Mystery Trend/Nagle mascot, "another [mentally challenged] guy like Eddie in 'Frank's Store.' He'd fallen off a streetcar in the Twin Peaks tunnel as a kid. As he got older he became more agitated and violent. He used to scare people, and they finally put him in a group home. But he used to laugh at everything, and he represented something to me: he *had* something, there was no pretense, no bullshit, he acted on instinct. Like the Legendary Stardust Cowboy." Denny Bruce: "Johnny would come to Ron's studio. He loved the Stones, he'd sing 'Jumpin' Jack Flash,' but he didn't know the words, so he just yelled the chorus. Ron loved his raw energy. He played a recording of him for Charlie Watts, who didn't get it. Charlie's wife thought Ron was making fun of Johnny. But that wasn't it. Ron dug him."

- "Sleep for Me": Piano and harmonium pace a tempo-shifting tune that Nagle says "is about Tom Donahue. He was a very imposing figure. I was paranoid about him and his ability to influence my thinking. He had the deep voice, this 400-pound presence, he'd hold court in his bedroom. There was a secret fear that I'd become mesmerized by his powers. There's a line in it, 'It's all that we've done /that's put you here where you are, son.' I mean, they *did* call him 'Big Daddy.' I have a different feeling for what Donahue did for me now, a more charitable view."

- "Alice Valentine": If it's lyrically a bit more diffuse, it's nonetheless an attractive first cousin to "Dolores," its soaring chorus pulling the listener toward an unlikely place: an impassioned defense of nostalgic recollection. Nagle's always been as genuinely sentimental as he is skeptical and candid, and who else would admit it with such grace? "Saxophones and violins/ Have got me in the shape I'm in/ They don't make 'em like that anymore." "It's interesting how songs evolve. 'Alice Valentine' turned into 'Moonlight Melancholy,' which is gonna be on my next record."

- "Wasted Paper": "It's about a guy who wants to say something but just can't get it together to do it. I played it for Jack, but he didn't like it, so we left it off *Bad Rice*. Probably, it was me reflecting on my divorce."
- "Rudy My Man": An utterly enticing excerpt from a song only Nagle could write. "Yeah, it's about a dog. I like to go back and revisit things and maybe change perspective on them. When I was a kid, I wanted a dog so bad my father said, 'OK, if you're a good boy I'll get you a dog.' He worked heavily on the bribery system; I got a '48 Ford 'cause I got straight A's one year. So he gets me a dog, a cute little Boston terrier. Basically, I knew nothing of the concept of the alpha male 'cause I was only about 8 at the time, and my father took over. The dog became his. And he *still* brags about it, at age 95, 'Oh that puppy!' I wanted to name him Butch, but my dad said, 'No! When you call him, it'll sound like "bitch." We can't do that.' He taught him all the classic tricks, 'Roll over and play dead,' he put a little hat on him. And I'm thinking, 'Fuck, where do *I* come into this? I thought it was my dog!' Tragedy plus time equals comedy. I kind of see them simultaneously."
- "Saving It All Up for Larry": One of the best and funniest entries in the Nagle canon, the finished version shines in full Spectorian girl-group glory on the Durocs album, with different lyrics on the verse. "The story came from this friend of mine, Larry. He had this girl he'd fallen in love with in high school. Larry was broke, and there was this other guy who wanted to hook up with Larry's chick. So Larry asks his girl, 'Will you go out on a date with this guy and try to get some money from him any way you can? Just try.' So the girl says, 'OK, Larry. Because I love you, I'll do it.' So she went out with this guy, and the guy wanted to screw her, and she goes, 'I'm sorry. I'll only [give you a blow-job] 'cause I'm saving for Larry.' True story. It went through a lot of changes. We finally made Larry a Navy man and it worked." (The video clip for the Durocs' version, featuring sailor Scott and stalker Ron [in an absurd mask] has popped up on YouTube from time to time.)

Like I said, this reissue of *Bad Rice* is an event. Not just for those who've long cherished its charms, but for the unique opportunity it offers 'newcomers': those who get to discover for the first time all the wit, joy and pathos that Ron Nagle first put into the world 40 years ago. I envy them.

Afterword: These Days

Yes, but what have you done lately? *These days I annotate albums (re-issues mainly), write the occasional article, and gear up to resume my still-on-hiatus radio show,* Atomic Cocktail. *And listen to a lot of radio in general, most enjoyably New Jersey's WFMU-FM, where Bob Brainen's wildly eclectic show plays. As far as contemporary music, pals are always pulling my coat to some worthy new act, for which I'm grateful, though I have to admit that my tastes remain conservative; the most appealing new tracks tend to be those that exhibit the kinds of qualities displayed by the best records of the Fifties, Sixties and Seventies. You can add my name to the chorus of listeners (not all of them graybeards) who find a continuing quality drop in mainstream pop over the last two decades. The upbeat stuff strikes me as desperate: hyper-driven—and far less tuneful—attempts to do what Real McCoy did 20 years ago with "Another Night," an almost illicitly effervescent hit single. Ballads? Dreary, over-empowered anthems, slow-mo cousins of "I Will Survive." (Like Dylan, I'm "waiting to find out what price/ I have to pay to get out of/ Going through all these things twice.")*

As far as today's music criticism, the "Overcovering Pop" and "Who Killed Rock 'n' Roll?" essays largely summed up my feelings on the subject. Zappa's classic definition of rock journalism as "people who can't write, doing interviews with people who can't think, in order to prepare articles for people who can't read" unjustly simplifies it, but by how much? Most of those who cover the subject in the mainstream media can write their asses off, but in service of what? Hasn't anyone told them there's really not much of a market for an atomic-powered toothbrush? But Kool-Aid sales are way up. The unquestioning, often reverential way many 'serious' critics approach musicians and their music seems to have migrated over from fan posts on social media. I can't recall one review that veered from the credulous official line that Beyonce's Superbowl 50 performance constituted a masterful blast at racial oppression. You mean that, this far into pop's dominance and our basic understanding of how it works, no one thought that maybe the Black Panther berets and raised fists were fully, or even partly, a fashion move, accessories designed to help pop do what it always does: grab our attention by any means necessary? Who's zoomin' who here?

In the past year there was a point where it seemed like I was actually losing my affection for stuff I've never not loved, like punk and doowop. The fear gripped hard, like the intimation of Alzheimer's that shakes all oldsters when the car keys aren't resting where we thought we'd left them. Then it receded: the Heartbreakers and Dion & the Belmonts sounded as good as ever. Whew!

Made in the USA
San Bernardino, CA
21 September 2016